CW00517851

THE MYSTERI

Praise for Kim Donovan

'A gripping story of a cold-blooded murder in a sleepy seaside resort which baffled Scotland Yard and enthralled Victorian society, unravelled with a forensic eye for detail. This is true crime at its best'
Wendy Moore

'A quicksand of a true-crime thriller that pulls you in and a unique murder mystery, impeccably researched and intelligently crafted – with drama so addictive it should be illegal'
Sam Christer

'An intriguing and gripping real-life murder case, with a tragic family story at its heart. This well-researched and beautifully written debut is a fast-paced and engrossing read – I couldn't put it down! Highly recommended for all lovers of both Victorian true crime and detective fiction'
Angela Buckley

'Donovan offers up impressively detailed research into the case of her ancestor's murder and a gripping moment-by-moment account of the High Court trial that followed, evoking a powerful sense of life around 1900 and getting behind the sensational newspaper headlines of the day to reveal the real struggles – and mistakes – of the characters involved. A strange, sad and enigmatic story that stays with you long after you've finished it'
Victoria Shepherd

THE MYSTERIOUS MRS HOOD

A TRUE VICTORIAN MYSTERY OF SCANDAL, ARSON, MURDER AND BETRAYAL

KIM DONOVAN

SEVEN DIALS

First published in Great Britain in 2024 by Seven Dials,
an imprint of The Orion Publishing Group Ltd
Carmelite House, 50 Victoria Embankment
London EC4Y 0DZ

An Hachette UK Company

1 3 5 7 9 10 8 6 4 2

Copyright © Kim Donovan 2024

The moral right of Kim Donovan to be identified as
the author of this work has been asserted in accordance
with the Copyright, Designs and Patents Act of 1988.

All rights reserved. No part of this publication may be
reproduced, stored in a retrieval system, or transmitted
in any form or by any means, electronic, mechanical,
photocopying, recording, or otherwise, without the
prior permission of both the copyright owner and the
above publisher of this book.

A CIP catalogue record for this book is
available from the British Library.

ISBN (Paperback) 978 1 3996 1538 9
ISBN (eBook) 978 1 3996 1539 6
ISBN (Audio) 978 1 3996 1540 2

Typeset by Input Data Services Ltd, Somerset

Printed in Great Britain by Clays Ltd, Elcograf S.p.A.

MIX
Paper from
responsible sources
FSC® C104740

www.orionbooks.co.uk

For Mary Jane.

And for Elsie and Harrison, who keep the Clark line burning bright.

Contents

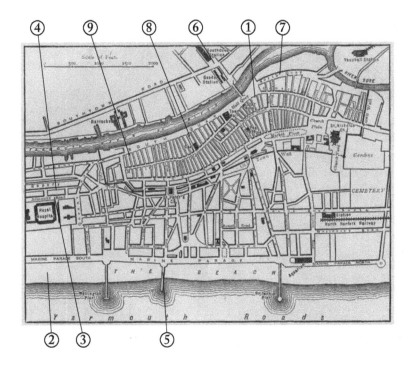

1. Crown and Anchor Hotel
2. Approx. location of where the body was found
3. Admiralty Road (where Alfred Mason lived)
4. Ordnance Road (where John went to fetch the horse and cart)
5. The jetty (where John found PC Manship)
6. South Town station (where Mary Jane arrived)
7. North Quay mortuary
8. The Rudrums' house (number 3)
9. South Quay Distillery

Clark family tree

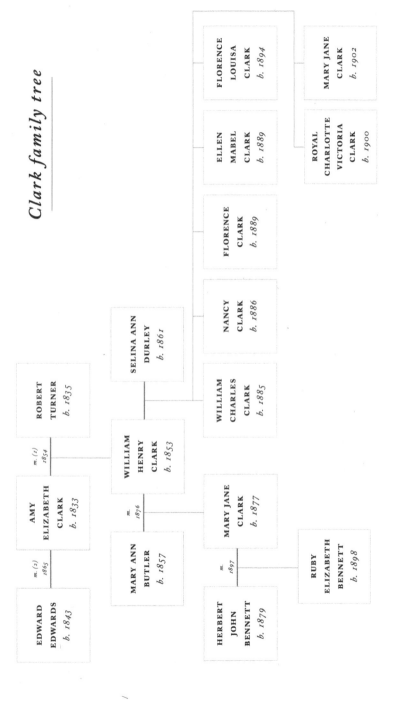

EDWARD EDWARDS
b. 1843

m. (2) 1865

AMY ELIZABETH CLARK
b. 1833

m. (1) 1854

ROBERT TURNER
b. 1835

SELINA ANN DURLEY
b. 1861

WILLIAM HENRY CLARK
b. 1853

m. 1876

MARY ANN BUTLER
b. 1857

WILLIAM CHARLES CLARK
b. 1885

NANCY CLARK
b. 1886

FLORENCE CLARK
b. 1889

ELLEN MABEL CLARK
b. 1889

FLORENCE LOUISA CLARK
b. 1894

ROYAL CHARLOTTE VICTORIA CLARK
b. 1900

MARY JANE CLARK
b. 1902

MARY JANE CLARK
b. 1877

m. 1897

HERBERT JOHN BENNETT
b. 1879

RUBY ELIZABETH BENNETT
b. 1898

Bennett family tree

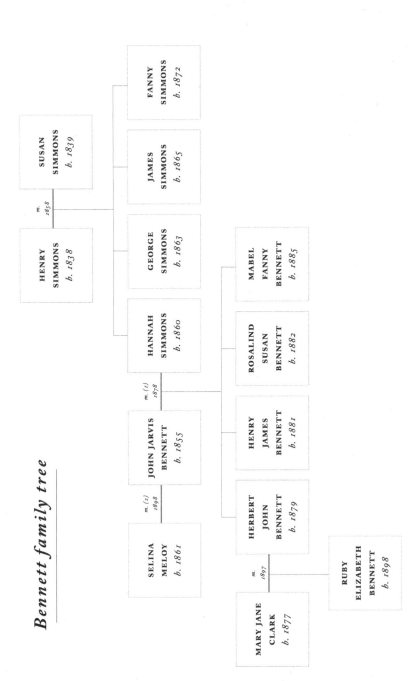

HENRY SIMMONS b. 1838 — m. 1858 — SUSAN SIMMONS b. 1839

Children: HANNAH SIMMONS b. 1860, GEORGE SIMMONS b. 1863, JAMES SIMMONS b. 1865, FANNY SIMMONS b. 1872

JOHN JARVIS BENNETT b. 1855 — m. (1) 1878 — HANNAH SIMMONS b. 1860
JOHN JARVIS BENNETT b. 1855 — m. (2) 1898 — SELINA MELOY b. 1861

Children: HERBERT JOHN BENNETT b. 1879, HENRY JAMES BENNETT b. 1881, ROSALIND SUSAN BENNETT b. 1882, MABEL FANNY BENNETT b. 1885

HERBERT JOHN BENNETT b. 1879 — m. 1897 — MARY JANE CLARK b. 1877

Child: RUBY ELIZABETH BENNETT b. 1898

THIS IS A TRUE STORY.

Introduction: My Family Album

This is the last surviving photograph of my great-great-aunt[1] and her husband. It was taken at around the time of their marriage in 1897, and originally belonged to my great-great-grandfather, William Clark, my great-great-aunt's father. After William's death, the photograph was handed down the Clark family line until it reached my grandmother, Beryl.

Our family album was chaotic. The photographs were kept in an old, disintegrating plastic carrier bag in a cupboard in my grandparents' bungalow. As a child, I recall emptying the bag out and sifting through the images, fascinated by what I found. Some of the photographs had pencil marks scrawled on their backs: names I didn't recognise and dates long since past. My grandparents told me stories about some of the people in the images. One photograph depicted a sailor – William Clark Junior – who fought in the Navy during the First World War. He died at thirty-one in the Battle of Jutland; the only major battle to be fought at sea during the conflict. And he was not the first of my great-great-grandfather's children to be killed by another's hand ...

One particular image always called out to me. It was this black-and-white photograph of a man and a woman, posing for a formal portrait in a photographer's studio. The first time I noticed it, the photograph's cardboard mount had started to crumble at the edges. I recall picking it up and watching as tiny flakes of dust fell away from it into the pile of photographs beneath. 'Who are these people?' I asked my grandmother.

She pointed to the woman. 'That's my mother's half-sister.' My grandmother paused, before adding: 'She was murdered just before my mother was born.' As it turned out, my grandmother knew very little about her aunt's death. Even as a young child, I was intrigued.

I rediscovered my family album when I was an undergraduate photography student in the late noughties. I was reading the seminal work of the French theorist Roland Barthes when I was instantly transported back to the photograph of my great-great-aunt and her husband. It was Barthes's description of what he called a 'punctum' – an 'element that rises from the scene, shoots out of it like an arrow and pierces [you]'[2] – that made me return to the image. As I examined it, my gaze continued to travel back to my great-great-aunt's face. I tried to figure out what drew me in. Was there a family resemblance to myself, perhaps? Something in her eyes? Her expression?

Eventually, I realised what it was that kept drawing me back to the photograph: a sense of sadness. As I gazed at the face of the young woman who sat contentedly in front of the camera with her husband by her side, I did so with the knowledge of what would come to pass. In three years, she would be dead.

That feeling of sadness compelled me to seek the long-forgotten truth that lay at the heart of my great-great-aunt's death. What I uncovered was more sensational than fiction.

She was Mary Jane Bennett, and this is her story.

THE BODY ON THE BEACH

'Horrible Discovery at Yarmouth!'[1]

A t 6.10 on the morning of Sunday, 23 September 1900, fourteen-year-old John Norton left his house on Boreham Road and made his way to Great Yarmouth's South Beach. John worked as an attendant at Hewett's Bathing Chalet under the watchful eye of the caretaker, Mr Grief. After a busy summer season, the long, warm days that had attracted the bathers to the seaside resort were beginning to fade away. As the sun began to rise sluggishly in the east, the young lad walked along the New Road before joining South Parade – the roadway that ran parallel to the coast. He squinted out across the beach.

As his eyes adjusted to the increasing light, he noticed what looked like a bundle of garments lying in the hollow of one of the dunes. The heap was partially concealed by the long marram grass that grew in tufts along the stretch of beach closest to the parade. This part of town had been largely untouched by development, and its secluded nature made it popular with courting couples. Curious, John jumped down from the raised path of the parade and climbed across the dunes to investigate. His feet sank into the sand, and the golden flower spikes of the marram grass brushed against his legs.

When he reached the bundle of clothing a few seconds later, John found himself standing over the lifeless body of a young woman. He stared at her bruised face before noticing the bootlace that was tied tightly around her neck. Her eyes were wide and sightless. In a panic, John turned and scrambled back up the beach. He ran desperately along Marine Parade until he reached the jetty. It was there, standing by the lifeboat station, that he stumbled across PC Edwin Manship.

Breathing heavily from shock and exertion, John relayed the news of his grim discovery. A few minutes later, with PC Manship by his side, he found himself gazing down at the unfortunate woman for a second time. The police constable swiftly took charge of the scene, sending John off to fetch a horse and cart from the local carter and fish transporter, William

Woods, at 59 Ordnance Road. PC Manship was an observant yet inexperienced officer. He had left the Royal Navy three and a half years earlier to join the Great Yarmouth Police Force, where he had received little formal training, as was standard at the time.

England's first modern police force, the Metropolitan Police Service, had been established in 1829 by Home Secretary Sir Robert Peel, and replaced the previous system of parish constables and watchmen. The success of the Metropolitan Police Service led to the establishment of the County Police Act ten years later. The Norfolk rural police force was the first of its kind and was well established by the time the County and Borough Police Act made county police forces compulsory in 1856. Its jurisdiction was divided into 12 areas, each supervised by a superintendent, with 120 PCs covering the whole county.

By 1900, the number of police officers in England, Wales and Scotland totalled 46,800, working in 243 separate forces.[2] At this time, the Great Yarmouth Borough Police Force was led by Chief Constable Parker, a solid, broad-shouldered man in his early fifties. (Parker was also superintendent of the fire brigade, inspector of hackney carriages and inspector of fish.) The local station was on Middlegate Street, a central location close to the town hall, and the force consisted of four inspectors, seventeen sergeants, and forty-five constables. Public perception and attitudes towards the police and policing had changed dramatically over the course of the nineteenth century and the once-despised 'blue locust' had become the much more popular 'bobby'.[3] Police constables, who were often drawn from the working classes, received minimal training, and were expected to learn most of their skills on the job. More senior police officers usually rose through the ranks, having started their careers as constables.

That morning, PC Manship's only thought was to remove the body from public view. It did not occur to him to preserve the scene. At the time, forensic science was in its infancy, and the police relied heavily on visual clues to investigate and solve crime. Photography had been used since the mid-1800s to record the faces of criminals ('mug shots'), and by the end of the century it was being used as a means of recording crime scenes. One of the earliest examples of photographic crime scene documentation was in 1888, when police photographed the body of Mary Jane Kelly, Jack the Ripper's last known victim. Photography was also being used as a way of recording the faces of corpses to aid identification. Despite its ability to more accurately record crime scenes, photography would not fully replace sketches as the main method of documentation until later in the twentieth century. Gradually, from 1902 onwards, expert testimony from scientists studying blood and fingerprint analysis would slowly be introduced into courtrooms. By the turn of the century, public interest and confidence in scientific testimony had already increased thanks to the fictional stories of scientifically based detection that had been popular during the 1890s. Arthur Conan Doyle's short stories published in the *Strand* magazine were chief among these, and by the end of the nineteenth century, his renowned amateur detective Sherlock Holmes had become a household name. Sherlock Holmes was not the first of the amateur detectives, but he was the first to employ forensic techniques in his detection of crime.

By now, it was 6.30 a.m. and the early-morning bathers, unperturbed by the September chill, would soon begin to arrive at the beach. PC Manship looked around. He was standing opposite the New Road, between the Royal Artillery Barracks and the Naval Hospital, approximately 20 yards from the pavement. The body lay almost directly in the path of Hewett's Bathing Chalet. He could see the bright stripes of the huts further along the beach to his left. He turned back to the woman. As he waited for John to return with the cart, he made a mental note of the scene.

The sand around the body had been disturbed and there were signs of a struggle. A white straw sailor hat lay beside the woman's head; its spotted net veil twisted neatly around the crown. PC Manship picked up the hat and found that its pins had been placed carefully in their holes. He noted that the woman appeared young; no more than thirty years old at his estimate. She lay on her back with her head to the south, her golden hair falling in curls around her shoulders. She was wearing a dove-coloured skirt and matching jacket, trimmed with decorative white braiding. The jacket, which was lined with crimson satin, had been unfastened but was pulled closely across her chest. Her skirt had been drawn up, and her bloomers – brown calico knickerbockers – had been unbuttoned and pulled down to her ankles. The crotch of the bloomers was torn, and the hem of the skirt had become unstitched.

Studying the scene more closely, PC Manship noticed a small amount of blood on the woman's chemise and other undergarments. Her left leg was slightly raised and bent at the knee. The woman wore three rings on the third finger of her left hand – one of which was a wedding ring – and another two on the third finger of her right hand. She was wearing a pair of new leather shoes, fastened by straps. The bootlace now digging into her neck was evidently not from one of her own shoes.

PC Manship reached into the pockets of the woman's skirt and pulled out a pair of brown kid gloves. Not thinking about disrupting the scene, he turned the body over to check underneath. Beneath her, he found a rolled-up white pocket handkerchief. He noticed that the woman wore a belt with a satchel suspender, but the satchel was missing. He found nothing on the body that could immediately identify her. It was plain that the woman had died a violent death, and that she had been sexually assaulted.

It was almost 7 a.m. by the time John Norton returned with William Woods' cart. He was accompanied by two more policemen, who helped PC Manship load the body. A few minutes later, the grim procession began its journey to the North Quay mortuary.

Across town in one of Great Yarmouth's lodging houses, the Rudrum family awoke to the sounds of a child crying out for its mother.

THE KILLER IN HER EYES

'It is a well-known scientific fact that the eyes of a person meeting with a sudden and violent end may retain a faithful impression of the last object on which their gaze has been fastened'[1]

I t was 7.45 a.m. by the time the horse-drawn cart with its grisly cargo reached the large wooden doors of the mortuary. The stone building stood on the bank of the River Yare, close to the Vauxhall railway station, one of Yarmouth's three stations. PC Manship, now assisted by Sergeant Johnsson, unloaded the body and laid it out on one of the slate slabs in the morgue. Suspicious deaths did not often occur in the quiet seaside resort of Great Yarmouth, and the lack of experience of the local police in dealing with such cases quickly became evident through their fumbled handling of the crime scene. The hasty removal of the body and the total abandonment of the scene likely resulted in the loss of vital evidence.

It had just gone 8 a.m. when the police surgeon – Doctor Thomas Lettis – arrived from his house in nearby Regent Road. Dr Lettis had been the town's police surgeon for thirty-four years, having joined the Royal College of Surgeons in 1866, at the age of twenty. A year later, he had been granted the Licence of the Society of Apothecaries (LSA), which enabled him to engage in general practice. As well as police surgeon, he was also Great Yarmouth's parish surgeon and general practitioner (GP). He was a competent and well-respected doctor.

That morning, Dr Lettis performed a preliminary external examination of the body, noting all outward signs of injury. His attention was immediately drawn to the ligature around the dead woman's neck. The bootlace bit so deeply into her flesh that Dr Lettis could barely get his fingernail underneath it. He examined the injuries to the woman's face and neck under a microscope and noted that there were scratches under the eyes and on the sides of her nose, as well as abrasions under her jaw. The abrasions were connected by a line across the chin that was almost the width of the ligature. Dr Lettis left the bootlace in place so it could be seen by the senior investigating officer. Then, assisted by Sergeant Johnsson and PC Manship, the doctor examined the woman's clothing for evidence and characteristic marks that could lead to identification. They found the number 599 written in thick black marking ink on the inside of the woman's blood-splattered chemise. By now, the body was showing signs of rigor mortis, and Dr Lettis estimated that the young woman had been dead for six or seven hours. He had no doubt that she had been brutally murdered.

Meanwhile, in nearby King's Street, Frank Sayers had just returned to his photographic studio after a morning swim when he was approached by two detectives. They asked him to accompany them to the mortuary to photograph the corpse of a woman. That morning, Sayers had passed very close to the spot where the body was found but had no idea that anything untoward had happened. The photographer was unnerved by the request – he had never been asked to undertake any such work before – but he agreed to do as the detectives asked and went with them to the mortuary. They arrived just as Dr Lettis was concluding his examination.

Sayers was asked to take a number of photographs of the woman, including close-up images of her eyes. At the time, optography – the process of viewing or retrieving an optogram, or image on the retina – was used by police as an investigative technique in murder cases. It was widely believed that the last image a person saw before death would be imprinted on their retina, like the negative of a photograph. Over a decade earlier, reporters had repeatedly suggested that the technique should be used as a means of identifying Jack the Ripper. Optography had ultimately been attempted in the Mary Jane Kelly case, but without success. Photographic images of the faces of corpses from other notorious murders had hung on the walls of the infamous Black Museum at New Scotland Yard since the mid-1800s, but the practice consistently failed to reveal anything useful. Its failure in the Yarmouth case would be attributed to the fact that the deceased was 'done to death while it was dark'.

As work to establish the circumstances surrounding the woman's death continued in the mortuary, the Yarmouth police took to the streets to ascertain the dead woman's identity.

Across town in one of Yarmouth's lodging houses, Mrs Eliza Rudrum, who had been awoken by the sounds of her lodger's baby crying, rose from her bed to investigate. When she opened the door to her lodger's bedroom, she was surprised to find the child sitting up alone in bed. Her amazement quickly turned to disapproval, on the assumption that the child's mother must have spent the night in a hotel with her brother-in-law. The landlady scooped the child up and went to tell her husband, John, that their lodger had not returned home the previous evening. Gossip had a way of spreading in Yarmouth's sprawling thoroughfares, and it was not long before the news of the Rudrums' missing lodger had reached the ears of the detective inspector now assigned to the dead woman's case. Robert Lingwood, a well-respected, chubby-faced man with a walrus moustache, who was often seen sporting a bowler hat, was one of Chief Constable Parker's four detective inspectors. He held the dubious accolade of 'spotting' more army deserters than any other officer in the country, despite looking, according to one reporter, 'more like a rural tradesman than a lynx-eyed limb of the law'.[2]

The Rudrums' house – Number 3, Row 104 – was located along the South Quay, just south of the town hall. Great Yarmouth's famous Rows – a series of narrow alleyways running parallel to one another – date back to the 1280s but were not numbered until 1804. They were previously known by the name of the person whose house fronted the Row.[3] Row 104 had at one time been Swannard's Row, named after the keeper of the town's swans, who had lived in it. Over the years, the Rows expanded southwards along the River Yare, until there were 145 in total. Once home to rich merchants, the Row houses had become increasingly dank and squalid places.

By 1926, living conditions would have become so poor that many of the houses were threatened with demolition. The area sustained heavy bombing during the Second World War, as the Luftwaffe dropped their unspent bombs on the town as they flew back out to sea. In 1941 alone, there were 167 raids, and over 7,000 incendiary bombs and 803 high explosives were dropped on the town.[4] The area between the South Quay and Middlegate Street sustained the most damage, and many of the Row houses were destroyed. Only the western end of Row 104 remains today and there is a gaping hole where the Rudrums' house once stood.

By 1900, the Rows were densely built-up and many of the houses had been sub-divided and let to multiple families. The Rudrums supplemented John's modest income as a shoemaker by taking in lodgers over the summer months. Most of their visitors came from the working classes and could not afford to stay in the hotels that had sprung up along the seafront. The Rudrums charged 14s. a week for a room, 6d. for breakfast, 1s. for dinner and 6d. for supper. They lived in a four-storey house with sash windows, which stood 20 yards from the western end of Row 104. Eliza Rudrum, a 'motherly-looking lady, with a kind face',[5] was the family's matriarch. She was barely literate, so it was her daughter, Alice, who dealt with all the family's correspondence. Alice, in her early twenties, was the Rudrums' third child, and she had inherited her mother's strength of character. Seven of the Rudrums' ten surviving children lived in the house, along with Eliza's elderly mother, Eliza Duffield.

It was DI Lingwood who informed the Rudrums of the morning's discovery. On his way to the mortuary, he had received a report of a woman missing from Row 104 from a police constable on duty in the town and had made straight for the Rudrums' house to investigate. The news shocked Mrs Rudrum deeply, but she managed to recover enough to show DI Lingwood upstairs to her lodger's bedroom. She had been staying in what Mrs Rudrum considered her best room, a small apartment on the first floor, which was just big enough for a single bed, wash basin and dressing table. Mrs Rudrum picked up a tiny tintype photograph from the dressing table, which she handed to the detective inspector, explaining that it was a photograph of her lodger, Mrs Hood, and her daughter, Rose. DI Lingwood looked down at the image. The photograph fitted comfortably in the palm of his hand. He could just about make out the woman's features and her clothing. Hanging from her neck was a long gold chain.

As DI Lingwood set about searching the room, he quizzed Mrs Rudrum for information about her lodger. The landlady talked freely, telling the detective inspector everything she knew about the young woman. She was a widow from York, Mrs Rudrum said, who had gone out the previous evening to meet her elusive brother-in-law. None of the Rudrums had met him, but Mrs Hood had told them that he was a jealous man and she suspected that he was following her about. On the surface, Mrs Hood appeared no different from any of the other holidaymakers that flocked to Great Yarmouth's hotels and lodging houses during the summer months. By 1900, visitors were coming from across the country, but particularly from the factory towns in the Midlands and the North of England. Walk-in guests at Great Yarmouth's many lodging houses were not generally required to provide their names or addresses, and most lodging houses did not keep detailed records about their visitors.

Great Yarmouth had started out as a port town, famous for its trade in herring, thanks to the 'silver darlings' that arrived in great shoals off the coast of Norfolk every autumn,[6] but during the 1800s, the town had started to develop into a seaside resort. By the middle of the century, the railway network had connected the town to the rest of the country, and an esplanade, two new piers and numerous hotels and entertainment venues had sprung up along the promenade. By 1870, Great Yarmouth was attracting more than 78,000 holidaymakers each year – 63,000 by rail and 15,000 by passenger steamer.[7] By 1900, it was a thriving seaside resort. The smell from Yarmouth's smokehouses filled the air and factory workers and their families lined the promenade. The attic rooms, once only rented to the 'fisher girls' who travelled to the area during the herring season to gut and pack the fish, were now let out to holidaymakers during the summer months. If the weather held, visitors would continue to come until the end of September, but the season was generally thought to be coming to an end by the middle of the month. It was at this point that the hotels along the promenade began to close their dining rooms and lay off their summer staff. The change in pace was also felt in Great Yarmouth's lodging houses.

When the detective inspector asked how long the woman had been staying, Mrs Rudrum replied that she had arrived with her child the previous Saturday evening, with very few belongings. That much was evident from the detective inspector's search. He found very little of any consequence. Among the exhibits he recovered that day was a small purse, which he found in one of the dressing-table drawers. Inside it he found a latchkey, a return railway ticket to London Liverpool Street station, and a small gold brooch with the word 'Baby' engraved on it. The railway ticket was due to expire the following Tuesday, 25 September.

Despite an extensive search, DI Lingwood found no papers or correspondence; nothing to confirm the young woman's name or identity. According to Mrs Rudrum, the only letter her lodger received had arrived two nights before. She could not say for sure, but she suspected that Mrs Hood kept it in a small satchel that attached to her belt. When DI Lingwood had finished searching the room, Mrs Rudrum handed him two items of baby clothing. The detective inspector examined the clothing and found that each bore the numbers 599, written in thick black ink.

By this point, DI Lingwood was confident that the dead woman found on the beach that morning was the Rudrums' missing lodger. His theory would soon be confirmed by John Rudrum, who would have the grim task of identifying the body in the mortuary. It had taken little more than two hours for the police to trace the dead woman to the Rudrums' house, but it would be a further six weeks before they would finally uncover her true identity.

THE LETTER IN THE BLUE ENVELOPE

'She didn't seem to want people to know too much about her'[1]

On the evening of Saturday, 15 September 1900, at 8.50, a young woman turned into Row 104 from the South Quay and approached the Rudrums' lodging house. She had come from the South Town railway station but had no luggage apart from a small brown paper parcel. It is likely that she had been accompanied at least part of the way by a man, but she was now alone, save for a small child, who was asleep on her shoulder. The woman's clothes, a light dove-coloured jacket and grey skirt, were noticeably new, and she wore a white straw sailor hat over her golden hair. She stopped outside number 3 and knocked on the front door. It was Mrs Rudrum who answered. She was delighted to find yet another late-season visitor on her doorstep. The Rudrums' only other lodger had arrived by boat earlier that day with his two young boys. The young woman asked the landlady if she had any vacant rooms. 'Yes, my best room is available,' Mrs Rudrum replied, enthusiastically ushering her into the house. The landlady showed the young woman to a room on the first floor, which was reached by a narrow spiral staircase. Her visitor agreed to take the room, remarking that Mrs Rudrum's house had been recommended to her by a 'friend's friend'.

The young woman began to undress the child, who she said was called Rose, while Mrs Rudrum put fresh sheets on the bed. When she had settled her daughter, the young mother asked her new landlady if she would like a deposit for the room. Mrs Rudrum said she would leave it to her to decide. The woman handed her 10s. She said she would be staying for a week and any longer would 'depend' on her brother-in-law. 'My brother-in-law brought me up from London – I'm a widow, you see,' she explained, 'and he's waiting to meet me as soon as I have put the child to bed, as he is going away by train this evening.' By that time, it was 9 p.m. and the last train to London had left the station at 6.50 p.m. It is unlikely that Mrs Rudrum knew the train times, and if she thought it curious that the woman's brother-in-law had not accompanied her to the door with the child, she kept her counsel. In fact, it seems the landlady was fairly relaxed about the whole affair, because she let her new lodger leave the house without so much as asking her name. Rose was sound asleep, and the young woman assured her that she should not worry, as she would never go far without her baby.[2]

Mrs Rudrum started to grow anxious when the young woman had not returned almost three hours later. As it approached midnight, she sent her husband, John, out to look for her. He had got as far as the doorstep when he spotted a young woman turning into the Row from the South Quay. He noticed by the light of the streetlamp that she was accompanied by a man. Great Yarmouth had its first gas lights installed in 1824, and by 1900 gas-lit streetlamps had been erected in large parts of the town. Row 104 had two: one under the archway at the entrance, and another about the middle of the Row, just beyond the Rudrums' house. Not wanting to be seen for fear the woman would think he was watching for her, John darted back indoors and headed for the stairs, stopping only to tell his wife that their lodger was outside with a gentleman. Had he realised that the identity of the man would later play a key part in a murder investigation, he might have taken more notice, but it was late and he was tired. He never was able to describe the man.

When the young woman came into the house a few minutes later, Mrs Rudrum was sitting in the downstairs passageway that was used as a sitting room. The rest of the family had gone to bed, and the house was dark apart from the light she had prepared for her lodger. The young woman apologised for being late, and Mrs Rudrum noticed that she was 'a little the worse for drink'.[3] She said that her brother-in-law had missed his train, so they had gone for a fish supper, and she had had 'three drops of brandy'. According to Mrs Rudrum's later account, the young woman's brother-in-law had spent the night at one of the hotels on Hall Quay. Mrs Rudrum's lodger spoke quite freely, adding that the man she had spent the evening with was her late husband's brother, and that she had been a widow for two years, her husband having died a month before the baby was born.

Over the next few days, the young woman behaved like any other visitor to the seaside resort. Her initial indiscretion on the night she arrived was quickly forgotten about and she proved herself to be an exemplary lodger. According to Mrs Rudrum, she took her child out each morning, usually returning to the lodging house in time for dinner (the mid-day meal). In the evenings, she put Rose to bed before going out alone. She always returned at 9 p.m. or just before, in time for supper with the Rudrums.

However, as time went on, Mrs Rudrum began to suspect that her lodger was not exactly what she claimed to be. Both Mrs Rudrum and her daughter, Alice, noticed that the young woman regularly contradicted herself. She told Mrs Rudrum that she was twenty-seven years old, but to Alice she said she was twenty-six (she was actually twenty-three). She said on one occasion that she had been married for five years, and on another it was three. The only age she could get right was her daughter's, which, curiously, she was very precise about, telling the Rudrums that Rose was one year and eleven months old. Despite being almost two, the child never answered to her own name, and her mother was in the habit of calling her 'dearie'. What Mrs Rudrum found most peculiar was that the little girl regularly referred to her 'dadda'. The young woman said that Rose was her only child, but that she had been 'towards others'. She added that her own mother had died when she was two weeks old, and that she had been raised by her grandmother. The Rudrums, particularly Mrs Rudrum, quickly developed a deep affection for little Rose. Her cheery disposition and beautiful curly flaxen hair meant that 'you couldn't help loving her'.[4] The Rudrums also found it difficult to resist their lodger's attractive personality. The child's mother would later be described by Mrs Rudrum as a 'lady-like and respectable young woman'.

The main topic of conversation that September was the war in South Africa. The Second Boer War had been raging for just under a year, and as the 1900 general election – the first of several to be dubbed the 'khaki election' because of the wartime influence – loomed, the general belief was that the British had won. In fact, the war, which was being fought between the British and two independent Boer states – the South African Republic and the Orange Free State – would continue for almost another two years. In the years leading up to the conflict, the discovery of gold deposits on the Witwatersrand had heightened British political interest in the region. The gold rush had also led to a rapid population surge, and between 1886 and 1899, 75,500 people migrated to South Africa from Britain alone.[5] By 1900, the number of immigrants landing in the country had drastically reduced, and ships destined for South Africa were instead packed with British soldiers. The Rudrums' lodger, having recently returned from South Africa, considered herself something of an expert on the subject. She claimed to have lived in the country for four mouths, having only recently returned on a steamer full of soldiers fresh from the battlefields.

When the young lodger was not chatting to various members of the family, she could usually be found on the beach with Rose. She was certainly there on the morning of Thursday, 20 September, because that day she was approached by a roving photographer named James Conyers who was out with his camera, touting for business. Conyers, a small, balding man in his fifties, was an outdoor photographer known for setting up his camera along the shoreline or at other popular tourist destinations around the town. He produced tintypes – or ferrotypes, as they were also known – inexpensive,[6] while-you-wait souvenirs. The images were usually quite dark, and often of poor quality. Most were very small, at around two to three inches in height. When Conyers approached the young woman that Thursday morning, she was initially very reluctant to agree to having her photograph taken. The photographer eventually managed to persuade her, however, and when she later returned to the lodging house, she proudly showed off the photograph before placing it on the dressing table in her bedroom, where it would remain until DI Lingwood took possession of it three days later. Unbeknown to the young woman, the tiny tintype, which would eventually become known as the 'beach photograph', was set to become one of the most famous images of the time.

On the Thursday evening, Mrs Rudrum accompanied her lodger to the circus. Despite being a permanent feature of Great Yarmouth's entertainment scene since 1845, the travelling circus was forced to perform in a semi-permanent wooden structure until Great Yarmouth's Hippodrome was eventually built in 1903.[7] On the way to the circus, the young woman told her landlady that she was expecting a letter. It would be addressed to 'Mrs Hood', she said. This was the first time Mrs Rudrum had heard her lodger's name. She later recalled the conversation because she remembered making a comment about 'Hood's Sarsaparilla', a popular drink in the late nineteenth and early twentieth centuries that claimed to purify the blood and cure a variety of disorders.

The letter arrived by the last post on the Friday evening. Mrs Rudrum took it from the postman and handed it to her daughter Alice. Both Alice and her grandmother examined the blue envelope and noted that the postmark was 'Woolwich'. When the three women had finished scrutinising it, they placed the letter on the supper table and waited for Mrs Hood to return home.

There was no sign of Mrs Hood, however, by the time Alice went upstairs to bed at around 11 p.m. Alice's bedroom was at the front of the house on the fourth floor. It was an attic room that was often warm and stuffy, and that evening was no exception. When Alice entered the room, she walked straight across to the window and pulled it open. As she did, she heard a man's voice drift up from outside. Curious, she leaned out of the window and looked down into the street below. She saw Mrs Hood standing just inside the Row, at the quay end. She appeared to be talking to a man. Alice could not see who it was because he was hidden from view by the angle of the archway. A few seconds later, Alice heard the man's voice for the second time – 'I am placed in an awkward position right now,' he said. It was a deep voice, but not otherwise distinctive. Not wanting to be seen, Alice quickly moved away from the window. She would later claim that she heard the sound of a kiss followed by footsteps.

Mrs Rudrum was alone in the sitting room when Mrs Hood came into the house a few minutes later. The young woman apologised for being late, claiming that she had lost her way. Mrs Rudrum told her not to worry and then handed her the letter that had arrived earlier that evening. The young woman opened it hurriedly. 'It's from my brother-in-law,' she said, scanning the contents of the letter. 'Meet me at the big clock at 9 p.m. and put your babe to bed,' she mumbled, reading aloud. The young woman looked up at Mrs Rudrum, who was watching her inquisitively. 'I suppose by the "big clock" he means the town hall,' she continued. Mrs Rudrum agreed. Turning back to the letter, Mrs Hood said, 'The appointment is for tomorrow. Alice and I will have to rearrange our plans.' She and Alice had intended to see *The Great Ruby*, a melodrama that was showing at the Royal Aquarium Theatre on Marine Parade that evening. Mrs Hood threw the letter down onto the table just as Mrs Rudrum went to leave the room. As the landlady passed the table, she noticed the letter was signed 'Hood'.

That was the last anyone ever saw of the Hood letter. What became of it remains a mystery to this day.

When Mrs Hood awoke the next morning, she had only a few short hours to live. The day started out like any other. She went out with Rose as usual in the morning, returning to the Rudrums' house a few hours later in time for dinner. She spent the rest of the afternoon in her bedroom preparing for her evening appointment, before leaving the lodging house again between 6.30 and 7 p.m. According to Mrs Rudrum's mother, Eliza, Mrs Hood returned to the house briefly at around 8.30 p.m. She went straight upstairs and came down a short while later 'looking very nice'.[8] On her way out of the house, Mrs Hood passed through the Rudrums' yard, where she was seen by sixteen-year-old Louisa, a friend of the family, who would go on to marry one of the Rudrum boys.

Alice Rudrum was also in the vicinity of the house when Mrs Hood left that evening. Having been disappointed at not being able to go to the theatre, she had arranged to meet a friend, Miss Breeze, who lived two streets along. As it approached 9 p.m., the two young women were out walking when Alice spotted Mrs Hood standing on the pavement in front of the west side of the town hall. The new gothic-style building was a grand feature of Hall Plain and it stood an equal distance between the Rudrums' house in Row 104 and the South Town bridge, which connected the eastern part of the town to the western part. A grand clock tower sat atop the red-brick, sandstone and terracotta building, with a decorative ogeed lantern above. Inside, there was an impressive assembly hall, and a large courtroom that functioned as a magistrates' court. At 5 foot 3 inches, Mrs Hood looked a small figure beside the imposing tower.

It is safe to assume that it was curiosity rather than coincidence that had led Alice to the very same spot where Mrs Hood was due to meet her mysterious brother-in-law that evening, but if she was hoping for a glimpse of the man, she would be disappointed. When Mrs Hood saw Alice, she apologised again for having to cancel their plans – 'I hope we can go to the theatre next week instead,' she said. Alice agreed and then Mrs Hood said something about expecting her brother-in-law down by train. Alice was later unable to say for certain exactly what she had said, as she 'didn't pay much attention',[9] but given that the London corridor train had pulled into the South Town station a short time earlier, at precisely 8.28 p.m., it is likely that Mrs Hood was expecting her brother-in-law on that. The train was full, and neither the guard nor the inside attendant were later able to identify any of its passengers.

A few minutes later, Alice walked away with her friend, leaving Mrs Hood standing alone. That was the last time any of the Rudrums saw their lodger alive.

Across town to the south, nineteen-year-old Alfred Mason was sitting in a shelter on Kimberley Terrace opposite the Victoria Hotel[10] with his sweetheart, seventeen-year-old Blanche Smith. The shelter was adjacent to Marine Parade and the South Beach Gardens, a picturesque area adjoining the Wellington Pier, the first of Great Yarmouth's two piers. Both Alfred and Blanche lived and worked locally: Alfred was a moulder at Crabtree & Co. engineering works and Blanche worked as a machinist at Johnson

& Sons, a factory that manufactured oilskin clothing for fishermen and merchant seamen.

It had just gone 10 p.m. when Alfred and Blanche decided to leave the relative sanctuary of the shelter to walk along the Parade.[11] As they emerged from underneath its protective cover, they were immediately exposed to the cold night air. They shivered from the chill as they walked south along the parade. When they reached the turning to the New Road, they decided to walk the short distance to Admiralty Road where Alfred lived so they could fetch his overcoat before venturing down to the beach. Alfred's house, number 52, stood at the junction of the two roads and it took them less than five minutes to walk there. When Alfred had collected his overcoat, he and Blanche walked back up the New Road, along exactly the same route that young John Norton would take the next morning. Unlike John, however, the young couple saw nothing out of the ordinary when they stepped onto the beach that evening. They had arrived at the most secluded part of South Beach, and it appeared to be deserted on this dark, moonless night.

By now, it was 10.45 p.m. Looking for somewhere to sit, Alfred and Blanche walked about 30 yards down the beach towards the sea, and then turned to the north and walked another 40 yards. When they had found an appropriately secluded hollow, they stopped and sat down. The long marram grass that grew in the sand around them afforded them plenty of privacy and the next few minutes passed by in blissful isolation. Fifteen minutes later, the stillness of the night was punctuated by the sudden appearance of a man and woman, who were walking purposefully onto the beach from the direction of the New Road. They were talking loudly, as if quarrelling. They came to a stop on an area of sloping ground about 30 yards to the south of Alfred and Blanche and sat down.

Ten minutes later, Blanche heard the woman cry out.

'Mercy!'

Blanche grabbed Alfred's arm and motioned for him to listen. The first cry was closely followed by another two desperate pleas, in a manner that the couple would later describe as a 'sort of dying exclamation'.

'MERCY, MERCY!'

Blanche looked at Alfred in alarm. The woman's cries turned into groans and then – seconds later – the night fell still once again. The couple listened in silence for a few minutes as they sat frozen in their hollow. The chill in the air had intensified. Alfred tried to convince an unnerved Blanche that the couple were just skylarking – he could see the man and the woman moving very dimly in the darkness.

'Did you do anything?' Alfred would later be asked.

'No, I remained where I was. I thought some man was having connection with the woman.' At the time, rape within marriage was not considered a crime,[12] but public tolerance for men's violence against women was declining.[13] Gender issues had become a major preoccupation in the 1890s and society was beginning to address gender inequality. Societal conventions, however, still dictated that a woman was the 'property' of her husband. The Victorians were also, on the surface, very prudish about sex and Alfred would undoubtedly have felt it was not 'his place' to intervene in another couple's affairs.

Fifteen minutes passed before Alfred and Blanche eventually got up to leave. On their way back up the beach, Alfred passed within 5 yards of the couple. In the darkness, he could just about make out their shapes. He noticed that the woman was lying flat on her back. The man was astride her, with his right arm resting on her chest. The woman was silent, motionless. Alfred's attention was drawn to her dress, which appeared 'shiny – very shiny'. As he passed by, the man sensed his presence and turned to face him. He looked up at Alfred, but it was too dark to see his face or to make out any of his features. Alfred carried on walking. Blanche, who had kept her distance, would later say that it looked to her as if the man was kneeling on the woman.

Having left the beach, Alfred accompanied his sweetheart to the door of her house where he left her at around 11.15 or 11.30 p.m. He then made his way home, where he arrived just before midnight.

When Alfred Mason heard the startling news of the grim discovery the following morning, his mind immediately lurched back to the scene he and Blanche had witnessed the previous evening. News of the body had circulated like wildfire in the part of town closest to the South Beach. Admiralty Road backed on to Ordnance Road, which had been the scene of much commotion earlier that morning when John Norton had hurtled down the street in search of the Woods' house. Alfred was haunted by the images of the man and the woman, and his mind replayed them over and over again. With a feeling of great unease, he recounted the events of the previous evening to his older brother, Walter. Alfred recalled the woman's piercing cries for mercy and described the chilling image of the man as he loomed over her still and silent body. Walter, who was fourteen years

Alfred's senior, cautioned his brother against making a statement to the police until they had gathered more information.

It was under this guise that the two brothers found themselves standing on the South Beach opposite the New Road later that Sunday morning. By now, it was 10.30 a.m. and the beach was crowded with people. Alfred's attention was immediately drawn to a man who was 'walking about in a very agitated manner'. He appeared to have a companion – a second man, who stood close by, looking directly at the spot where the body had been found. Alfred called his brother's attention to the two men. Now suspicious, the brothers watched as the men turned and walked away from the scene in the direction of the town. Convinced they were up to no good, but reluctant to approach them, Alfred and Walter followed them for a short distance before losing them in a crowd near the South Beach Gardens.

Alfred Mason made a report to DI Lingwood later that day. Blanche was also interviewed by the police, and Chief Constable Parker arranged for two policemen to accompany her to the South Beach to have her point out the spot where she had seen the man and woman the previous evening. Instead, however, the policemen took Blanche to the exact spot where the body had been found and pointed it out to her. By that time, there were close to 200 people on the beach and Blanche found herself looking upon an entirely different scene to the one she had witnessed the previous evening. She was hesitant in her identification of the location – an uncertainty that would later follow her into the witness box.

Another visitor to the police station that afternoon was a local man named William Clay, who handed in a pair of gold-rimmed spectacles that he had found on the beach 30 yards from the edge of the Parade. The glasses were later identified by the Rudrums as belonging to their dead lodger.

Police investigations were limited to the local area that day. The police station was not connected to the telephone, and the telegraph lines, housed at the local post office, were only open for an hour on a Sunday, between 5 and 6 p.m. The focus of the day's enquiries was an attempt to locate Mrs Hood's mysterious 'brother-in-law'. Enquiries were initially concentrated around Hall Quay, a parade of hotels that overlooked the River Yare and were conveniently positioned close to the South Town railway station. PC Platten called at the Crown and Anchor Hotel, and spoke to the hotel's 'boots' (general dogsbody), a man named Edward Goodrum. The police constable asked Goodrum if they had a guest named 'Hood'. He told the officer that they had a walk-in guest who had arrived late the previous evening and left first thing that morning, but he had not taken his name as it was not customary to keep records of walk-in guests. PC Platten made a note of the information and then left the hotel. It would be some weeks before the police thought to investigate the Crown and Anchor's mysterious walk-in guest any further.

THE MISSING BOOTLACE

'A boot without a lace was suspicious'[1]

When the telegraph lines reopened the following day, Chief Constable Parker sent word of the murder to twelve police districts across the country. The briefing included details of the crime, copies of Sayers' photographs and a description of Mrs Hood's clothing. 'The portraits,' reported the *News of the World*,[2] 'will travel to some two or three hundred towns in all before returning to Yarmouth.' The police focused their efforts on London, Leeds and York; all places where Mrs Hood was thought to have had a connection. At the time, they believed that formally identifying the dead woman would be a fairly simple case of tracking down her friends or relatives.

That day, by order of the borough coroner – John Tolver-Waters – Dr Lettis performed a full post-mortem examination on the body of Mrs Hood.[3] He was assisted by the medical officer for the north district of the borough, Mr Charles O'Farrell, who had held the position for almost thirteen years. Dr Lettis began by cutting away the ligature, taking care to leave the knots intact. He struggled to remove the bootlace without cutting the skin and when it eventually came away from the woman's neck, it left a tinged band of red discoloration. He passed the lace to Mr O'Farrell to measure. The medical men were shocked to discover that the bootlace, which measured 9 inches in length, was 4 inches shorter than the circumference of the woman's neck.[4] Great force would have been required to tie the ligature in place. Examining the bootlace more closely, the doctors determined that it was made of mohair. A double reef knot had been used to tie it, with a 'granny' (grandmother) knot on top to keep it in place. Curiously, the lace appeared to have been broken, or else two pieces of lace had been knotted together to make a longer ligature.

The two doctors now examined the marks on the woman's chin and the abrasions on either side of her face and found evidence to suggest that the lace had, at one point, been tied tightly over the chin. The medical men hypothesised that the woman's assailant had caught the bootlace on her chin before realising their mistake and had then quickly slipped it down over her neck before tightening it and tying the death knot in place. The woman's jaw was clenched tightly shut, and it took some force before Dr Lettis was able to prise it open. Her tongue was pressed firmly against her bottom teeth. Dr Lettis examined the woman's hands under a microscope but found no scratches or abrasions and no evidence to suggest that they had been forcibly held. He found no sign of skin underneath her finger-nails, which indicated that the marks on the woman's face had been caused by her attacker.

The doctors now looked for signs of rape and found evidence of sexual assault. Studying the blood first noticed by PC Manship on the woman's linen, Dr Lettis found a mix of arterial blood – which was likely to have originated from a small tear in the woman's vagina – and menstrual blood. There was bruising on the front and outside of the woman's right thigh, as if it had been pressed, or someone had lain on it. Examining the rest of the woman's organs, the doctors found clear signs of asphyxia.

When they had finished the post-mortem examination, Dr Lettis and Mr O'Farrell reviewed their findings. They unequivocally agreed that the cause of death was strangulation, brought about by the mohair bootlace. They discounted a theory of suicide, which had been posited by PC Man-ship, due to the elaborate knotting of the lace and the force with which it had been applied. The doctors concluded that the unfortunate young woman would have been unconscious within a minute, and dead within two minutes of the lace being tightened around her throat. They had found no evidence of a blow to the head, which led them to believe that the dead woman had been conscious when her assailant had applied the bootlace. The force with which it had been applied would have made it impossible for her to scream as soon as it was around her throat. The medical men prepared the body for further viewing and awaited instructions from the coroner.

Meanwhile, the police were continuing their enquiries at Great Yarmouth's hotels and lodging houses. They were also conducting door-to-door inter-views of residents living in the vicinity of the South Beach. One such resident was a retired lieutenant with the Royal Garrison Artillery, a man named Richard Cole. Lieutenant Cole lived in a red-brick house at the extreme northeast corner of the Royal Artillery Barracks grounds, close to the New Road. He told the police that he was at home all evening on the night of the murder, but that he had heard nothing out of the ordinary. In fact, the police found no one in the local area who saw or heard anything unusual on that fateful night, and Alfred Mason and Blanche Smith remained the only two potential witnesses to Mrs Hood's untimely demise. The police also made enquiries at the railway booking office and found that another first-class return ticket was purchased alongside Mrs Hood's. They attempted to trace the person who had bought the tickets but were unsuccessful. Every ticket used on the railways had to go through the Railway Clearing House, which was set up in 1842 to manage the allocation of revenue between the different railway companies, in a process that took weeks.

On the Tuesday following the murder, DI Lingwood discovered another witness in the form of local man William Borking. Having had no luck hunting down leads at Great Yarmouth's hotels and lodging houses, the detective inspector had extended the search to include the neighbourhood's bars and taverns. That day, his enquiries had taken him to the Mariner's Compass, a small bar attached to the South Quay Distillery at 61 South Quay, on the southwest corner of Row 142.[5] The manager, William Borking, was a man in his early sixties, who wore a heavy moustache and a beard that was so long and dense that it obscured his shirt front. Borking lived at number 4, Row 113, a short distance from Row 104 on the opposite side of Middlegate Street. His bar, a small, shabby establishment, was about a ten-minute walk from the town hall, along the South Quay. Like most of the other residents and visitors to the town, news of the murder had first reached Borking on the day the body had been discovered.

When DI Lingwood showed the landlord a copy of the beach photograph, Borking immediately recognised the woman as someone he had seen in his bar. He claimed to have seen the woman in the company of a man on the night of the murder at around 9.45 p.m. Borking, who was described by a *Star* reporter as 'a man of few words, keen as a ferret,'[6] was able to recall the time as he was due to close the bar at 10 p.m. and was annoyed that the couple had come in so near to closing time. His description of the events as he remembered them proved of great interest to DI Lingwood.[7]

On the evening of the murder, William Borking had been standing behind the bar of the Mariner's Compass when a man and woman walked into the public house. It was a tall bar – about chest height – with a brass rail above, but Borking could see enough to note that the man was wearing a steel-coloured suit and a trilby hat, and the woman had on a dove-coloured jacket. The couple approached the bar and the man ordered two drinks – a gin and a Johnnie Walker. The man 'looked worried and nervous', said Borking, 'whereas the lady looked calm, and I think pleased'. The man paid a shilling for the drinks. When the woman turned her back to the bar, Borking was struck by how fair her hair was. He also noticed the detailed braiding on the back of her jacket. 'I was attracted by the pretty scroll,' Borking said, 'and it so took my fancy that I sketched it, so I could keep it as a pattern.' Continuing his story, the landlord said the woman had removed one of her brown kid gloves and adjusted her gold-rimmed spectacles. When he had served the drinks, she placed one of her gloves on the bar, then lifted the veil attached to her straw sailor hat so she could take a drink. Her companion picked up a copy of the Great Eastern Railway timetable – which had been hanging on a hook beside the bar – and opened it out on the counter. 'He had a rather heavy moustache,' recalled Borking, 'and kept twisting the ends between his finger and thumb. He did it so frequently that I stood and watched him.' A few minutes later, the couple finished their drinks and turned to leave. As they walked towards the door, Borking realised that the woman had left her glove on the bar. He called out to her. The man walked back and took the glove from Borking, nodding his appreciation. The couple left the distillery at about 9.55 p.m. and walked down the Row in the direction of the Quay. They then turned south and walked past the front window of the bar.

When Borking had finished recalling the events of that evening, he produced the sketch he had made of the scrollwork on the woman's jacket and handed it to Lingwood. The detective tucked it into the pocket of his jacket and then asked if anyone else had been in the bar at the same time as the couple. Borking said that his washerwoman, Elizabeth Gibson, had come in with her child to deliver some clean linen and had stayed for part of the evening.

William Borking would later claim to have kept the glasses that Mrs Hood and her male companion had drunk from on the evening of the murder. A couple of years later, these exhibits might have proved useful in the police investigation. Although techniques for fingerprint identification and classification had been developed in the late nineteenth century, fingerprint evidence would not be accepted in British courts until 1901 – the same year that the fingerprint branch of the Metropolitan Police was formed – and the fingerprinting system would not be thoroughly established in England until 1904.[8]

Later that day, William Borking called at the police station to give a formal statement. While there, he saw the dead woman's jacket hanging on the door of the detectives' office. He recognised it immediately. Mrs

Hood's clothing had been delivered to the police station to be examined for clues following the post-mortem examination. The police had found the name of the makers on the bodice of the jacket and had traced the firm to London. They were preparing to send the garment to them in the hope that the makers would be able to identify its owner. The company were ultimately unable to trace the purchaser from their records.

On the following evening, Wednesday, 26 September, at just past 9 p.m., a man walked into a wholesale stationer's shop in the small town of Lowestoft. The occurrence, in itself, was in no way remarkable. Had it not been for the recent murder of a woman in the neighbouring town of Great Yarmouth, the incident would inevitably have passed by without further thought. As it was, the shopkeeper, a man named Mr John Rochford O'Driscoll, was, like everyone else, on high alert for unusual behaviour. O'Driscoll's shop was in Lowestoft's main street, close to the railway station, on the ground floor of Dagmar House. Mr O'Driscoll lived above the shop with his wife, Eva, and a young servant named Elizabeth. The shopkeeper, variously described as a printer, stationer and tobacconist, was a well-respected businessman in his late thirties, but his bald head and neat grey beard made him appear older.

The man who now entered O'Driscoll's shop was 5 foot 9 inches, with a big black moustache, and scratches that were several days old on his face. He appeared to be between twenty-five and thirty years of age and wore a long grey overcoat and greasy cap. He approached O'Driscoll, who was standing in front of the counter. O'Driscoll's shop assistant, William 'Bill' Overy, a quiet young man in his early twenties, was standing behind the counter. Both men noticed the scratches on their customer's face. The man asked for a newspaper with the best account of the Yarmouth murder – 'I've been trying to get one everywhere but cannot,' he said. He was well spoken and – had it not been for his greasy cap – he would have had a gentlemanly appearance. 'Would you like a local or London paper?' O'Driscoll asked. The customer replied that he did not mind as long as it was the best account of the murder. O'Driscoll handed him a copy of the *Ipswich Star*. The man snatched the newspaper and then unbuttoned his coat to fumble in the pocket of his waistcoat for a halfpenny. As he did so, O'Driscoll noticed that his hands were scratched. Several grazes on his right hand had been patched up with white adhesive paper and the skin on his right thumb had been cut. The man handed O'Driscoll the halfpenny and then took up the newspaper and hurriedly turned it over and over, searching for the report. It was at this point that O'Driscoll noticed that the leather tongue of one of the man's boots was hanging out, which led him to think that it was missing its bootlace.

'Where is it? Where is it?' O'Driscoll's customer exclaimed, frantically turning the pages of the newspaper. He was clearly agitated. O'Driscoll calmly pointed out the article and the man started scanning the report eagerly. The newspaper trembled violently in his hands. He let out a groan before suddenly becoming aware that he was being watched. He looked up from the newspaper before crumpling it up and rushing out of the shop.

O'Driscoll asked Overy if he had noticed that the man was missing a bootlace. Overy replied no but agreed that he had been acting oddly. Startled by the incident, the two men agreed to report their strange customer to the police, and a few minutes later O'Driscoll had shut up the shop and rushed off in search of a police officer. '[The customer] gave me the impression something was wrong,' O'Driscoll would later say. 'It struck me that a boot without a lace was suspicious.'[9] O'Driscoll recounted the incident to a policeman on point duty outside a nearby hotel and the officer immediately hurried after the strange man. The police officer, unable to trace him, called at the shop later that evening to take further particulars. The report from the Lowestoft police was conveyed to the Great Yarmouth police force for further investigation a few days later. It joined a pile of hundreds of similar reports.

The coroner, Mr Tolver-Waters, had originally intended for the inquest to take place on the Tuesday after the murder, but he had adjourned it twice to give the police more time to investigate the dead woman's identity. By the Thursday, however, it had become obvious that the inquest needed to take place so that the body could be buried. At the time, it was common for bodies to be laid out (sometimes for days at a time) after death so that family members could say their final farewells. Modern methods of preserving bodies would not be introduced until much later in the twentieth century, however, so decaying bodies was a common (albeit distressing) sight. Flowers and scented candles were used to mask the unpleasant odours of decomposition.

The inquest was held in the magistrates' court, a grand room on the first floor of the town hall. The foreman of the jury was a man named Mr George Norton – no relation to the young lad who had found the body. Norton, along with most of the other members of the jury, were well-known local tradesmen. At the opening of the inquest, the coroner confirmed that the body remained unclaimed. As the woman had not been formally identified by relatives or friends, the inquest would be conducted on the basis that she was 'unknown'. He went on to describe the events surrounding the discovery of the woman's body, pausing only to chastise PC Manship for his handling of the crime scene – 'It was somewhat unfortunate that the constable did not leave the body in place and seek further assistance so the scene could be photographed,' he said. Murder was not a common occurrence in the quiet seaside town, so it is likely that the officer's superiors forgave his shortcomings. The coroner advised PC Manship to learn from his mistake, should he find himself in a similar position in the future.

The spot on the beach where the body had been found had been photographed by local photographer Frank Sayers and the image was now entered into evidence. The coroner proceeded to describe the murdered woman's injuries and the efforts the police had taken in attempting to identify her. He then accompanied the jury to the mortuary, where the two medical men – Dr Lettis and Mr O'Farrell – highlighted the injuries, marks and wounds that they would later refer to in evidence. This was usual practice at the time, and jurors would often light their pipes before entering the mortuary in an attempt to keep the smells of decay at bay.

When the grim expedition returned to the town hall, the Rudrum family were called one by one to give evidence. John Rudrum was first into the box. He was closely followed by his wife, who was able to give a far more detailed account of their lodger. Finally came their daughter, Alice, who had been the last to see Mrs Hood alive. John Norton then gave evidence of the finding of the body before the inquest was adjourned until the next day.

The following morning, the keeper of the mortuary and the guardian's undertaker placed the lifeless body of the mysterious young woman, known only as Mrs Hood, into a redwood coffin. She had been dressed in her blood-splattered chemise. At the time, the chemise carried cultural overtones of purity.[10] The garment was likely chosen as the young woman's burial outfit because it was one of the few items of clothing she owned that had not been entered into evidence, but it also happened to be the only item of the woman's clothing that carried the mysterious 599 mark. Mrs Hood's funeral had been arranged and paid for by the borough, but the coffin was of better quality than those usually reserved for pauper's funerals. The lid of the coffin was decorated with two ornamental metal shields. It bore no name plate. Interest in the woman's death was intense and the police had gone to great lengths to conceal the date of her interment. In response to repeated enquiries from the press, they had announced that the woman would be buried the next morning. With the lid of the coffin securely fastened, the keeper of the mortuary, the guardian's undertaker and the caretaker from the workhouse carried it carefully out of the morgue. A hand ambulance – a small cart big enough to transport one person, or in this case a coffin – was waiting outside the large wooden doors of the mortuary. The pallbearers, who were all wearing conventional black mourning dress, placed the coffin on the cart and the morbid procession began its slow journey along the North Quay, up Fuller's Hill to the parish church. As the funeral cortege passed through George Street, the significance of the convoy soon became clear and news that the murdered woman was about to be buried began to circulate. Within minutes, a curious crowd of some 200 people had gathered, joining the back of the procession as mourners.

The funeral service was read by the Reverend J. Rimmington and was attended by Eliza and Alice Rudrum, Detective Inspector Lingwood and several other officers. The tolling of a muffled bell from the tower of St Nicholas's Church indicated that the funeral had taken place. The coffin was then transported to the far northwest section of the Kitchener Road cemetery where Reverend Rimmington read the committal rites. The deceased was recorded in the church and cemetery register as 'Unknown', with the name Hood in parentheses.

The sombreness of the day was not lost on those who congregated for the resumed inquest that evening. PC Manship was called to describe the murder scene as he recalled it, and he was closely followed by the two medical men. Dr Lettis was questioned extensively by the coroner. 'In your opinion,' asked the coroner, 'would it have been possible for the woman herself to have tied the lace?'

'No,' replied Dr Lettis, 'I don't think so for a moment . . . she could never have drawn it so tight.'

'Are you quite satisfied from all these appearances that it was not a case of suicide?' persisted Tolver-Waters.

'Oh, certainly,' insisted Dr Lettis. 'Death in that form could not have been self-inflicted. Someone else must have tied the bootlace.'

The inquest was then adjourned until Monday, 29 October, when it was hoped the police would have made further progress with their enquiries.

Meanwhile, Mrs Hood's murderer continued to roam free.

A MURDER A DAY

Will the 'Dispatch' solve the crime?

The first accounts of Mrs Hood's murder reached the newspaper-reading public the day after the body was discovered.[1] Following an interview with PC Manship, local newspaper the *Eastern Evening News* produced a particularly thorough account of the crime, which included detailed facts about the circumstances surrounding the young woman's death – '. . . a bootlace was tightly knotted round the woman's neck, immediately below the chin . . .'[2] Later that day, the specifics were also printed in some of the London evening newspapers, notably the *Star*: '. . . there were trampled footmarks round the spot where, stark and stiff, the young woman lay flat on her back . . .'[3]

The murder of Mrs Hood quickly became the principal topic of conversation in Great Yarmouth and its neighbouring districts. Throughout the week following the murder – while the police were busily engaged in hunting down the slenderest of clues – the town's bars and taverns were abuzz with talk of the crime. Interest in the case was fuelled by this extensive newspaper coverage. The development of a more affordable and less regulated press over the latter part of the nineteenth century had coincided with an increase in literacy levels, which had led to a dramatic rise in newspaper readership. By 1900, the adult literacy rate had risen to 97 per cent, an increase of 28 per cent from the middle of the previous century.[4]

During the same period, there had also been a significant shift in the way crimes were reported and, by the turn of the twentieth century, crime news had become a staple feature of the popular press. The railways had made it possible to quickly distribute large quantities of newspapers over wide areas and, from the 1840s, London newspapers had been distributed across the country on the day of publication.[5] The first 'newspaper train' had been commissioned in August 1845 by *The Times* and, by 1875, *The Times* was running specially equipped trains to transport its papers across the country.[6] Other newspapers soon followed suit, and W.H. Smith emerged as a leading distributor and newsvendor. The Victorians regarded crime, both fictional and real-life, as a form of entertainment and many popular leisure activities centred around representations of crime, particularly murder.

The reporting of crime was heavily sensationalised, and early accounts were often exaggerated and inaccurate. Although it would be some years before journalist Eric Pooley would coin the phrase 'If it bleeds, it leads', in reference to the prominent news coverage and sensational reporting of gory crime stories, the phrase was never truer than in the Victorian era of newspaper reporting.

During the latter part of the nineteenth century, journalists and police detectives had developed strong links and interdependencies that helped them to perform their respective duties. This reciprocal relationship was at times uneasy and was often marked by tension and conflict.[7] When the police failed to solve the Whitechapel murders in the late 1880s, the press had adopted an approach of alternately blaming and praising – lashing out at detectives when they failed to solve a case and praising them when they were successful.[8] At around the same time, the police became more reticent in sharing information about ongoing investigations, which often resulted in journalists employing less conventional ways of information gathering. In their search for clues and information, reporters 'interviewed witnesses, bystanders and anybody who could provide details; followed detectives at work, used informers and speculated about suspects'.[9] Some journalists assumed the role of detective and conducted their own investigations, and others insinuated that they themselves could crack the crime if they had all the information.[10]

By the end of that week, the more factual accounts of the crime, which had quickly been dubbed the 'Yarmouth Beach Murder' by the press, had been supplemented by a number of sensationalist reports. One newspaper reported that the 'meagre facts' of the case were being added to considerably and this became even more apparent when reports containing two distorted versions of the events began circulating. One account claimed that the body of the dead woman had been stabbed in numerous places and was smothered in blood when young John Norton had discovered it,[11] and another reported that the body had been 'shockingly mutilated after death'.[12] Both claims, which had begun to gain traction, were eventually debunked by the reporter for the *Star*, who, having attended the inquest, wrote that the medical examination had found that the only injuries (other than the bootlace) were relatively minor wounds to the face'.[13] By then, journalists were regularly attending coroners' court proceedings, as they were seen as a useful source of information. The scientific or medical expert testimony would not always, however, be used as a source of fact, but was at times used as an opportunity to sensationalise.[14] Court proceedings were often reported in detail, which at times proved problematic, even prejudicial, to subsequent trials.

Among the other reports that were published in the days following the murder was one that recounted a morbid event that had unfolded the previous summer, when a midnight attack on a woman by an unknown man had been interrupted by the woman's husband before the stranger could cause any physical harm. The man, panicking in the ensuing scuffle, had run into the sea and drowned. He was never identified.[15] The deep mystery surrounding these crimes led two newspapers to compare the murder of Mrs Hood to the 'complex detective stories' of the bestselling Victorian mystery novelist Fergus Hume:

> This latest [death] is no ordinary sensation, and has an element of mystery, perhaps of intrigue . . . In many respects it bears a close resemblance to those entertaining fictional problems . . . what better material could Fergus Hume or anyone else desire for some shilling 'shocker' to be entitled 'The Strangler of the Sea' or 'A Seashore Mystery'?[16]

Other reports likened the crime to a Sherlock Holmes mystery.[17] By this time, detective stories had emerged as a popular genre and newspapers had started to publish serialised fiction, which had first been introduced in the ordinary press in the 1870s, and had, by the end of the century, become a firm feature of the Sunday and daily newspapers. When one story concluded, another started in the same issue, a ploy used by newspaper editors to hook readers so that they would be compelled to buy the newspaper on a daily basis in order to read the next instalment. The serials had their roots in cheap fiction, namely the penny dreadfuls of the 1830s, adventure stories of pirates and highwaymen, and then, later, crime stories. One of the most notable of these penny dreadfuls was *The String of Pearls*, which was the literary debut for Sweeny Todd, 'the Demon Barber of Fleet Street'. The publication, which began in 1846, would later be adapted for the stage and eventually the screen. In 1891, the *Star* serialised British author Israel Zangwill's *The Big Bow Mystery*. The serial was met with great acclaim and is widely regarded as the first full-length locked-room mystery. In the same year, Arthur Conan Doyle began publishing his Sherlock Holmes detective stories in the *Strand* magazine. Conan Doyle took a keen interest in true crime and would go on to advocate the exoneration of two men convicted of crimes, whom he believed to be innocent.

Mrs Hood's murder was reported for the first time in the Sunday newspapers exactly a week after her death. By then, Sunday papers had become known for their mix of crime, scandal and sensationalism. They outsold the London dailies by some margin. Readership likely surpassed circulation, as the working-classes regularly pooled resources to buy and share newspapers, particularly on a Sunday, which was the only day of leisure for many working people. *Lloyd's Weekly Newspaper* was the most popular of the Sunday papers, and by 1886, 50 per cent of stories in the newspaper comprised murder, crime and other thrilling events.[18]

On Sunday, 30 September, the *Yarmouth Mercury* and the *Yarmouth Independent*, two local newspapers, printed halftone reproductions of the beach photograph and Sayers' image of the spot on the beach where the body had been found. The photographs were accompanied by detailed reports of the evidence given at the inquest. The cost of printing images was high, and many of the London newspapers had been slow to adopt the new technology. By the early twentieth century, the halftone process was being used on high-speed rotary presses, and by 1903, the telegraphic transmission of photographs would be possible. In 1904, the *Daily Mirror* would become the first daily newspaper to feature photographs on its front and back pages and in the centre spread, paving the way for the age of photojournalism.[19]

Unable to reproduce the photographs in a legible form, the London newspapers printed rudimentary line drawings, which were intended to represent the victim and the crime scene. They were in no way faithful to the originals.

By 1900, the *Weekly Dispatch* – established almost a century earlier – had become well known for its crude representations of crime. Like many of the other newspapers that reported on the Yarmouth Beach Murder, the '*Dispatch*', as it was known, published crude sketches of the dead woman alongside sensational accounts of the crime. It was the only newspaper, however, to offer its readers a reward for information concerning the identity of either the deceased woman or her child. A sum of £5 for the 'payment of expenses incurred' was proposed: 'If this woman can be identified,' the report stated, 'the arrest of her murderer is but a question of time.'[20]

As a result of the extensive newspaper coverage, the police received enquiries from across the country, including from three men whose wives were missing.

> A man in London who had missed his wife and child, was absolutely sure that [the] deceased must be the former – but on examining the photograph at Scotland Yard, he had to confess there was no likeness. On Wednesday, a man came down from Woolwich with some similar suspicion in his mind – but that suspicion faded when he saw the gruesome form in the mortuary.[21]

6

CALL IN SCOTLAND YARD!

'No one has come forward to claim her'

By mid-October, Chief Constable Parker had concluded that the local police force was not making sufficient headway in resolving the case and decided to call in Scotland Yard.

The Yarmouth Beach Murder case was assigned to Chief Inspector Alfred Leach of the Criminal Investigation Department (CID). Leach was a hard-working officer with over twenty-six years' experience. He had joined a long line of family members who had been upholding the law for over 100 years. Leach lived in Islington, inner London, with his wife, Sarah, and their six children. The eldest, Charles, then aged nineteen, would later claim to have been 'employed' by his father as a child to tail men that he was 'interested' in. At aged twelve, claimed Charles, he was forced to 'pace the streets ... from early morning until close on midnight with neither food nor the wherewithal to purchase it',[1] because of his father's gruelling work schedule. Leach was assisted by a team of officers, including fellow Yard detective Gummer. The officers quickly established that there were two key pieces of evidence that warranted further investigation: the 599 mark – by now identified as a laundry mark, and Mrs Hood's mysterious voyage to South Africa. Chief Constable Parker had done little to investigate either.

At around the time the Scotland Yard officers were launching their enquiries in London, the inquest was reopening in Great Yarmouth. No progress had been made in identifying the woman, or her assailant, and the coroner was now forced to relay this news to the small group that was gathered in the town hall courtroom. 'Despite persistent enquiries by the police,' Tolver-Walters said, 'nothing has been discovered that could throw fresh light on the woman's death, no further letters have come for her and no one has come forward to claim her as a friend, relative or acquaintance.' The coroner then proceeded to read over the depositions of the witnesses. Finally, turning to the jury, with George Norton again at the fore, he asked them to consider their verdict. It took less than a minute for them to agree on an open verdict of 'wilful murder against some person or persons unknown'. As George Norton delivered the verdict, Mr Tolver-Walters nodded his head in agreement. 'It will be left to the police to continue their enquiries,' he said, 'and I only hope that the man – if he could be called a man – who has committed this foul and brutal crime will be speedily brought to justice.'[2]

'What of the woman's child?' a juryman asked.

'The deceased's child remains with the Rudrums,' replied the coroner, 'but she will probably ultimately be sent to a Home – I have already received a letter from an institution.' At the time, orphaned children who were not otherwise claimed by relatives usually ended up in the workhouse or a similar institution. Some children benefited from educational schemes that were designed to teach them a trade or to prepare them for service. It was not an easy life and Rose's future was uncertain.

The press reported that the inquest had closed under as dense an atmosphere of mystery as it had begun and returned to the capital.

Back in London, the police were making systematic enquiries at laundries across the city. During the latter half of the nineteenth century, there had been a massive expansion in the demand for laundry services – a consequence of the enormous growth in the country's service industry and infrastructure. To meet the demand, laundries had sprung up across the country and the number of laundry workers had grown from 167,607 in 1861 to around 200,000 by the turn of the century.[3] It was arduous work that was traditionally considered women's labour.

Leach had instructed his officers to start their search for the laundry mark in Woolwich, due to the postmark on the blue envelope. They identified many customers across a number of laundries who had been assigned the number 599. Each person – including current and former domestic servants who shared the mark with their employers – had to be traced and eliminated from their enquiries. Progress was slow. When the police had exhausted all of the Woolwich laundries, they were ordered to fan out to the neighbouring districts. The London outgrowth of Bexley was assigned to fifty-four-year-old Detective Sergeant Bartle. Following intensive investigations at Bexley's nine laundries, DS Bartle found that only one used the number 599: Kingdom's Laundry on the Broadway, Bexley Heath's main High Street. The proprietor was a man named Mr John Savage.

When DS Bartle eventually called in to Kingdom's Laundry, he was carrying a photograph of the laundry mark, which had been reproduced from an item of the child's linen, after Mrs Hood had been buried in the only piece of clothing she owned that had borne the mark: her bloodstained chemise. He also carried a copy of the beach photograph. When DS Bartle enquired after the owner, he was told that Mr Savage was not there, but was instead referred to the manageress. She was unable to identify either the mark or the photograph. DS Bartle asked if they had a customer named 'Hood' with the requisite number who had recently stopped sending in washing. The manageress explained that the only customer assigned the number 599 was a Mrs Bennett, of number 1, Glencoe Villas, Bexley Heath (now Bexleyheath). Looking at her records, Mrs Bennett had been sending in washing every week, as usual. Convinced that Kingdom's customer was not the woman he was enquiring after, DS Bartle left. He made his report and thought no more of it.

At around the same time, a newspaper published a facsimile of the 599 laundry mark, alongside a crude sketch of the brooch with the 'Baby' engraving and the latchkey that were found among Mrs Hood's possessions at the Rudrums' lodging house. The report implored readers 'who are in any way connected with laundry work to carefully examine their books and find if they have a customer whose clothing would be numbered 599'.[4]

While DS Bartle was investigating the laundries, other officers were scrutinising passenger lists from ships to and from South Africa for people named Hood. It was laborious work, but the officers ploughed on methodically. They had traced and accounted for a number of 'Hoods' before at last coming to a Mr and Mrs Hood who had sailed to Cape Town on the *Gaika* on 17 March 1900. When initial searches to locate the couple failed, detectives questioned several employees of the Union-Castle Steamship Company. One – a clerk in the accountants' department, named Walter Penton – remembered Mr and Mrs Hood. In fact, Penton not only remembered the Hoods, but he also recalled that Mr Hood had an old label on his portmanteau that had been partly torn to reveal the name 'Bennett' written in pencil underneath. The Union-Castle Steamship Company put the police in touch with Jacob & Co. passenger agents, the travel agency who had sold the Hoods their tickets. The sale was traced back to an employee named Henry Finch, who was questioned and recalled selling two tickets for the *Gaika* on 7 March, which had been booked in the name of Mr and Mrs Hood. The tickets had been priced at £48. 6s., and had been paid for in seven £5 notes, one £10 note and some coins. Finch had kept a record of the numbers of the banknotes, and they were duly traced back to the Woolwich branch of Lloyds Bank. Records showed that the cash had been withdrawn on 23 February by a man named Bennett.

The repeated occurrence of the name Bennett in connection with the mystery prompted Leach to order a fresh investigation into the woman named 'Bennett' in Bexley Heath. DS Bartle was dispatched to Kingdom's Laundry in Bexley Heath for a repeat visit and this time he spoke to the owner, Mr Savage.

Shown a copy of the beach photograph, Mr Savage immediately exclaimed, 'Why, that is Mrs Bennett!'

24, DOCK ROW

'He was always a good boy'

The laundry proprietor explained to the police that Mrs Bennett had been away since mid-September. At that time, there had been a break in the washing, but laundry had started coming in again at the end of September. Instead of women's and child's clothes, men's collars and shirts were sent in from a number of locations, including Woolwich. Mr Savage explained that, by some extraordinary coincidence, he and his wife had lived next door to Mrs Bennett and her daughter, *Ruby*, until 25 September – ten days after Mrs Bennett had gone away on holiday.

The unfortunate 'Mrs Hood' was in fact Mary Jane Bennett, a married woman last known to be residing in Bexley Heath, Kent. Sensing a new chapter was about to unfold in the saga, the press quickly relit the dying embers of the story and within days, the Bennetts' affairs had been splashed across the newspapers.

Mary Jane Bennett was born on 28 August 1877 (the year Queen Victoria was proclaimed Empress of India) to a young couple named William and Mary Ann Clark.[1] The family lived in Bow Street, East London, close to the local cement works where William worked as a labourer until two months after Mary Jane was born. At that point, her mother, Mary Ann, left the family home under mysterious circumstances and never returned. She was later thought to have been living with another man. Struggling to cope, William handed his infant daughter over to her grandparents, his mother, Amy Elizabeth Edwards and Amy's husband, Edward.[2] At the time, working men were not expected to undertake the sole care of small children, so the offspring of absentee or deceased mothers were often left with relations, or even committed to the care of the local workhouse.[3]

For a number of years following, William worked on board a ship, first as a deckhand and then as a steward. He saw very little of his daughter during her formative years. When he eventually returned to land, he rejoined the manual working classes as a bricklayer in London. Large-scale building operations were in full swing across the capital, particularly in Streatham, and demand for manual labourers had increased. By 1885, William had a new 'wife' named Selina, and an infant son named William Charles. Mary Jane was eight years old and had been informally adopted by her grandparents.[4] Mary Jane's grandfather, Edward, a carpenter and joiner by trade, now owned a butcher's shop in Northfleet, a small town in the borough of Gravesend. The Edwards family lived above the shop, which stood at 24, Dock Row.

Edward was a keen musician and encouraged Mary Jane's interest in both the violin and the pianoforte. As a young girl, she was taught music and quickly developed a talent for performing. In her youth, she played as a soloist at a number of concert halls, including the Prince of Wales Theatre of Varieties in Gravesend. The theatre, which occupied a prime position on Harmer Street, was close to the River Thames and boasted a 'handsome auditorium, with pit and gallery floors, private boxes and an excellent stage and dressing room'.[5] For Mary Jane, it was a world away from playing music in her grandparents' flat above the butcher's shop, and it must – at least initially – have been a very daunting experience. The tuition Mary Jane received was intensive: when she was not playing one instrument, she was playing the other.

William always spoke proudly of his daughter's musical achievements. Although he and Mary Jane had reconnected, their relationship remained strained. In an attempt to demonstrate his regard for her, William brought Mary Jane a small silver pocket watch for her twelfth birthday. At the time, he was living in West London with Selina and their three children but working in Poplar. He purchased the watch from a pawnbroker named Josef Hall in East India Dock Road. The watch cost £1 – which was no small sum in 1889, particularly for a labourer – and was paid for in instalments: 6d. a week for 40 weeks. Mary Jane was suitably impressed by the gesture and took great pride in wearing the watch.

By the time she was eighteen, Mary Jane was an established teacher of music. She had become an enterprising young woman, who made money in her own right at a time when society expected women to be dependent. Her lessons cost 9d. an hour and took place in her grandmother's front parlour above the butcher's shop. Edward Edwards had by now died, leaving his wife to run the business. William occasionally visited his mother and daughter but spent most of his spare time with his new family in West London – but Mary Jane loved her grandmother and Amy held a deep affection for her granddaughter.

This was the year Mary Jane met her future husband. Sixteen-year-old Herbert John Bennett worked as a shop assistant at the Northfleet branch of the Royal Arsenal Co-operative Society (RACS), where he made 14*s.* a week.[6] It was a rather meagre wage; Mary Jane had only to teach for nineteen hours a week to earn the same amount. Also working at the Co-operative stores at that time was Herbert's good friend, William Parritt, who was the twenty-two-year-old eldest son of a local painter and paper hanger. Both he and Herbert had noticed the petite young woman who visited the stores at the behest of her grandmother and were soon vying for her attention. Herbert, who was six years Parritt's junior, was far more assertive than his more introverted friend, and he had soon charmed his way into Mary Jane's affections.

The young couple's initial meetings were conducted in secret, but it was not long before Herbert had convinced his young sweetheart to allow him to pose as one of her students so that he could be alone with her. Mary Jane charged him a reduced price of 6*d.* an hour instead of the usual 9*d.* Herbert took up the violin, an instrument that would have an ongoing significance for the couple. He would never become proficient, presumably because so little of his 'music lesson' was spent actually learning music.

Herbert John Bennett was the eldest son of John Jarvis Bennett, who worked as a labourer at one of the local cement manufacturing plants, whose tall chimneys and black smoke dominated the district. For most of his working life, John had been employed by Portland cement works in Swanscombe, J.B. White & Brothers, often known as 'White's Works'. The company was the longest operating cement works in Swanscombe and one of the biggest in the UK. The Bennett family were of modest means, and lived in a small cottage in Bloomfield Road, Galley Hill, in the parish of Swanscombe, about two miles west of Northfleet. A news reporter would describe the place as 'dreary and desolate ... perched right on the top of a mighty hill, where the wind blows in tornados and the rain makes the road impassable in winter'.[7]

Herbert, who was born on 9 August 1879 in Stone, Kent, had led a much more conventional life in childhood than Mary Jane. He lived with his parents, John and Hannah, and three younger siblings, Henry, Rosalind and Mabel. As was customary at the time, the Bennetts took in boarders to supplement John's wages. Herbert got on well with his two sisters, but there were tensions between him and his brother, who was two years younger. Henry was named after the boys' maternal grandfather, Henry Simmons, who lived next door with his wife, Susan, and their three children.

As a boy, Herbert attended the local National School. Schooling had been compulsory since 1876, and the network of National Schools had been established by the Anglican Church, primarily for families who could not afford to pay for their children's education. Despite holding the position of class monitor – the highest rank in the school – Herbert was later described by his headmaster, Mr Legg, as 'in no way distinguished beyond the rest of his fellow pupils, either on account of his good or bad conduct'.[8] According to his father, the young Herbert was quite agreeable at home: 'He was always a good boy . . . I never remember having any serious quarrel with him.'[9] Herbert left school at thirteen and delivered papers locally before finding employment at the Co-operative stores in Northfleet, where his father was a member.

In the winter of 1896, Herbert's life changed for ever when his beloved mother, Hannah, died at the age of thirty-five. According to John Bennett, 'She just fell over in the kitchen one day and was dead.'[10] Naturally, her death came as quite a shock to the young Herbert.

By now, Herbert and Mary Jane had been holding clandestine meetings for over a year and had become secretly engaged. Herbert knew there was little chance that his father would agree to the marriage because of his paltry wage, which was not enough to support a family, so the couple continued to meet in secret all through the rest of that year and into the next. In the spring of 1897, Mary Jane suddenly found herself pregnant. In the nineteenth century, the freedom of behaviour within male/female relationships was determined by one element: the 'promise of marriage'. It was only under these circumstances that pre-marital sexual relations were considered slightly more acceptable.[11] An engagement bound a man by his word of honour but would only be official when the fiancé was introduced to the girl's family, and marriage was expected to follow swiftly.

With no choice but to tell her grandmother about the pregnancy, Mary Jane confessed to the engagement. Amy and Mary Jane's father, William – neither one a stranger to the then-unfortunate circumstance of an unwed mother – quickly agreed to the marriage. William, whose surname was his mother's maiden name, had been born out of wedlock himself, and he was, at that time, 'living in sin' with Selina, unable to remarry because he had no idea whether his wife was alive or dead. At the time, separation among working-class couples was not uncommon. Divorce was legal, but expensive – and was impossible for those who were the object of desertion. Most working-class couples turned, instead, to 'irregular unions', choosing to cohabit with new partners. It was common for a woman in these circumstances to adopt the name of her common law husband in an attempt to protect her respectability.

Tradition dictated that marriages were celebrated in the woman's parish, and so, on the first Sunday of July 1897, the wedding banns were read at the Northfleet chapel. Herbert was still concealing his impending nuptials from his family and hoped that the reading of the banns in a different district from his own home would go unnoticed by his father. Unfortunately for him, John learned of the proposed marriage and went to the church on the second Sunday of 'asking' in order to stop the banns[12] – 'My reasons were good enough,' he said; 'it was absurd for the boy to marry, for he was only just 18,[13] and the wages he was getting were no more than 14s. a week. Think of marrying on that!'[14]

But Herbert Bennett was a determined and resourceful young man. He moved out of his father's house and took lodgings at number 1, Addison Road, Tidal Basin – in the heart of the Royal Victoria Docks – where he was joined by Mary Jane. The couple applied for a marriage licence from their new address and were married at Leytonstone Register Office on 22 July 1897. On the marriage certificate, Herbert overstated his age by four years, and – in the ultimate act of defiance against his father – he registered John as 'deceased'. The marriage was witnessed by William and Selina, both of whom signed the official register as 'Clark'.

Contrary to his father's assertion, Herbert turned eighteen the following month. Despite his boyish features he could easily pass for twenty-one. Mary Jane, who had just turned twenty, also looked older than her years. Herbert was a tall, thin young man with dark-brown wavy hair that he combed into a quiff. He had brown eyes and his ears were rather large and 'unshapely'.[15] He was never able to grow much facial hair apart from a rather 'insipid moustache'. Appearance was important to them both and they shared a particular fondness for fashionable clothing. Herbert insisted on wearing crisp white shirts – despite the dirty work of his trade – no doubt because they were the mark of a gentleman. It was likely that he had decided that the working man's equivalent – a checked or striped shirt – was not for him.

Having exhausted their meagre savings on renting the small dwelling in Addison Road, the newlyweds moved back to Dock Row to live with Amy. Shortly afterwards, Herbert lost his job at the Co-operative stores. Free from the obligation of having to provide for his family, thanks to Amy's hospitality, Herbert spent most of his days pottering around the Northfleet marshes with a rifle, taking pot-shots at small animals. Despite being heavily pregnant, Mary Jane continued to teach music, until the November, when the child that had necessitated the marriage was stillborn. By early 1898, Mary Jane had conceived again. Life continued at a similar pace until 10 June that year, when Amy Edwards died. Mary Jane was shattered by the loss of her grandmother and entered a deep state of mourning. Societal expectations for mourning had been set almost four decades earlier by Queen Victoria herself following the death of her beloved husband, Prince Albert, who had died in the winter of 1861, at the age of forty-two. Queen Victoria had entered a two-year period of mourning and subsequently wore black for the rest of her life. Along with the pea-soup fog and harsh shadows cast in the gaslit streets, Queen Victoria's bleak dress code epitomises the darker side of the Victorian era, a side that Mary Jane and Herbert would soon come close to experiencing for themselves.

VIOLINS AND VIOLENCE

'They were in great straits . . . they couldn't make a living'¹

I t quickly transpired that Amy had bequeathed the butcher's shop premises and most of the furniture to her son. William, who had long considered his son-in-law a layabout, promptly evicted the young Bennetts. William, by now forty-seven, would have viewed taking on his mother's business as an opportunity to escape the back-breaking work of a labourer and the constant money worries that were so entrenched in the lives of many working-class people.

The Bennetts, however, were barely a year into their marriage, homeless and in dire need of money. Mary Jane was five months pregnant, and William's apparent indifference to the couple's plight marked a decline in her relationship with her father, which would never recover. Amy had left Mary Jane a modest sum of money, precisely £15, which they used to rent a small house in Stockwood Street, a dingy thoroughfare off Plough Street, near Clapham Junction. It was in 'down at heels' Battersea, in the London borough of Wandsworth. The ground floor had been converted into a makeshift shop selling coal, fruit, vegetables, sweets and other articles. Amy had also left her granddaughter the piano, a valuable antique violin, a few trinkets and sticks of furniture and a solid gold chain. William gave his daughter the necklace the week after Amy died but refused to give up the piano and furniture until the couple had settled into a suitable new home.

Herbert, thus far free from the burden of traditional husbandly duty, suddenly found himself solely responsible for the upkeep of a family. He did not adapt well, and the couple quickly fell on hard times. Home life was not as Herbert had imagined, and he did not like being tied down. Born out of this resentment came a spark of volatility that was set to weave its way through the Bennetts' relationship. Herbert begrudged being forced back into work, and it soon became apparent that his idle nature did not lend itself well to running a business. He constantly complained about the need to get up at four o'clock each morning to buy produce from the markets, and he soon gave up the 'beastly nuisance' altogether, opting instead to buy second-hand from a local wholesaler. The additional expenditure incurred through this practice quickly ate into the takings, and the shop, which had been turning a profit before the Bennetts took it on, fell into decline. The Bennetts had also started losing customers thanks to the shop's erratic opening hours – one day it would be open, and the next it was closed, sometimes for a day or two, sometimes more. To help with their struggling finances, Mary Jane attempted to relaunch her music lessons, but her advertisements went unanswered.

Around this time, the Bennetts became friendly with a couple named Mr and Mrs Gregory, who lived opposite. Mrs Gregory would later recall the circumstances the Bennetts were living under at the time. 'They were in great straits,' she said; '. . . although Mrs Bennett used to go out with the cart, they couldn't make a living. Mr Bennett used to say he didn't know what he would do, and at one time talked of going to work as a carman [delivery driver].'[2]

Meanwhile, William had taken over the butcher's business and now lived in the apartments above the shop with his family. They certainly seemed to take to their new surroundings, and would even name their sixth child – Royal Charlotte Victoria Clark – after the hotel at the end of the road.[3] The couple's eldest, William Jr, now thirteen, was living with Mary Jane and Herbert, and had been put to work in the greengrocer's. Perhaps 'lending' his son to Mary Jane and Herbert was William Sr's way of helping the young Bennetts out. It was not, however, an easy life for William Jr. He witnessed many a stormy scene take place between his half-sister and his brother-in-law, and he would often find Mary Jane crying and unhappy at the way her husband was treating her.[4] William Jr claimed that Herbert had prevented him from going home to his father, and on one occasion he witnessed Herbert smack his sister in the face. Afterwards, Mrs Gregory noticed that Mary Jane had a black eye, but the young woman told her that she had fallen down the stairs. William Jr also witnessed Herbert point a revolver at his wife's face and then pull the trigger while knowing that one of the barrels was loaded. Terrified, William Jr begged Herbert to give the weapon up and eventually rushed at him, turning the revolver away before the loaded barrel could reach the trigger point.

Running out of ideas to save his ailing shop, Herbert decided to claim the valuable piano that Mary Jane had been left by her grandmother, and he travelled to Northfleet with the intention of persuading his father-in-law to give it up. William refused. His reasons were just: he knew that his son-in-law was in poor circumstances and suspected that he only wanted the piano so he could sell it to make some money. Herbert refused to leave without it, and the situation quickly turned violent.

Suddenly, Herbert pulled a revolver out of the pocket of his waistcoat and pointed it at his father-in-law. 'Look here, this is what I have brought down especially for you!' he shouted in a rage.[5] The quarrel brought Selina rushing into the room. She at once seized Herbert and, with William's help, managed to overpower him. When they eventually released him, however, Herbert was still bent on shooting his father-in-law. William fled to his bedroom, where he quickly slammed the door and pulled the bolt. Herbert waited for some time, revolver in hand, for William to come out. Eventually, he grew tired and went away. Shaken by the ordeal, William went to the magistrate to obtain a warrant against his son-in-law.

The Bennetts' circumstances had become desperate. Back in Battersea, the couple lost most of their possessions before eventually losing their business, which was sold for the price of the fixtures.[6] Herbert was forced to take work at Johnson's, a local provision shop. By this point, Mary Jane was heavily pregnant, and had started to worry about the birth of her baby. Acting on advice from Mrs Gregory, she joined a dispensary 'so that she would not have a doctor's bill to pay'. Dispensaries were charitable organisations that provided free medical care for the poor. To join as a free member would have brought with it a significant social stigma. Mary Jane, in particular, would have found this change in domestic circumstances very difficult to adapt to when she had, up until now, lived her life in relative comfort. She would inevitably have worried about bringing a child into the world when its parents were teetering on the edge of poverty. The following year, Arthur L. Baxter, who was assisting Charles Booth in his survey of London's working class, would visit Stockwood Street and describe it as awash with 'drunken, rowdy and troublesome people', displaying firm signs of squalor and litter in the streets.[7] If by 1898 it was not already there, it was well on its way to becoming one of the 'lowest class, vicious and semi-criminal' streets in Victorian England.[8]

However, just before the baby was born, the Bennetts moved into a £30-per-year flat at 216, Wandsworth Bridge Road.[9] Their sudden rise in circumstances left many people, including the Gregorys, puzzled. One of the first things the Bennetts did was engage the services of a private doctor, a local man by the name of Dr Townsend Barker. The doctor called on them at least once in the weeks preceding the birth of the baby. They were so

keen to keep their mysterious change in fortune quiet from Herbert's employer that, when the doctor had occasion to write out a certificate, Mary
Jane stopped him from writing the Wandsworth Bridge Road address.[10]
A short time later, Dr Townsend Barker attended Mary Jane's labour, and
the baby – a girl – was born without complications on 13 October 1898, and
later christened Ruby Elizabeth Bennett.

Not long after the baby was born, Herbert's father remarried. Mary
Jane, who had a naturally endearing character, got on considerably well
with her husband's new stepmother, also called Selina, and took to calling
her 'Ma'. Herbert, on the other hand, resented his father for remarrying
and immediately took against his stepmother.

The Bennetts' new address was in the London borough of Hammer-
smith and Fulham. Despite the necessary journey across the river from
Stockwood Street, Mrs Gregory continued to visit Mary Jane. It was on
one of these occasions that she discovered where the Bennetts' money was
coming from – they were trading in violins. Although the Bennetts' desire
to escape the destitution of Stockwood Street was understandable, it appears that they were willing to do it by any means possible. It is likely that
the idea to sell violins had come from Mary Jane. As a music teacher, she
was known to have sold the odd instrument to make a bit of extra money.
At that time, her intentions would have been fairly honourable. This new
venture, however, was far from honest.

The couple bought cheap violins and mis-advertised them as antiques
to inflate the prices. Mary Jane's musical knowledge helped convince many
customers that the violins were worth much more than they actually were.
When selling the instruments, she would pose as a vulnerable and desperate woman on the brink of destitution, an 'orphan', a 'young widow, selling
the last relic of her late husband for bread', a 'musical student, driven to sell
her violin to pay the rent' or a 'clergy man's daughter'.[11] The shop windows
that had previously been home to adverts touting for violin students were
now awash with 'for sale' ads, and before long, advertisements started pop-
ping up in the *Exchange and Mart*:

> Widow lady offers fine old violin, bow, case, strings, tuning fork, chin rest,
> &c, property deceased professor. Worth £10; accept 19/6 if immediate. Ap-
> proval. Mrs. B., c/o Lee, Culmore-rd, Balham.[12]

Herbert purchased their stock in bulk from Woolf's wholesale store,
buying twenty or thirty violins at a time for 4*s*. 6*d*. each. The couple sold

them for an average of 30s. each. At the peak of their sales, the Bennetts were reportedly making £5 or £6 a day.[13,14] Herbert endeavoured to keep a job alongside the violin trade but failed to keep up the pretence that his shop work was the main source of his income. He carried around small bags of gold, boasting to his friends about the money he was earning. 'Why do you work so hard?' he would ask. 'Why don't you do as I do? I can always lay my hand on £1,200 or so when I want it.'[15] The violin trade suited Herbert perfectly. It required limited effort, and he made far more money than he would ever have made from honest work.

In April 1899, the Bennetts left their lodgings in Wandsworth Bridge Road and moved back across the river to 23a Geddes Road, East Hill. They were within close proximity of their previous two addresses, which suggests that Herbert was still working at Mr Johnson's provision store at the time. They stayed for six months before moving to Rossiter Road, in the adjacent neighbourhood of Balham. Here, they rented two ground-floor rooms in a bow-fronted house from a woman named Mrs Susan Kato.[16] Her husband, Edgar, hailed from Sweden and worked as a tailor. The couple had three young children, all under five. Mrs Kato had very fair hair – much like Mary Jane's – and a reputation for being a sycophant.

By now, Herbert had worked out that he could obtain violins and other goods on credit and disappear with the merchandise and any profits from the sales before his creditors realised and demanded payment. The Bennetts were still dealing primarily in violins, but Mrs Kato believed that their business transactions extended to jewellery, furniture and pianos. Trade was good, and the couple were making a great deal of money. Mary Jane openly gossiped with Mrs Kato about the couple's business, and it appears that she also confided in her extensively about other personal matters. Clearly believing that she held the moral high ground, Mrs Kato objected to the deceitful nature of the business, and Mary Jane agreed that she felt 'a bit sorry for the fools' she had taken money from. Despite this, it seems she was ultimately willing to go along with the schemes as they paid for the comfortable life to which she had become accustomed.

Herbert, on the other hand, displayed no remorse. By now, he had given up waiting for customers to come to him and spent his spare time scouring the 'wanted' columns of the *Exchange and Mart* for the addresses of people who were looking to purchase musical instruments. He then sent his wife to their lodgings, offering a violin for sale. On some days, Mary Jane would go out laden with as many as half a dozen instruments and would rarely return with one unsold. Their advertisements had continued to appear in the *Exchange and Mart* on an almost weekly basis since the previous year, under a series of different names and accommodation addresses. Sometimes Mary Jane was Mrs B., Mrs X.B., and then Mrs W. and Mrs McD. Herbert also placed ads – boldly using his own name and address – in *Lloyd's Weekly Newspaper*, a popular Sunday newspaper, which dedicated around half of its editorial space to advertisements:

> VIOLIN – Excellent Strad model; cost £7. 7s. od.; suit professional; in 10s. 6d. case, with 12s. 6d. artiste's bow and 5s. tutor; must sell; cash needed; sacrifice 25s.; no rubbish. Grand bargain; approval anywhere – W. Bennett, Ullswater, Rossiter Road, Balham, Surrey.[17]

According to Mrs Kato, Mary Jane had 'the most to do' with the business, and she claimed that her lodger had once told her that a male friend saved her from getting into trouble for trading as a single woman. 'I asked her if her husband knew anything about this man,' Mrs Kato recalled, 'and she said, "oh no". She then added, rather cryptically, that Bennett was jealous of her "brother-in-law".'[18]

Mrs Kato always spoke critically of Mary Jane. She described her lodger as a 'loveable little creature' but claimed that she lacked the habits of a 'good wife'. At the time, many women derived pride and self-esteem from the way they managed their households, and their domestic behaviour was strongly implicated in working-class constructions of respectability.[19] Any woman who was thought to have failed in her role of wife or mother was thought to have failed in life. Mary Jane was, admittedly, ill-prepared for the responsibility of running a household. Most working-class girls of the time gained domestic experience by lending a 'helping hand' to their mothers or by entering into domestic service for a few years before marriage. Growing up in her grandparents' house as an only child, Mary Jane would not have developed any of the essential skills – cooking, cleaning, mending, looking after children – that were considered to be characteristic of a 'decent' wife.

As an example of Mary Jane's failure to properly care for her husband, Mrs Kato would later recall a time when she had attempted to teach her how to make a poultice – a warm mass of material made with crushed linseed – to treat Herbert's foot, which had become sore and inflamed. Mrs Kato soon became frustrated with Mary Jane's ineptitude and dressed Herbert's toe herself. The landlady also complained that Mary Jane did not take good enough care of her baby, claiming that the child's condition was 'filthy'. Mrs Kato clearly considered herself to be the superior wife and mother and would certainly have made Mary Jane's 'shortcomings' known to her. As motherhood and the ability to be a 'good' wife were major structuring forces within the lives of working-class women – and a vital component in the construction of contemporary feminine virtues – Mary Jane would, no doubt, have felt these criticisms keenly.[20]

It was around this time that significant cracks began to appear in the Bennetts' relationship. Mary Jane had apparently become consumed with doubt over the legality of her marriage – 'she told me her husband was only seventeen when they married, although he had pretended to be four years older. She said the certificate had been signed by a woman with a false name,' said Mrs Kato.

It appears that Herbert also confided in his landlady: 'I remember Bennett saying he would be better off living in lodgings,' Mrs Kato recalled. 'He asked me what I thought a woman could comfortably live on alone.' According to the Poor Law, the upkeep of a woman was the responsibility of her husband and if an able-bodied man refused to pay for his wife's maintenance, the poor law guardians would seek to recover the costs.[21]

Herbert was then employed as 'first bacon hand' at J. Sainsbury of 87–89 High Road, Balham, where he made 30s. per week (more than double what he had been earning as a shop assistant at the Northfleet Co-operative). He had taken to bartering with his colleagues and had become a keen gambler. He regularly absconded from work, and his absences were generally found to coincide with big race meetings that were taking place within easy reach of London. Herbert found it difficult to maintain the motivation for his 'day job' and was dismissed following a period of absence, less than two months after starting in the role.

The Bennetts spent Christmas 1899 with Herbert's family in Swanscombe. It was Ruby's second Christmas and – at just over a year old – she would have had her first taste of Christmas dinner. That year, the Royal Family dined on woodcock pie, roast beef, chine of pork and boar's head. The Bennetts' meal would have been a considerably pared-down affair, but they may have, like the Royals, indulged in plum pudding – a rich, heavily fruited dessert, inspired by Prince Albert's German childhood. At this point, the Bennett family appear to have been on fairly good terms. Herbert's once-simmering animosity towards his stepmother had significantly subsided – or was at least put to one side for the festivities. Mary Jane was, by now, estranged from her own family, due to her husband's broken relationship with her father. As a consequence, she would have sought to make positive connections with Herbert's family so that she had some support raising her child.

Mary Jane and Herbert returned to Rossiter Road with Ruby in time for the New Year. Herbert began discussing plans to open a music shop in the small town of Taunton in Somerset and, by the end of the month, the Bennetts had moved out of the Katos' house. They left a forwarding address of 5 Morecambe Terrace, Taunton. The music shop idea was presumably Herbert's way of throwing Mrs Kato (and anyone else who would be interested to learn where the Bennetts had moved to) off their scent. It would appear that Herbert was right to be cautious – letters supposedly 'poured in' for the Bennetts after they left, from people they had allegedly swindled. Some were from firms of Birmingham jewellers still looking for the samples of stock that Herbert had taken from them and never returned.[22]

Unsurprisingly, the Bennetts did not go to Somerset. Instead, they travelled to Westgate-on-Sea, a seaside town in northeast Kent, where they had purchased a greengrocer's from a man named Theodore Murton. It was their chance at a fresh start, but wherever the Bennetts went, trouble was never too far behind . . .

9

A GRAVEYARD OF CANARIES AND A
CURIOUS CASE OF ARSON

'I require one lady's wig and one gentleman's, for private use'

Theodore Murton had recently been appointed chief of the fire brigade in the neighbouring town of Faversham and – no longer able to run his business – was offering it for sale for £545. Murton's Kent Supply Stores was advertised as a 'high class grocery and provision store'. Early in the new year, Herbert had contacted the agents to arrange a viewing. When he met Murton, he immediately asked how much the business was insured for. Murton was taken aback by the question – 'For the full valuation,' he replied – 'about £545'.

'You are underinsured,' declared Herbert. 'My furniture in London is insured for £800.'

After some negotiation, Murton agreed to accept £535 for the business. Herbert paid £375 upfront, by way of a cheque that was honoured by letter from the London manager of Lloyds Bank. The two men agreed that Herbert would pay the remaining £160 in two instalments over the ensuing six months. When the cheque had cleared, the lease, stock and insurance were duly transferred into Herbert's name. Murton's Kent Supply Stores offered the Bennetts the opportunity to start afresh and lead an honest life. Or so it would seem.

The shop – 5, Station Road – was one of a parade of shops situated a short walk from the Westgate-on-Sea railway station. It was well patronised when the Bennetts purchased it and they would likely have continued to trade well under Murton's good name. Murton had one shop assistant in his employ – a man named Seamark – whom Herbert kept on.

Almost as soon as they arrived in Westgate that January, Herbert hastily took out several insurance policies. One of these insured his furniture for £500 and another covered his produce against loss. He failed to pay the first instalment on the policy relating to his furniture, which immediately invalidated it.

On Thursday, 8 February, just over a week after the Bennetts arrived in Westgate-on-Sea, disaster struck. Seamark was preparing to leave work for the evening when he noticed that the gas fire was still lit. He called Herbert's attention to it, but he was told to go home. Shortly after Seamark left, Herbert and Mary Jane took Ruby out for a walk. At approximately 8.10 p.m., a fire ripped through the empty shop. Coincidentally, Captain Weston of the local fire brigade lived a few doors down from the store. He was at home when the fire broke out and reached the shop within minutes. By then it was well ablaze. The fire gutted the ground floor and caused extensive smoke damage throughout the property. The flat above the shop was spared, but the smoke suffocated most of the caged birds that had filled a large atrium on the top floor. Among the wrecked produce in the downstairs rooms were around forty to fifty violins and a large quantity of 'rather basic' furniture. The scene would later be described as a 'graveyard of canaries and burnt-out violins'.[1]

To say that Herbert reacted well to the news is an understatement. About an hour after the fire, he was seen drinking and singing at the local tradesmen's club. The circumstances surrounding the blaze immediately brought Herbert under suspicion of arson. As soon as the news of the fire reached Theodore Murton, he started his own investigation into the blaze. 'When I made my examinations,' he later recalled, 'husband and wife tried to tell me that the fire had broken out through a defective flue downstairs. But, with a fireman's eye, I saw that it had originated among a pile of rubbish swept under the counter.'[2] Undeterred by Murton's investigations, Herbert promptly made a claim to the Kent Fire Insurance Company for a reported £390.

A few days later, the Bennetts reopened their business. Capitalising on the sympathy of their patrons, they traded from a vacant shop next door to their burnt-out premises. They auctioned off their damaged stock for £107, before procuring additional produce on credit from several traders. They raised £250 by selling off their new produce and a further £50 from the sale of a horse and wagon and a piano belonging to Mary Jane. By the end of February, Herbert had raised £315 of the £375 he had paid out to Murton at the end of January, with £160 still owing. Anyone who witnessed the Bennetts' feverish attempts to make money from the ashes of their ruined business were likely to have applauded their resilience.

Following a thorough investigation into the fire, the Kent Fire Insurance Company concluded at the end of February that the fire was 'unsatisfactory'. However, given that there was not enough evidence to establish its origin, the company declined to take any further action and agreed to settle the claim for £208. Herbert promptly received a cheque. By mid-March, Herbert had made a profit of £240 on his original purchase.

Shortly after 6 a.m. on Saturday, 17 March, the Bennetts decamped, abandoning the charred shell of Murton's Kent Supply Stores. Naturally, they left no forwarding address. It did not take long for news of the Bennetts' departure to reach Theodore Murton, who went straight to the store. He let himself in and began picking through the detritus of his once-prosperous business. Among the possessions the Bennetts had left behind were several letters from Willy Clarkson, a London-based theatrical wig-maker and costumier. Murton wrote to Clarkson later that day and it soon became apparent that the Bennetts had been preparing to leave Westgate-on-Sea since the middle of the previous month. Herbert had first written to Clarkson five days after the fire, requesting a price list for ladies' and gentlemen's wigs. Herbert's letter, which Clarkson later passed to the press, was written on headed notepaper in a 'swift, flowing hand', with an engraved coat of arms and a grand claim that his shop was 'Patronised by H.R.H. the Duchess of Fife and the Duke of Fife':

> Dear Sir, – Yours to hand re wigs, etc. I require one lady's wig and one gentleman's for private use. Lady's wig to be done up in the latest fashion, blonde in colour; gentleman's black and curly, with parting at side, both of best hair and workmanship. Size of lady's head in circumference 21 In., size of gentleman's head in circumference 22 In. (own hair, hardly any).
>
> I should like you to give me an estimate for supplying me with these and also black moustache to match wig. Any further particulars you may require I shall be pleased to send.
>
> I hope you will give me your early attention, as I require them this week.
> Yours faithfully,
> H.J. Bennett.[3]

Then followed a letter from Mary Jane. She enclosed a lock of her own hair with a request that the lady's wig be made a shade lighter. A second letter instructed Clarkson to send the wigs and the moustache privately to the address provided, reinforcing the 'immediate' need for them, and a third countermanded this request, stating that Mrs Bennett would collect the order in person.

Mary Jane had collected the wigs on Tuesday, 6 March. Clarkson would later recall 'the petite blonde with the fair skin'[4] and her 'excessive delight' when she saw the wigs. When she had finished at Clarkson's, Mary Jane travelled to Swanscombe to meet Herbert and Ruby. They then called in on Herbert's family at Galley Hill. The visit was unexpected, as was Mary Jane's request. She asked Herbert's stepmother, Selina, if she would take Ruby for a month or two – 'Herbert and I have decided to go to America,' she explained. 'We have booked our passage on board the *Margetta*, which will sail on the 17th.' The request caught Selina unawares, but she agreed without hesitation. At the time, Herbert's brother, Henry (eighteen), and sister, Mabel (fifteen), were still living in the house, but Selina had no children of her own, so was likely to have welcomed the opportunity to care for her stepson's young daughter. As Mary Jane was preparing to leave, she asked Selina, 'If anything happens to me, Ma, you will look after my little Ruby, won't you?'

'Of course!' replied Selina. It was a promise that she, undoubtably, never thought she would actually have to keep.

Herbert's relationship with his stepmother, although now improved, still warranted plenty of distance, so while Mary Jane was settling Ruby and gossiping with Selina, Herbert was next door at number 4, with his grandfather. Henry, who was sixty-one but still in perfect health, received much the same story.

When Herbert and Mary Jane Bennett left Westgate-on-Sea in the early hours of 17 March, they would have donned the wigs that Clarkson had made for them. They set a course for Southampton, a journey that would have taken much of the day. That evening – under the cover of darkness – they boarded the SS *Gaika* – not the *Margetta*, as they had told Herbert's family. The SS *Gaika*, which was part of the Union-Castle Steamship Company shipping line, was being used to transport troops from Britain to South Africa. That day, 53 officers and 1,556 men boarded the vessel, all destined for the Cape. Among the 42 'ordinary' passengers were a bewigged couple named Mr and Mrs 'Hood'. In 1900, ships were required to keep passenger lists that were certified by immigration and customs officials, but those travelling overseas were not required to have a passport. Most travellers had no formal documents to prove their identity, which made it much easier for people to travel under aliases.

Exactly what impelled the 'Hoods' to make the journey that day remains a mystery, but it is safe to assume that Herbert sensed that the most recent of his fraudulent activities posed a significant threat to his liberty. He may also have considered the trip an opportunity to investigate the lucrative gold-mining industry that was flourishing in South Africa at the time. Mary Jane, no doubt, would have been drawn to the promise of the 'restorative benefits' of a sea voyage. The Victorians believed that sea air offered health benefits and a 'short pleasure trip to the Cape' was recommended for those who required a 'change of air' – '. . . *after three weeks of perfect rest in a mail steamer having all the regularity and dependency of an express train on a well-appointed line, you find yourself refreshed and renewed by a period of quintessence unobtainable on land'.*[5]

Towards the end of March, the Bennetts' creditors held a meeting in London to discuss Herbert's debts. The majority of those in attendance voted to see him declared bankrupt. Murton vetoed the proposal, arguing that there would then be nothing to collect. As the largest creditor, his vote was carried. Any hopes he may have had of securing repayment were fruitless as, by then, the Bennetts were halfway to Cape Town.

Another month passed before news of the couple reached Herbert's family in Swanscombe. On 3 May, a letter arrived at John and Selina Bennett's house in Galley Hill. It had been written by Mary Jane and simply asked for news of the baby. Enclosed was a note from Herbert sending 'lots of love and kisses for little Ruby'. It had been posted on 10 April, the day the Bennetts had arrived in Cape Town. John and Selina were surprised to see the South African postmark, as they had been expecting news from America. There was no explanation for the change of plans and a postcard received by Herbert's grandfather Henry Simmons on the same day was just as vague.

Herbert and Mary Jane did not stay long in South Africa. Four days after they had disembarked from the SS *Gaika* in Cape Town, they were boarding the SS *Avondale Castle*, which was due to set sail for England on 14 April. Whatever the threat that had impelled them to travel under an assumed name on their outward journey had obviously passed by the time they boarded the *Avondale Castle*, as they travelled back to England as Mr and Mrs Bennett.[6] Herbert even listed his occupation as 'grocer's assistant'. The vessel reached Southampton on 9 May, and the Bennetts secured lodgings at 78, Harwood Road, Walham Green, which was about half a mile north of their old Wandsworth Bridge Road address, on 10 May. They were there for two nights before Herbert instructed his wife to seek cheaper lodgings elsewhere.

10

GOLD

'I wish you were dead'

On Saturday, 12 May, Mary Jane travelled to the outlying town of Plumstead, a quiet Victorian outgrowth of Woolwich, looking for somewhere else to rent, and visited the house of Mrs Sarah Elliston. Sarah, who went by her middle name, 'Emma', was the thirty-three-year-old wife of a local police constable named Herman Elliston. The couple had five daughters, and their eight-roomed house was at 64, Wickham Lane, just off Plumstead High Street. The area was home to many young families and the cries of children could be heard drifting into the streets from the yards and small gardens that stood behind many of the houses.[1]

The Bennetts' new landlady was a thin, pale woman who spent much of her day running after her children. That day, Mary Jane secured two furnished rooms for 10s. a week and when she took out her purse to pay the deposit, her new landlady noted that it was 'well filled with gold'.[2] 'My husband is returning from South Africa today,' Mary Jane said as she handed Mrs Elliston some money. 'He will be here tonight. I have to go to Yarmouth to get my baby, and I will be back here on Monday or Tuesday.'[3] Mrs Elliston nodded and then watched as her new lodger left the house. As anticipated, a man appeared at the Ellistons' front door that evening, introducing himself as Mr Bennett. He stayed alone in the house on the Saturday and Sunday.

Meanwhile, Mary Jane had returned to the boarding house in Walham Green, where she stayed for the remainder of the weekend. On the Monday, she travelled to Swanscombe (not Yarmouth) to collect Ruby. Having just received Mary Jane and Herbert's letters eleven days before, Selina was surprised to see her stepdaughter-in-law when she appeared on her doorstep. 'Well, Ma, I've come back for the baby!' Mary Jane announced. Selina asked her why she and her husband had gone to South Africa instead of America. 'Oh!' replied Mary Jane, 'we changed our plans at the very last moment. Herbert did take tickets for the *Margetta*, and everything else was arranged for America . . . but we went to Africa instead.'

'And that', Selina would later recall, 'was all the explanation she gave . . .'4 Mary Jane then distracted Selina from any further questioning by producing several presents, including a painted ostrich egg and a wall tidy, which was decorated with 'pretty' feathers and other ornaments. Perhaps Mary Jane also showed her 'ma' the little shovel, pickaxe and bucket brooch that Herbert had bought her in Cape Town, which was reminiscent of the South African mining industry. In reference to her letter – which had arrived just days before – Mary Jane said that she had chased it back to England from Cape Town by mail-boat.

What she failed to mention was that she had actually been back in the country for the better part of a week and that her husband had returned with her. It had been more than two months since Ruby had seen her mother and she did not recognise her at first. She took some persuading before she would go away with her, but when at last she did, Mary Jane said they were off to meet Herbert in Cape Town. She promised to write as soon as they arrived. That was the last time Selina Bennett would see her stepdaughter-in-law alive.

Naturally, Mary Jane's proclamation that she was 'off to Cape Town' was a lie. Instead, she travelled to Plumstead with Ruby. When they arrived at the door to the Ellistons' house, Mary Jane set down the small portmanteau she had been carrying and readjusted Ruby, who she had balanced on her hip. Herbert met them at the door. He appeared visibly irritated – 'What makes you so late?' he snapped.

'Herbert, dear,' began Mary Jane, 'the baby was so heavy, also the portmanteau. I could not get here before. You knew the time I was coming, why didn't you meet me?'

'Shut your great mouth!' Herbert retorted roughly. 'Damn you and Ruby too!'

'Oh, Herbert, do look at Ruby. Don't you think she has grown? Don't you think she looks better?'

Herbert was indifferent to his child – 'Oh, damn Ruby!' he responded. 'Considering the Bovril I left her, she ought to have got on well.'

Herbert's foul mood continued into the evening. Mrs Elliston, who had been listening to the Bennetts' rough exchange from the kitchen, would likely have felt sympathy for Mary Jane. The Bennetts' apartments were in the front and back parlours, which were a mere two or three yards from the kitchen. Mrs Elliston – like many other working-class women of her time – spent a large part of her day preparing meals and cooking and cleaning in the kitchen. As a result, she would go on to overhear most of the Bennetts' exchanges. She later claimed that it was sometimes hard not to overhear her lodgers, as Herbert had a habit of speaking loudly on account of Mary Jane's 'deafness'. Mrs Elliston's claim would later be somewhat confirmed by Mary Jane's father, William Clark, who stated that his daughter was 'slightly' deaf. Mrs Elliston was in the kitchen that evening when Mary Jane walked in. Her lodger explained that she had come to fetch some hot water for her husband's bad foot. When Mary Jane returned to the parlour a short time later, Herbert immediately demanded to know what she had been speaking to their landlady about. 'I told her you had a bad toe,' replied Mary Jane. 'Well, shut your great mouth,' retorted Herbert, 'and don't talk about me!'

All throughout the following week, Herbert left the house at 8.30 a.m. each morning, presumably in search of employment. He returned in the afternoon to sit in the parlour and scowl at the latest issue of the *Exchange and Mart*. Despite her husband's instruction not to talk about him, Mary Jane told their landlady that her husband was a commercial traveller who dealt in pianos. By now, the advertisements that Herbert had placed in the Sunday newspaper *Lloyd's Weekly Newspaper* had dried up and the couple showed no indications of returning to their trade in violins.

Estranged from her family and without friends, Mary Jane sought solace in motherhood. Ruby was by now eighteen months old. Herbert took no notice of the baby and had lost all interest in his wife. Despite this, Mary Jane was still 'passionately fond' of him.[5] She obviously sensed the need to give him space, however, spending most of her days in Greenwich Park with Ruby.

Herbert, meanwhile, had obtained a six-week temporary contract working at the grocery counter at the Co-operative's main stores on Powis Street, Woolwich. To secure the job, he had provided a reference from a grocer in Putney, which – unsurprisingly – was forged. Herbert worked his first shift on Saturday, 19 May. Working at the counter next to Herbert's was a twenty-six-year-old man named Robert Allen. Allen had married his sweetheart, Annie, the previous month and the two men regularly discussed their wives. Herbert described Mary Jane as a 'great help'. Also working at the stores at that time was a tall, slimly built twenty-year-old man named John Cameron. It would not be long before both Allen and Cameron would fall victim to Herbert's lies.

Shortly after Herbert began working at the stores, Mrs Elliston noticed that Mary Jane started bringing home tinned salmon, Bovril, ham, jam and smoked sausages, at the behest of her husband, leading her to suspect that Herbert was stealing from the stores. On one occasion, the landlady overheard Herbert telling Mary Jane to meet him outside the Co-op at 5 p.m. John Cameron witnessed one of these meetings and later asked Herbert if the golden-haired woman 'in the blue dress and gold-rimmed spectacles' that he had seen him with outside the stores was his wife. 'No,' replied Herbert, 'she is one of the good girls I know.' He went on to say that she was a teacher of music from Putney. This was no surprise to Cameron, who would later claim that Herbert was 'constantly going with loose women'.[6]

In June, Herbert visited Allen at his home to purchase a sewing machine and child's mail cart (a nineteenth-century baby carriage or pram, designed to carry a toddler in a seated position). Herbert was with a woman who he introduced as his wife. He had already told Allen that his wife and child lived in Putney, but that he had a lodging for himself at Wickham Lane. The fact that Herbert had started to describe himself as living apart from Mary Jane and Ruby was an indication of his future intentions.

By this point, the Bennetts' marriage was fast deteriorating. Herbert's foul moods had intensified, and he was now utterly frustrated by the trappings of domesticity. According to Mrs Elliston, he regularly referred to his family as a burden, complaining that they were 'hanging about his neck' all day and all night. The Bennetts' quarrelling had continued non-stop since they'd moved into the Ellistons' house. Herbert 'flared up and abused' his wife and child over the smallest things. He was 'cross and savage' and his temper often left Mary Jane in tears. On one occasion, Mary Jane confided in her landlady that her husband had smacked her in the face. When Mrs Elliston spoke to her about it afterwards, Mary Jane had tried to shield her husband by telling her landlady how good he had been to her – 'Oh, I'm alright,' she said, 'he gives me plenty of money and takes me about a lot, and I have good clothes. Of course, he does look rather disagreeable, but that's only a way he's got into lately.'[7] Mrs Elliston would also claim that Herbert referred to Ruby with a series of 'nasty names' and was generally unkind to her. He called her a bastard at least once and, on another occasion, he slapped her in the face. Mrs Elliston supported her young lodger where she could; she offered advice on raising Ruby – she had plenty to share, having five girls of her own – and when Ruby broke the precious gold chain that Mary Jane had inherited from her grandmother, she helped her to fix it with a piece of white cotton thread.

About four weeks after the Bennetts had moved in, Mrs Elliston overheard the couple talking about moving – 'You are to go and look out for a house at Bexley Heath,' Herbert instructed his wife. He then asked Mary Jane what name she would take, but Mrs Elliston – listening from the kitchen – was unable to make out the answer.

Shortly afterwards, Mary Jane had secured a top-floor flat that was being offered for rent in a house in Woolwich Road, Bexley.

The night before they were due to leave the Ellistons' house, Herbert and Mary Jane had a particularly loud argument. It all started, Mrs Elliston would later claim, over Herbert's toe – 'she [Mary Jane] put a poultice on too hot . . .' Herbert lost his temper and swore at his wife. He shouted at her to go to bed, which she did, leaving him alone in the front parlour. A short time afterwards, Herbert strode into the back parlour – the room they used as a bedroom – and laid down on the floor to go to sleep. Mrs Elliston had noticed in recent days that Herbert had taken to sleeping on the floor at night. Mary Jane looked at Ruby, who was in bed with her: 'Tell Daddy to come to bed and love Ruby,' she said playfully. Her attempt to coax Herbert into bed was unsuccessful.

'Bugger Ruby and you too!' Herbert shouted angrily. 'You're nothing to me and she is no more to me than you are. I don't intend to sleep with you or live with you any more. I have taken a room at Woolwich. You go to the house at Bexley and leave my luggage behind.' Herbert's outburst caused Mary Jane to start crying.

'Herbert,' she said, between sobs, 'I will follow you for the sake of the baby and if you're not careful I shall get you fifteen years.'

'I wish you were dead,' Herbert replied, 'and if you are not careful, you soon will be.'

The next morning, Mary Jane gathered her things and took Ruby to catch a horse-bus to Bexley. Their new home was the upstairs flat in the London suburb of Bexley Heath. Three weeks after they had moved in, a lady named Emma McDonald moved into the building with her husband, Charles, a labourer at Woolwich Arsenal. Mary Jane introduced herself to the McDonalds as Mrs 'Bartlett'.[8] Mrs 'Bartlett' told the McDonalds that her husband was a commercial traveller, and others that her husband was 'a detective with a lot of work'. Letters came to the house addressed to 'H.J. Bartlett Esq' and Herbert – calling himself Bartlett – visited on several occasions, staying overnight once.

From Mrs McDonald's perspective, the Bennetts appeared to get along fairly well and seemed happy most of the time. She only overheard them argue once – a disagreement that ended abruptly when Herbert shouted, 'It is not what you want, it is what I want to give you!' She heard Mary Jane crying on another occasion, but for the most part it appeared that the Bennetts' separation had done their relationship some good.

Mrs Elliston later claimed that Mary Jane visited Plumstead several times after she left, the last occasion being in July. On one of these occasions, Mary Jane remarked sadly, 'I am by myself a good deal now; my husband only visits me once a week ... I've not a soul or friend in the world.'

In late July, Mary Jane procured a notice to view another property in Bexley Heath. Number 1 Glencoe Villas was a small, two-storey, semi-detached property with bay windows and the main door at the side. It was exactly the type of home that Mary Jane would have desired in an effort to end her nomadic lifestyle. At the end of the nineteenth century, Bexley Heath was much smaller than it is today, with a population of only 6,000.[9] As one resident would later observe, it was a very quiet part of the world, where people naturally took an interest in their neighbours.[10] The house stood in Izane Road, on a relatively uncharted estate where the roads were poorly defined.

The keys to the house were held by one of the residents of number 2: a thirty-year-old woman named Mrs Edith Savage. Edith was wife to John Savage who owned Kingdom's Laundry on the Broadway – the very laundry that would ultimately prove the key to unlocking Mary Jane's identity. Edith had recently given birth to her first child, a daughter. Consequently, most of her days were spent at home caring for the baby. It was no surprise, then, that she was at home when the Bennetts knocked on her front door that day. When she answered, Herbert handed her the notice to view the vacant property and Edith handed him the keys in return. Mary Jane took to the house immediately. Herbert agreed to rent the house for £18 a year and paid £2. 5s. for half a quarter's rent.

It was early August when the Bennetts moved in. Edith watched from the front window of her house – 2 Glencoe Villas – which adjoined the Bennetts' property by a thin dividing wall. That day, Edith would have noticed the young child that Mary Jane carried in her arms and would have thought that she had something in common with her new neighbour. Mary Jane was wearing a gold chain and Edith watched as the little fox terrier they had with them jumped up and broke it. Herbert kicked the dog in response.

Edith and Mary Jane quickly became firm friends. At this time, Mary Jane mostly went by the name Bennett, but some of the tradespeople she used knew her as Mrs 'Good'. She told them that her husband was a detective. Mary Jane told the Savages a similar story to the one she had told the Ellistons and the McDonalds – that her husband was a commercial traveller who was only able to visit once a week on account of his work. She told the house agent, Walter Hudson, however, that Herbert was a sailor. It would have been important for Mary Jane to have established herself as a married woman, as there was an enormous stigma attached to women who were separated from their husbands.

Living in the house to the left of Mary Jane's – number 3 – was a family called the Langmans. They had recently moved to the capital from their native Cornwall. John Langman – a carpenter – and his wife, Catherine, had several children, including two daughters named Lilian and Elizabeth. At twenty-one, Lilian was closest to Mary Jane in age, but the two young women had led very different lives. Elizabeth 'Lizzie' Langman was the youngest and was especially taken with little Ruby. Both sisters spent a lot of time with Mary Jane, as did their mother. Mary Jane settled into quiet village life quickly and was often in bed by half-past seven or quarter to eight of an evening. She had no visitors apart from her husband, who visited once a week, usually on a Wednesday. For the most part, these visits were uneventful, apart from on one occasion, when Edith overheard the couple arguing about money – 'You're always dragging money out of me,' Herbert shouted. 'You know the fix I'm in now.' It is likely that he was referring to having to pay out for two sets of lodgings. Edith moved to another room in the house to avoid hearing the rest of the Bennetts' argument. By now, Mary Jane was completely reliant on Herbert's allowance, and it seems she was starting to struggle to make ends meet.

Shortly after moving, Mary Jane fell desperately ill. By the end of the first week of August, she had taken to her sickbed. At the time, diseases such as pulmonary tuberculosis, also known as 'consumption', were endemic. At the start of the nineteenth century, tuberculosis killed at least one in seven people in England.[11] The disease raged on throughout the century, ripping through families and sending children and adults alike to the grave. It was more common among the urban poor, who lived in squalid, close-quarter environments. A public-health campaign that was designed to slow the spread of the disease was launched following Robert Koch's identification of the organisms responsible for the disease in the 1880s, but the illness continued to cause widespread public concern into the early twentieth century. By then, death was a common result of the disease. When Edith discovered that her neighbour had become 'dangerously ill', tuberculosis may have been her immediate concern. She begged Mary Jane to allow her to call a doctor, but her neighbour refused. Eventually, Edith managed to persuade her to send for her husband. By this point, Mary Jane was too weak to write the message out herself, so she dictated it and Edith scribbled down the message on telegraph paper:

TRY COME HOME M VERY ILL.

She signed it 'BEXLEY'.

Mary Jane gave Edith an address in Union Street, Woolwich, where she said her husband could be reached, and then the telegram was handed to Lizzie Langman, who rushed off in the direction of Board Street and the post office.

Edith would later claim that Mary Jane was so ill that she was 'terrified she would die'. Describing the circumstances leading up to Mary Jane's illness, she would recall, '. . . she was very poorly off. She hardly ever cooked any food and lived on the cheapest she could buy. During the whole three weeks she was in bed all she bought was a dozen eggs and a small bottle of Bovril.'[12] Mary Jane was ultimately found to be suffering from influenza, which had been largely absent from England from around 1848 to 1889 but had reappeared in the 1890s. Both 1895 and 1900 were considered to be particularly bad years for the flu.[13]

Herbert arrived at Glencoe Villas late that evening having received the telegram from Bexley earlier in the day. It was raining and he was covered in mud from a cycle ride. He looked in on Mary Jane, all the while grumbling that she had 'cost him £200', as he had had to hand over an important 'case' to a 'colleague'. Before leaving that evening, he gave Mary Jane a small amount of money. It was enough to pay Lizzie 3s. ½d. for running errands for her while she had been ill in bed. It was another two weeks before Mary Jane had fully regained her strength. When she had recovered, she decided she needed a holiday. Surprisingly, Herbert agreed to the idea quite readily, and one afternoon in early September Mary Jane excitedly announced to her neighbours that her 'old man' was going to take her on a holiday to 'Yorkshire'.

When Herbert visited his wife on Friday, 14 September, he gave her some money for new clothes. After he left that day, Mary Jane took Ruby and went shopping in Bexley with Lilian, where she bought a dove-grey coloured jacket and skirt. That evening she had supper with the Langmans. She spoke about her plans for the holiday and Lilian and Lizzie both offered to help her pack. The following day, Lizzie sorted Mary Jane's linen, while Lilian washed and dressed the baby. Lizzie then accompanied Mary Jane and Ruby to Woolwich. They called at Garrett's drapery store on Powis Street, Woolwich's premier shopping centre.[14] At the time, Powis Street and its neighbouring Hare Street were considered to contain the best 'drapery stores, grocers, public houses, boot shops, and bacon and cheese shops' in Woolwich and the crowds that lined the busy streets could always be relied upon to be of a 'good tempered and sober' disposition.[15] That day, Mary Jane bought a blouse, veil and straw hat. Her purchases were tucked away carefully into little parcels, which Lizzie helped her to carry home.

At around three o'clock that afternoon, Mary Jane left Glencoe Villas with Ruby. She was wearing the blouse that she had purchased earlier in the day, along with the dove-grey costume she had bought the previous day. Hanging from her neck was a long gold chain and carefully stowed in her pocket was a small silver pocket watch. She carried a small brown paper parcel with a change of linen for her and the baby. Lizzie watched Mary Jane shut the house up and then accompanied her and Ruby to Liverpool Street station. It was certainly not the first time Mary Jane Bennett had stepped effortlessly from one life into another, but it would be the last.

⌒11⌒

THE OTHER WOMAN

'With fondest love, from your ever loving and affectionate, Herbert'

Herbert had moved out of the Ellistons' house the day after Mary Jane left with the baby in June 1900. He had already secured lodgings in Woolwich; his new landlady on Union Street was a middle-aged woman named Comfort Pankhurst.[1] Her husband, Walter, worked as a foreman examiner at the Woolwich Royal Naval Dockyard. By 1900, the dockyard was a functioning equipment storage facility for the War Department, with a primary function of equipping ships for expedition to South Africa to support the British war effort. The house was close to the docks in the riverside district in an area that had once formed part of the notorious 'Dusthole', named on account of the coal dust that hung in the air.[2]

The former inhabitants of the street had by now 'scattered' and a series of new two-storey houses had been built in an attempt to improve the area, which had been known for high levels of crime, poverty and prostitution. As the sociologist George Arkell remarked of this street in 1900, 'New houses don't at once give a street a new name.'[3] The Pankhursts occupied one of the newer, 'fairly decent' houses at the end of the road and took in lodgers from among the 20,000-strong workforce of the nearby Royal Arsenal.

At the time, the Woolwich Royal Arsenal was a key producer of the country's artillery. The Arsenal factories produced a wide range of ordnance and military equipment for the battlefield, including rifled guns, ammunition, torpedoes, artillery fittings, gun mountings and shields.[4] The sounds of industry reverberated throughout the town, and residents were used to the occasional flashes out on the marshes, which signalled guns being tested. It was more difficult to adapt to the loud crashes caused by the bigger guns, the force of which caused nearby windows to rattle in their frames.[5]

Conditions inside the factories themselves were intense – the stifling heat made the arduous work of the labourers more gruelling, and everyone worked under a constant threat of danger from explosions. A 'frightful explosion' in the rocket factories in 1883 had killed two men,[6] and an explosion in 1907 would be forceful enough to shatter 30,000 windowpanes across the district.[7]

Employee numbers ebbed and flowed along with war- or peace-time conditions. In 1900, the workforce was at the highest it had been since the start of the Crimean War in 1853. Gambling was rife. Betting was more indulged in than drink and bookies would loiter in the square outside Beresford Gate, the main entrance, ready to pounce on workers as they left for their lunch hour. Paper boys selling the 'news' mingled in the crowd, and the large coffee house at the corner of Cross Street, a few paces from the Arsenal entrance, did a roaring trade.

It was this workforce that Herbert Bennett joined on 6 July 1900, having left his job at the Co-operative store a week earlier. Although Herbert would go on to claim that he worked as a clerk at the Arsenal (the type of exaggeration that was typical of Herbert's character), in actuality he had taken a job as a labourer in 'K' shop, the building repairs department, where he was paid 30s. a week. Herbert had never worked as a labourer before and the sudden change in direction led some to believe that there was more to Herbert's work at the Arsenal than meets the eye.[8]

Despite paying for two sets of lodgings, and an (albeit small) stipend to his wife, it seems that Herbert was not short of money at this point. The day after he started work, he purchased a new light-grey suit. The suit, which cost 65s. (more than double his weekly wage), was tailor-made in the upper-floor workshop of the five-storey flagship store, Messrs Arding & Hobbs in Clapham Junction. By 1900, the ready-to-wear clothing industry was well established, offering cheaper options for working-class men while the wealthier continued to visit tailors. A tailor-made suit fitted snugly and evened out any oddities of body shape, whereas a ready-made suit was looser on the body and had a tendency to look worn within a few weeks of purchase.[9] For a man like Herbert, a ready-made suit was not befitting of his self-image, which was at odds with the social position that his job at the Arsenal dictated. He wore the suit with a bowler hat, which by now had become a symbol of middle-class status within towns and cities.

The reasons behind Herbert taking the job (if there were any aside from it being an attempt at honest work) may be unclear, but he was likely to have secured it by recommendation of one of his two fellow lodgers, both of whom worked at the Arsenal. Herbert shared a room with a twenty-two-year-old man named Albert Eardley, who worked as an engine and machine maker. Eardley, who hailed from Staffordshire, had left the clay pits and black coal smoke of his hometown for the capital in search of employment. A third man, John Stevens, slept in an adjoining room. Herbert and Stevens quickly became firm friends, which suggests that Stevens was the more likely of the two to have found Herbert the job.

When Herbert first went to live with the Pankhursts, he had told them that he was a single man – a lie that he would successfully maintain for some months. He spoke regularly about his family, particularly of his female 'cousin' who lived in Bexley with her husband and child. He told Mrs Pankhurst not to worry about his washing and mending, as his 'cousin' did it all for nothing, and that if he was out late, he was probably there. In reality, he was more likely to have been frequenting one of the many brothels that lined Rope Yard Rails, two streets away from his lodgings. Mrs Pankhurst took to her new lodger very quickly and would later describe him as the 'perfect gentleman', and one of the 'nicest lodgers' she had ever had. Her account of Herbert's temperament during this period differs significantly from what others said about his past conduct. Perhaps his character mellowed the more time he spent apart from his wife and child.

Herbert spent most of his spare time with Stevens, who was seeing a young woman named Kitty Treadwell who worked as a cook in a house in the West End of London. Stevens introduced Kitty to Herbert on the last Sunday in June, and Kitty was said to have been so taken with him that she suggested they meet again the following weekend. On the following Sunday, 1 July, Herbert was introduced by Kitty to Alice Meadows, a young parlourmaid who worked in the same house as Kitty on Hyde Park Terrace. The houses, known as Hyde Park Gardens, had been built in the 1800s and were home to a series of 'well-to-do' families.

Herbert was immediately attracted to Alice. Just five days after their initial meeting, he wrote what would become the first in a long stream of love letters, and the couple began meeting regularly. Herbert was so taken with Alice that he signed off this first letter with his 'fondest love':

My darling Alice, – Just a small note to say that I arrived home safe last night, or rather this morning . . . I wish you were down here today, dearest . . . I hope it keeps fine next Sunday so that it may not spoil the few happy hours we may have together . . . I must now close, with fondest love, from your ever loving and affectionate, Herbert.

As a parlourmaid, Alice would have expected to make anything between £18 and £30 a year.[10] During the latter part of the nineteenth century, parlourmaids had taken the place of manservants, because they were less expensive to keep, did more work and asked for lower wages.[11] The main duty of a parlourmaid was to wait at the family's table, but they were also responsible for opening the door to visitors, bringing up afternoon tea and laying the table for meal times. In addition, Alice would have 'kept the linen in repair, waited upon her mistress, assisted her to dress when required, looked after the fire, made the beds, dusted, and washed up'.[12] The work of a parlourmaid was gruelling, arduous and often dreary. Alice's day would have started at around 6.30 a.m., and she would not have been permitted to retire in the evening until her mistress had gone to bed, usually at around 10.30 p.m. Alice would later describe Hyde Park Terrace as a 'hard place' to work. By 1900, servants benefited from slightly more time off, and Alice was permitted to leave the house on Thursday afternoons and on some Sundays, when she usually returned home to her mother's house in Stepney.

The Meadows family lived at 22 York Road (now Yorkshire Road), in Stepney, East London, in the borough of Tower Hamlets, historically one of the poorest areas of London. The house stood close to the Ratcliffe Highway (now the Highway), which had been the scene of seven murders in 1811, in what is now widely considered to be one of England's first serial killings. The London docks were to the west, with Pennington Street above, where prostitutes were known to service the sailors that crewed the many passenger and trade ships that landed in the capital.

Alice was the second eldest of seven surviving children, including an adopted son, Sydney, aged two. Alice was particularly close to her sister, May Lenson, who had been widowed two months earlier, when her husband of two and a half years, John George Lenson, had died aged twenty-two. Their mother, Sarah Ann Meadows, had become head of the household in 1890, when her husband, William Henry, had died at the age of forty-five. William was a butcher, and Alice – just like Mary Jane – had grown up above the family's butcher's shop. Alice had turned thirteen the day before her father was buried. At the time, the family were living in a large house in York Square, just around the corner from York Road. They took in boarders, mainly seafaring men from across the country. The house would have been alive with the trill of accents from Scotland, Ireland and Wales. Following her father's death, Alice would have been expected to start contributing to the family's income, which meant joining the large numbers of teenage girls and young women who went into service every year. Alice's mother had been a live-in domestic by the age of thirteen, but Alice would have been expected to complete her education before she entered into work, most likely at around the age of fifteen.

By now, Alice was twenty-three years old, and Mrs Meadows had moved the family to the smaller house, adjacent to the railway line. A reporter would later describe Alice as a 'tall, good-looking young woman, with rather refined features'.[13] These were sought-after characteristics for a parlourmaid. As the first person seen by visitors, and the person who waited on the family over dinner, a parlourmaid's appearance was considered important. Women who had tall, trim figures were in greater demand, as they were thought to be more graceful in the way they waited tables.[14]

During the years that she had spent in service, Alice had learned to anticipate other people's wants and needs and had become accustomed to adhering to the strict rules and restrictions put in place by her mistress. As a result, she had developed a quiet, unassuming nature. She was rather naive and lacked the fighting spirit and astuteness that Mary Jane possessed. Perhaps it was these qualities that attracted Herbert. Thursday was Alice's half-day, and Herbert worked the night shift. So, on a Thursday afternoon, Alice would have discarded her bib apron and simple white cap and thrown on a cloak to go out and meet her sweetheart.

They wrote to each other in the days between. Naturally, Herbert told a few lies, mostly about his family. He had told his friend Stevens that his father owned a public house in Gravesend, a lie he kept up for Alice.[15] To her, he said that he had a grandfather, grandmother and sister in Gravesend, but that he was unable to introduce them since his father had remarried after his mother died and his stepmother – whom he described as a 'bad tempered woman' – disliked him. He also spoke of his 'cousin', Fred, who lived in Bexley with his wife and child. He tried to impress Alice by telling her stories about his recent visit to Cape Town.

Unlike his early courtship of Mary Jane, Herbert's relationship with Alice was an open one. He was quickly introduced to her family and became a firm favourite of her mother and sister, May. He was also popular with her two brothers, Fredrick, nineteen, and Harry, sixteen. Herbert became a regular visitor to the Meadows family's house on a Sunday, and sometimes stayed the night. At the weekends, he took Alice's brothers out rowing on the river and on other excursions around the city. Alice was quick to trust Herbert and she soon fell for him.

Less than a month after their first meeting, Herbert asked Alice to go away with him. She was hesitant at first, but his patient persistence soon convinced her – 'he was kind and gentle ... I became very attached to him ...' she later said. Alice would have been obliged to take her holiday when her mistress took hers, and she had been planning a trip to Great Yarmouth with her sister, May, for her main holiday. Herbert suggested that they go to Ireland instead, but so as not to disappoint her, he said they would spend the bank holiday weekend in Great Yarmouth. Alice agreed and gave Herbert the addresses of two boarding houses that had been recommended to her by Kitty, who had recently returned from a trip to the seaside resort.

On 30 July, Herbert wrote two letters. The first was to a landlady named Mrs Newman. The second was to the landlady of the house where Kitty had stayed. Her name was Mrs Rudrum and her address was number 3, Row 104, Great Yarmouth. The letter read as follows:

> Dear Madam,
>   Having been recommended by a Miss Treadwell who has stayed at your address, I wish to engage two bedrooms for next Saturday and Sunday night & should be obliged if you could put us up for the two nights, an early answer will oblige.
>   Yours Faithfully,
>   W.H. Bennett.

Neither place was able to offer accommodation so close to the bank holiday weekend. Undeterred, Herbert secured alternative lodgings at the Crown and Anchor Hotel on Hall Quay, and he and Alice travelled first class from Liverpool Street station to Great Yarmouth's South Town station on Saturday, 4 August 1900.[16] Alice would later claim that Herbert was a 'perfect gentleman' throughout their stay at the seaside resort. Her account describes them 'walking about a lot', weaving in and out of the dark, dingy alleyways between the Rows. On one occasion, as they walked along the Quay, they passed Row 104, which Herbert pointed out to Alice as the location of Mrs Rudrum's lodging house. Whether Herbert had deliberately guided them there, or they had simply stumbled across the Row by chance remains to be seen, but he took a keen interest, remarking, 'I wouldn't want anyone belonging to me to stay there, it's a horrid-looking place.'

During their trip, Herbert spent money freely, telling Alice that he had a business in second-hand violins, which brought in 'plenty of money'. Alice had no reason to suspect the trade was anything other than an honest one. He also told her that he had inherited £500 from his mother. The other half of her fortune, he said, had gone to his 'brother', a Captain Bennett, who was serving in the Army Medical Corps in Pretoria, South Africa. Eventually, Herbert would announce that his 'brother' had been killed, and the entirety of his mother's fortune would go to him. Alice had no reason to question any of this – she trusted Herbert completely – but her mother was slightly more discerning. Mrs Meadows would later say that she regretted not having insisted on meeting Herbert's family. She had tried to convince Alice to press him on the matter, but her daughter had been reluctant to do so for fear of offending him.

Herbert and Alice arrived back in London on the evening of Monday, 6 August, and on the Thursday of that week Herbert turned twenty-one. He received two telegrams. One was from Alice, wishing him 'many happy returns for the day', and the other, which has already been mentioned, called for him to go to Bexley Heath at once, as 'M' was very ill. Herbert was at work when the telegram arrived. Mrs Pankhurst opened it and, sensing the urgency behind it, rushed over to the Arsenal where she handed it to her lodger. She would later claim that when he read it, he looked 'really worried and anxious'.[17]

Herbert returned to Union Street sometime between six and seven that evening. Mrs Pankhurst asked him what the matter was, and he said his 'cousin' at Bexley was ill. Shortly afterwards, he went away on his bicycle, and his landlady did not see him again until the following morning. It was not unusual for Herbert to stay out all night – he did so 'frequently', according to Walter Pankhurst.

When Herbert returned home the next morning, he was on foot, and had acquired a woman's umbrella. Concerned, Mrs Pankhurst asked after his cousin, and he told her that she was very ill with influenza, and that she was not expected to live. He appeared annoyed and complained about being troubled by his cousin's illness, saying that he did not want to hear about it if she got any worse. Alice, too, learned that week that her sweetheart's cousin was ill. Eventually, he would tell Mrs Pankhurst that his cousin had recovered and that she and her husband planned to move to South Africa.

The next couple of weeks passed by without incident. Herbert bought another suit from Messrs Arding & Hobbs on 18 August. He had worn the light-grey suit on his holiday to Yarmouth, together with a bowler hat, and the new suit was purchased in preparation for his trip to Ireland, which was booked for 28 August.

Arsenal records show that Herbert was off work 'sick' between 25 August and 15 September. Employees did not get sick pay until they had worked at the factory for three years, so it is safe to assume that Herbert went without pay for those three weeks. The prospect of not getting paid did not deter him from spending money, however, and Alice describes him as having plenty during their trip to Ireland.

As the couple sat in their first-class train carriage ready to depart on 28 August, Herbert presented Alice with a diamond and ruby engagement ring. He was clearly overlooking the fact that he was still legally bound to Mary Jane, and – should he have gone through with the marriage under his current circumstances – he would have been committing bigamy. Although divorce had been legal since 1858, proof of adultery was required if a man was to rid himself of his wife. Unaware of Herbert's marital status, Alice accepted his proposal and they talked about marrying the following June.

When she later recalled their trip to Ireland, Alice spoke of it fondly, stating, 'He behaved to me just as I could have wished in every way. I trusted him to such an extent that I went away with him for fourteen days, and he never took advantage of me, behaving at all times as a gentleman.'[18] During their fortnight away, the couple 'travelled around a lot', staying in hotels and visiting various places, including Killarney, in County Kerry.

Alice and Herbert returned to London on 11 September and Alice went straight back to her employer's house. Herbert, however, was in no rush to return to work. He had arranged to meet Alice in Woolwich the following day, Wednesday, so he could introduce her to Mrs Pankhurst. While he waited for her to arrive that afternoon, he slipped into Rose's Distillery on Hare Street. The pub, also known as the 'Prince Albert' or simply the 'Distillery', was a striking three-storey building and one of a number of pubs in the area a short walk from Mrs Pankhurst's front door. By this point, London was teeming with pubs. During the latter half of the nineteenth century, their number had peaked at around 20,000,[19] and one pub for every thirty households was not unusual in working-class districts.[20] It was not only the promise of alcohol, but the warmth and comradeship that drew many of their customers in.

Curiously, 'Rose' was the name given to Ruby by Mary Jane when they travelled to Great Yarmouth. Perhaps it had been Herbert's suggestion. If so, it is likely that he had taken inspiration from the name of the public house he so regularly frequented. The licensee of Rose's Distillery was a young man named Austin Cutting. He employed five barmen, all in their late teens or early twenties. Perhaps it was the feeling that he was among his contemporaries that drew Herbert to Rose's Distillery. The atmosphere would certainly have been very different to that of the White Hart Tavern, two doors down, which was run by an older, family man by the name of Shippard.

When Herbert walked into Rose's that afternoon, he was surprised to find his old friend William Parritt sitting in the bar alongside John Cameron, whom he had worked with at the Woolwich Co-op. Parritt had also taken a job at the Woolwich branch of the stores the previous month. The stores closed at 1 p.m. on a Wednesday. That day, the two young men had headed straight to the pub from work. Two years had passed since Herbert and Parritt had last met and they now greeted one another warmly.

'Hullo, Herbert!' Parritt exclaimed. 'How are you?'

Parritt and Herbert exchanged pleasantries and then Parritt asked his old friend if he would join him and Cameron for a drink. Herbert accepted – his tipple of choice was spirits, usually whisky. Parritt then asked after Mary Jane and the baby. The question caused Herbert to become visibly uncomfortable. Alice's impending visit was likely to have been at the forefront of his mind. Perhaps it was this that fuelled his next statement – 'They died of fever in South Africa,' he said quietly. The statement hung in the air for a few seconds, as Parritt looked up at Herbert in shock. Herbert appeared upset. 'Don't say much about it,' he said, hurriedly. 'I feel it very much.' Then, referring to Mary Jane, he said, 'I miss her. She was my right hand.'

Parritt, who himself had harboured feelings for Mary Jane, sympathised with Herbert. He asked if he could have a photograph of her and Ruby to remember them by. Herbert promised to send him a photograph of himself and Mary Jane. Herbert staved off any further conversation on the topic with the remark that he had just returned from Ireland, and it was not long before he was entertaining his drinking companions with stories from his trip. The atmosphere had lightened considerably by the time Herbert left to meet Alice, whom he greeted heartily. He was obviously drunk, and Alice was far from impressed – 'The day after we got back from Ireland was the first time I noticed he'd had too much to drink,' she would later say. Nevertheless, Herbert introduced Alice to Mrs Pankhurst as his intended wife and they spent an enjoyable afternoon together.

A LIKELY STORY

'Don't get miserable'

O n the morning of Friday, 14 September, Herbert travelled to Bexley Heath to visit Mary Jane. It was after he left that his wife began making preparations to leave Glencoe Villas for a holiday. That same evening, Herbert visited Alice at Hyde Park Terrace. He told her that he would not be able to see her the following day as he had to go to Gravesend to visit his grandfather, whom he claimed had fallen ill. Herbert was referring to his mother's father, Henry Simmons, since his paternal grandfather had by now died. Alice reminded Herbert that he had made plans with her brothers on the Sunday and asked if he would be back in time to meet them. Herbert said he thought he would be but added – somewhat evasively – that he would let her know for sure when he had confirmed his plans.

The following day, as his wife was on her way to Liverpool Street station with Ruby, Herbert telephoned Hyde Park Terrace to tell Alice that he would not be back in time to take her brothers out after all, but that he would meet her outside her employer's house at 3.30 p.m. the following day. Alice recalled the conversation because she had to cut it short – 'I must ring off,' she said hastily, 'my lady is coming downstairs.' Servants were forbidden from using the telephone and Alice would have been wary of upsetting her mistress, who had just returned home that day from her summer holiday. When later asked, Alice said she thought Herbert had telephoned from Charing Cross station, as he had called her from there in the past.

The following day was Sunday, 16 September. As the Rudrums were scrutinising their new lodger in Great Yarmouth, Mrs Pankhurst in Woolwich was busily engaged in her morning chores. She had one less bed to make that morning as Herbert had told her the same story he had told Alice – that he would be staying the night with family in Gravesend. His bed, therefore, had not been slept in. When Herbert did materialise that day, he did so quite unexpectedly at the house of Alice's mother in Stepney.

May Lenson, Alice's sister, would later claim that he arrived at their door at 'about' 11.30 a.m. When later pressed, she was unable to swear to the exact time. She did, however, clearly recall that her sister's fiancé was not wearing his usual Sunday best, but what appeared to be a ready-made suit, consisting of a plain blue coat and waistcoat and striped trousers. May claimed that he had been there for 'some time – about twenty minutes' when she called her mother into the room.

Mrs Meadows was surprised to see Herbert as she had received a letter from Alice the previous evening telling her not to expect him. It was then that Herbert told Alice's mother and sister a peculiar story about his usual suit of clothes. 'Don't laugh,' he said, indicating his ready-made suit. He showed the two women his frockcoat, waistcoat and trousers, which were stained wet. He explained that his 'cousin' had hit him with a stick and broken a bottle of iodine that had been in the pocket. At the time, iodine was a commonly bought medication that was used to treat swelling or inflammation. It is likely that Herbert had begun using it when he had separated from his wife as a substitute for Mary Jane's well-meaning, yet bumbling, attempts at poulticing. His home treatments to manage the swelling and pain of his ingrowing toenail were by now becoming less effective, and it would not be long before his condition would become too much to bear.

Mrs Meadows hung Herbert's suit up to dry. She would forward it to Mrs Pankhurst the following day. Although the timing of Herbert's visit would later be subject to scrutiny, the fact that he was there that afternoon was never disputed. When Herbert left the house, he went straight away to meet Alice. He again drew attention to his clothes, telling Alice the same story about the broken bottle of iodine. The staining, had, in all likelihood, been caused by a broken bottle of iodine – as Herbert claimed – but the circumstances around the accident were less clear.

Herbert returned to work at the Arsenal on Monday, 17 September, following twenty-two days of 'sickness' absence. He was seen by one of the Arsenal doctors, who assessed his health and cleared him to return to work. He clocked on at the usual time of 8 a.m. and worked a full day, finishing at 5.40 p.m. That day, Alice gave notice to leave her employment, citing ill health. It was around this time that signs of a disagreement between Herbert and his roommate, John Stevens, began to emerge. Mrs Pankhurst would later state that the two men had 'some trouble before they parted ...' Any disagreement between them would inevitably

have affected Alice's relationship with Kitty, her friend and fellow servant. Under such conditions, life at Hyde Park Terrace would have become
difficult for Alice and this may have added to her decision to leave her
employment. The two men appear to have been estranged by the time
Herbert and Alice returned from Ireland, as Stevens would later claim
that he learned of Herbert's engagement from Kitty. In a letter to Alice,
which is dated Sunday, 23 September – the day after Mary Jane's murder
– Herbert writes, 'I hope you are feeling better, my darling, and I shall be
glad to see you out of that place all together. Do not take any notice of
Kitty and be sure and don't get miserable . . .'[1]

On Wednesday, 19 September, Herbert travelled to Bexley Heath and
stood for some time outside Glencoe Villas. Lilian Langman – Mary
Jane's neighbour – caught sight of him in the passageway between the
two houses and watched as he walked around to the back of the house.
He tapped at the Langmans' back window. Lilian spoke to him briefly. He
asked if anyone had called at the house since his wife had been away. Lilian
told him no – not as far as she was aware. He left not long afterwards
without going into the house. When Herbert met Alice the following
day, he told her that he would be unable to see her as usual on Sunday, as
he and his 'cousin' Fred were going to visit their grandfather, whose condition had worsened.

Meanwhile, in Great Yarmouth, Mary Jane had just told Mrs Rudrum
that she was expecting a letter. The elusive letter would need to have been
sent at some point on Thursday for it to have arrived in Yarmouth the
following evening.

Arsenal records show that Herbert worked a full day on the Friday,
starting at 6 a.m. and finishing at 7 p.m. Herbert, therefore, could not
have been in Great Yarmouth that evening when Alice Rudrum claimed
to overhear Mary Jane talking to a man in the Row outside the lodging house. That same day, Herbert wrote to Alice to tell her that Stevens
was leaving – '. . . and I am not sorry for I feel miserable with him in the
house . . .'[2]

In the year of 1900, the autumn was slow to reach London. The berry
harvest had been a bumper one, and the warm September sun continued
to ripen and colour the sloes, blackberries and other hedgerow fruits that
were still growing in the countryside surrounding the city.[3] Throughout
the month, news from South Africa had dominated the headlines, and
on the morning of Saturday, 22 September, the newspapers reported that

the British had overpowered a Boer convoy and captured guns, cattle and ammunition.

There was something reassuringly familiar about how that day started out for two of the central characters in this story. In London, Alice prepared breakfast for her mistress's family and Herbert toiled away at the Arsenal. Further north, however, dark clouds had begun to loom over the county of Norfolk, bringing with them the threat of rain.[4]

Herbert had arrived at the Arsenal at 6 a.m. and was due to leave at 12.40 p.m., the usual hours for a Saturday. When he returned home from work that afternoon, the first thing he did was change out of his work clothes into his grey suit and black bowler hat. He then went down to the kitchen, where he came across Mrs Pankhurst. By now, it was between 2.30 and 3 p.m. Herbert was carrying an ABC railway guide,[5] and he mumbled something about having missed a train. He said he would need to hurry if he was going to catch the next. About an hour later – at around 4 p.m. – Herbert telephoned Alice to tell her that he was on his way to Gravesend to visit his grandfather. He told her that someone was waiting for him, but Alice could not be sure if he had referred to 'them' or 'him'.

Herbert's absence from Union Street was noted by several people that evening. Unfortunately for Herbert, it was a memorable day in the Pankhursts' house. Walter Pankhurst's grandmother, Elizabeth, had just turned eighty-one. She was the same age as the queen, as Herbert himself had pointed out earlier in the week when old Mrs Pankhurst had visited her grandson's house. Herbert had promised to 'keep up' the birthday, so Elizabeth was expecting to see him that evening. Despite life expectancy at birth in England and Wales having risen by about ten years during the latter half of the nineteenth century, at that time still only 5 per cent of the population were aged sixty-five or over.[6] It was, therefore, considered quite an achievement to have reached such an auspicious age, and the younger Pankhursts had duly arranged to throw Elizabeth a small party at their house. The celebrations concluded at around 10 p.m. when Elizabeth left to go home. Herbert had not made an appearance and he was still not home by 11.30 p.m. when the Pankhursts went to bed.

At that time, 145 miles away to the northeast, Alfred Mason had just left his sweetheart, Blanche Smith, at the door to her house and was heading home to Admiralty Road. As he walked across town, we can assume that the scene he had just witnessed on Great Yarmouth's South Beach – the woman lying motionless in the sand, the man astride her – played heavily on his mind.

The morning of Sunday, 23 September, dawned brightly in Great Yarmouth. The dark clouds that had hung heavily over the county the previous day had shifted to make way for the sun, which now shone the first of its rays over the South Beach where young John Norton would soon stumble across the most frightful of scenes.

13

A GLASS TOO MANY

Back in London, Mrs Pankhurst was in the kitchen at Union Street preparing the morning's breakfast things. The landlady was in the habit of sending tea up to her lodgers on a Sunday morning to 'help get them up', so she could begin the day's chores. For working-class families living in the south, a cup of tea in the morning was generally accompanied by a chunk of bread. Middle-class families who were slightly better off could also afford a slice or two of bacon and possibly some eggs.

That morning, Mrs Pankhurst was assisted by her son, Walter Jr. At around 8 a.m., he took a cup of tea up to Herbert's room. Walter brought it back down almost immediately – Herbert was not there. Unlike the previous week, Herbert had not told his landlady that he would be out all night. Given that her lodger had not returned home before she and her husband had gone to bed the previous evening, Mrs Pankhurst was not surprised that Herbert's bed had remained empty all night.

At around 10 a.m. that morning, Alice was preparing to leave her mistress's house to meet her friend, Teresa Humphrey. The two women had arranged to meet in Hyde Park after Herbert had told Alice he could not see her. Central to their discussions that morning would undoubtedly have been Alice's plans for her wedding. She had already started to gather her trousseau, which, so far, consisted of a pair of 'little white shoes and a bridal veil', which were all safely stowed in a trunk that she kept underneath a table in her mother's front parlour.[1] At that time, the bridal veil was still a relatively new accessory, having replaced the bonnet around the mid-century. A trousseau not only consisted of wedding garments, but also of clothes suitable for a married woman, as well as household linen and bedding. Garments were traditionally sewn by the engaged woman herself and Alice would possibly, with the help of her sister, May, a tailoress, have made some of her own clothes.

Alice and Teresa were standing on the Oxford Street side of Hyde Park,

near to the Albion Gate, at around 1.50 p.m. that afternoon when Alice
spotted Herbert strolling purposefully towards them. She was surprised
to see him because she had expected him to be with his grandfather. As
he moved closer, she noticed that he was wearing the grey suit he had
purchased for their trip to Great Yarmouth, together with a black bowler
hat. It was a peculiar choice for a Sunday, as he never usually went out in
anything but a frock coat and silk hat. Everyone, no matter what their
class or social standing, made an effort on a Sunday. When he reached
them, Herbert explained that he had felt 'in the way' at his grandfather's
house: 'My father, sister and cousin were there,' Herbert explained. 'So, I
came here to see you instead. If the train hadn't been delayed,' he continued, 'I would have been at your place before you started out.' He said he
had been wandering around looking for her for some time – first at Bays-
water, then Cadogan Gardens, before finally ending up at Hyde Park. The
350-acre Royal Park would undoubtedly have been busy that day. From
mid-century onwards, the popularity of public parks had grown enor-
mously. Alice asked Herbert if he would go with her to have dinner at her
mother's house, but he declined, saying he had to go to Woolwich.

Herbert did not make it home to Union Street until around 5.30 p.m. It
is likely that he went straight to the pub after meeting Alice, as he stumbled a little when he walked into the kitchen. Mrs Pankhurst was surprised
by Herbert's 'untidy' appearance – 'He was not smart, like I like to see him
on a Sunday,' she would later say. 'You have never been to see Alice like
that?' she exclaimed.

'Rats to Alice!' Herbert replied jovially. 'She doesn't mind.'

Herbert went upstairs, washed, and changed into his frock coat, silk hat
and patent leather boots. Walter Pankhurst Sr saw him leave the house
shortly afterwards.

From that day, Mrs Pankhurst noticed a change in her lodger's behaviour. 'He drank more whisky than I liked to see,' she would later say. She
was not the only one – Alice was also concerned that her sweetheart had
started having a 'glass too many on occasions'.

By 1900, the Temperance Movement, which campaigned against the
consumption of alcoholic beverages, had gained a large following, particularly among women and children. The movement emphasised the negative
effects of alcohol and encouraged general abstinence (teetotalism). Alice,
no doubt, would have been concerned by the growing connection of drunk-
enness with degenerate or 'intemperate' personalities. In a letter Herbert

would write to Alice on 8 October, he addresses Alice's concerns about his drinking, promising to 'go straight and keep steady'.

Herbert went to work as usual on the morning of Monday, 24 September – the day after Mary Jane's body was discovered. He returned to his lodgings between 1 p.m. and 2 p.m. for dinner. For the working-class man, dinner was the main meal of the day and usually consisted of carbohydrates to keep him fuelled throughout his afternoon's work. At some point that day, Mrs Pankhurst showed Herbert John Stevens's old room, and he agreed to take it. That evening, Herbert wrote to Alice to tell her that his grandfather had died. The letter was dated 23 September,[2] but was most likely to have been written on the 24th:

> I have been to Bexley to night dear & am sorry to tell you that
> Grandfather passed away this morning at 3.30. a.m. & is to be buried on
> Monday next when I shall not be able to attend as I must not lose any
> more time at present. . . .

Herbert signed off with the promise that he would have 'lots of news' when they next saw each other.

By Tuesday, 25 September, news of the Yarmouth Beach Murder had reached the London newspaper-reading public. Herbert went to work as usual that day, returning to his lodgings in the evening. On the following day, Herbert left work early and headed straight to Bexley, where he called on Walter Hudson – the house agent – at Ralph & Sons Auctioneers' main office.

Herbert arrived at 5 p.m., just as Hudson was closing. He introduced himself as 'Herbert Bennett' and Hudson took him to be the husband of Mrs Bennett, who rented a house in Bexley Heath. He was aware that Mrs Bennett was married, but had never met her husband, as Mary Jane had always paid the rent herself. It was for this reason that he was taken by surprise by the man's next statement: 'I wish to give notice on the house I occupy in Izane Road.' Hudson explained that he was unable to accept the notice himself, and referred Herbert to the owners, two brothers named Butler.

When Herbert returned to Woolwich, he came across Elizabeth Pankhurst as he strolled down Powis Street. He stopped to say hello – 'How about the birthday?' he asked.

'I was there, but you were not,' replied Elizabeth.

*

When Herbert met Alice on the Thursday, he did not fall short on his promise of 'lots of news'. He also had a request. Quite unexpectedly, he asked Alice to consider moving their wedding forward to Christmas. Alice was surprised by the suggestion and asked why he had changed his mind. Herbert said that his cousin had 'gone straight away to South Africa', and that, with his grandfather gone and his relationship with his father strained because of his stepmother, he was all alone in the world. Besides, he said, he had made a deal to buy up all of his cousin's furniture and he wanted them to make a home together as soon as possible.

Mrs Pankhurst would later claim that Herbert had discussed the purchase of his cousin's furniture with her. When he had returned from Bexley Heath one evening, she noticed that he appeared upset, and when she had asked what the matter was, he announced that his cousin had gone to South Africa. In reference to him buying the furniture, he said, 'I have had some trouble with my cousin. She has already had £10, and she wants more. I said I would give £5, making £15 in all.'

Alice was hesitant about bringing the date of the wedding forward but agreed to think about it and eventually promised to give Herbert an answer the following Sunday. That evening, Herbert gave Alice a gold brooch in the design of a shovel, pickaxe and bucket . . .

This was the first time Alice had seen Herbert since his grandfather's death and she sympathised with him. As was customary for the Victorians at the time, Herbert wore mourning dress – black trousers and a black tie. The Victorian dress code for mourning was complicated. Rules were stricter for women, which was reflective of their role in society; widows, in particular, were required to mourn for longer than men and other family members. At the time, a woman's identity and sexuality were considered to be so subsumed in her husband's that when he died, she was thought to have died with him.[3] The acceptable period of mourning by a granddaughter for a grandparent was six to nine months,[4] but the same rules did not apply to men. When Mary Jane's grandmother had died in June 1898, she was photographed in deep mourning. According to the managing partner in the firm of photographers who had taken her portrait, Mr Seward, she was photographed again a year later, on 27 July 1899, in similar mourning clothes. Men's clothes, however, were not substantially altered by mourning requirements. After 1850, they had only to wear black gloves, hatbands and cravats for half the period of mourning prescribed for women.[5] The only exception was the widower, who was expected to wear a hatband and black suit for three months.[6]

While Alice was later unable to recall for exactly how long Herbert wore mourning dress, he was certainly suitably dressed the following day, Friday, 28 September, when his wife was buried in an unmarked grave in Great Yarmouth Old Cemetery on Kitchener Road. The 'sad and quiet ceremony'[7] was attended by Mrs Rudrum and her daughter Alice, and Detective Inspector Lingwood. Herbert, meanwhile, remained in London.

As news of the police's fruitless investigations into the crime began to spread across the country, Mary Jane Bennett's murderer would undoubtedly have been gaining confidence of escaping detection. On the Friday, Herbert posted a letter that he had written to the owners of Glencoe Villas, the Butler brothers, giving notice to leave the property:

Dear Sir,

...I am writing to inform you that I wish to give you three months notice from today Sept. 28th as I shall be leaving the premises No. 1. Glencoe Villas Izane Rd. in Dec. I am sorry to have to do so, but I have to leave England for America on Dec. 24th. Mrs Bennett is away on account of her health, so I will call & see you on Thursday afternoon next ...

Yours Respectfully,

H.W. Bennett

Herbert spent the evening with William Parritt and John Cameron in the Shakespeare pub. Parritt reminded Herbert that he had promised to give him a photograph of Mary Jane. Herbert again vowed to send him one.

A few days later, Herbert showed Mrs Pankhurst a portrait of himself and his wife, which he claimed to be of him and his sister. 'Don't tell Alice I have this,' he said, 'she might want it.'[8] The photograph had, in fact, been taken in Frank Sayers' studio in Great Yarmouth on a visit Herbert had taken with Mary Jane not long after they had married. The photographer – whether it was Sayers himself remains to be seen – had placed Mary Jane upon a chair, with Herbert standing beside her. The knuckles of Herbert's right hand were resting on a wooden plinth to steady him for the long exposure, and his left hand was placed behind his back. The photographer directed Mary Jane to allow her right arm to hang casually over the back of the chair. Her left hand was resting in her lap, revealing the wedding ring on her third finger. Both were wearing their Sunday best. The cabinet card had at one time sat proudly on the mantelpiece in the front room at Glencoe Villas. A copy had also been given to Mary Jane's father, William.

Having shown the photograph to Mrs Pankhurst, Herbert placed it in an envelope and sent it to the Woolwich Co-operative stores for Parritt's attention. It was a risk – Parritt would almost certainly have shown it to John Cameron, who may have recognised the woman as the 'golden haired lady'[9] he had seen Herbert talking to in Powis Street on two separate occasions. Parritt may also have shown it to Robert Allen, who would have been able to identify the woman as the lady Herbert had introduced to him as his wife. It is doubtful, however, that any of the men would have connected Herbert's 'dead' wife with the murdered 'Mrs Hood' in Great Yarmouth. Up until that point, the only images of the deceased woman to have appeared in the London newspapers were crude illustrations taken from the beach photograph, which were hardly recognisable.

On the following day – Sunday – Herbert went to Alice's mother's house as usual. It was settled that he and Alice would marry at Christmas. On this occasion, Alice told Herbert that she planned to buy a black coat and skirt. Herbert said his cousin had a nice blue coat and skirt that she no longer wanted as she would only need light clothes for South Africa. He told her that he would buy them for her, along with anything else that might be suitable.

Herbert visited Glencoe Villas, Mary Jane's house, on several occasions throughout October. On one of his earlier visits, he forced open the back window of the house with a knife he had borrowed from the Langmans. He claimed that he had left the key at home in the pocket of another pair of trousers. In reality, there was only one key to the house and that – having been found in Mary Jane's room at the Rudrums' lodging house – was now in the possession of the police. At this point, the police were no closer to unlocking the mystery surrounding the dead woman, let alone the door to Glencoe Villas. Having given notice to leave the property, Herbert seemed keen to empty the house as quickly as possible. He took away packages each time he visited. Some were intended for Alice, others he took home to Union Street. Following one of his visits to Bexley Heath, he showed Mrs Pankhurst the items he had 'purchased' from his cousin. They included a white satin tablecloth, two pieces of dress material, some music and two violins. One of the instruments was a valuable antique. It was the violin that Mr Edwards had gifted his granddaughter years before. Among the stack of music was a handwritten piece, which had been written, Herbert said proudly, by his cousin, who was a 'beautiful musician'.

The Savages had moved out of 2 Glencoe Villas on 25 September, which meant that Herbert had only to account for his wife's continued absence to one set of neighbours. He told the Langmans that Mary Jane had fallen ill while in Yorkshire and was not able to return home. Every time he took something from the house, he explained that he intended to send whatever it was – usually clothing – to Mary Jane. The Langmans were naturally concerned about their neighbour, and their thoughts would have travelled back to Mary Jane's illness in August when they had all feared for her life. Mary Jane's neighbours gratefully received Herbert's regular updates about his wife's recovery and never challenged his constant visits.

On Tuesday, 2 October, Herbert bumped into Robert Allen in Woolwich. Herbert happened to mention that he had a bicycle for sale and showed his friend the machine. By now Herbert was accustomed to inflating both the price and quality of even the most basic of things. He told Allen that the bicycle had cost him 15 guineas new. He quickly added that he could show him the receipt to prove it. During the conversation, Herbert told Allen that he also had a piano to sell. Allen said he would consider the purchase and the two men parted.

By the afternoon of the following day, Herbert was laid up at Union Street following an operation to remove an ingrowing toenail. He recounted his 'terrible day' to Alice in a self-pitying letter that he wrote when he returned home from the hospital:

My Own Darling Alice,

. . . I cannot get my foot to the ground dear &am in awful agony with it I went under Gas for 17 minutes, & I feel quite ill after it, I don't expect that I shall put my foot to the ground for about a week to come yet, I had to come home in a cab as I was in such pain . . . I should like to see you very much dearest tomorrow night if you can possibly come & see me if only for an hour or so, as I am now very miserable what with the pain & one thing & another I feel like going mad . . .'[10]

Alice, like many other people, would later wonder what Herbert was referring to when he wrote the closing sentence.

Despite telling Alice that he could not put his foot to the ground, Herbert travelled to Bexley the next day (as he had promised he would in his letter to the Butlers) to call on the owners of Glencoe Villas. The Butler brothers agreed to release Herbert from the lease on the house in exchange for a payment of £4. 10s. Herbert returned to Union Street in time for Alice's visit that evening. His mood had improved significantly by the time she had left, as evidenced in a letter he wrote to her in which he declared, 'I seem to love you ten times more, especially now that I have nothing to do but think of you dearest . . .'[11]

On Monday, 8 October, Herbert spent the entire day at Bexley Heath, packing up the house. He had written to Alice before breakfast that morning to say that he would forward her the coat and skirt and 'anything else that will be useful', adding that they would only be 'thrown away' otherwise. A second letter, written after his visit, confirms that he had also sent a sealskin cape, a piece of lace and a silver horseshoe brooch. Alice received the parcel the following day, and she sent him a letter on 9 October thanking him:

> My darling old boy,
>
> Just a line to let you know I received the parcel quite safely and thank you very much for the things, but I am sorry to say the coat does not fit me. It is much too short waisted for me and am afraid it cannot be altered, but darling, if you don't mind Florrie [another of her sisters] would like to buy the thing right out as it just fits her splendidly . . . but the cape dear is alright, I like that very much . . . the skirt is alright for me, but it would cost me as much as a new thing to have a coat made to match. I hope darling you are better. Write to me soon, there's a dear old boy. I shall be looking for a letter, must say goodbye now.
>
> With fondest love and kisses,
>
> Your devoted Alice[12]

On the following day, Herbert met Robert Allen, who was on his half-day. He had arranged for Allen to view Mary Jane's piano at Glencoe Villas. The two men travelled to Bexley Heath by horse-bus, which – alongside the railway – was the main method of public transport in London at the time. On the way, Herbert explained that Glencoe Villas was his 'cousin's' home and that he had recently 'bought up' his house, meaning that he had purchased the contents. Presumably by way of explaining any letters or documents that may have been lying around, he added that his cousin's name was also 'Bennett'. When the two men arrived at the house it was deserted apart from the little fox terrier that was in the back garden. Despite Herbert saying that no one was living in the house, Allen noticed signs of life: a woman's hat, a pair of lady's gloves and a child's pinafore. He assumed that the items belonged to Herbert's wife and child and asked if his wife was there. 'She is not here,' Herbert said, 'she is down home.' Then, having spent a few seconds considering the question, Herbert added: 'I have no wife; but I am about to be married.' He explained – rather lamely – that what he had previously said about being married was untrue. Allen's enquiry about his wife caught Herbert off-guard, much like Parritt's had the month before in Rose's Distillery. He reacted in much the same way as he had on that day: by giving a rather impetuous and ill-considered response. Noticing Allen looking at the garments that were strewn about the place, Herbert explained that his 'cousin' had left for South Africa in a hurry six weeks earlier, which was why the house was in such disorder.

Having viewed the piano, Allen said that he would give Herbert a decision about purchasing the instrument and the bicycle at the weekend. The two men travelled back to Woolwich and Herbert frequently tried to impress upon Allen that he had never been married, but that he was about to be. He then asked him 'two or three times' not to tell anyone that he was getting married. Herbert had clearly realised his mistake in taking Allen to Bexley Heath, and there was suddenly a very real danger that he would become tangled up in his own lies.

Herbert saw Alice in Woolwich again on Thursday, 11 October. On that occasion, he gave her the tablecloth and dress material that he had brought back from Glencoe Villas. Alice no doubt added the fabric to her trousseau, which by now also included a wedding dress of white satin. That evening, Herbert asked Alice to tell her mother that he would send her a child's cot, highchair and a mail cart for Alice's adopted brother, Sydney.

Meanwhile, Allen had been in touch with Herbert to ask if he could see the piano again before making up his mind. Clearly driven by the prospect of earning some easy money, Herbert agreed. The two men arranged to meet on the Sunday. Herbert paid an advance visit to the house on the Friday, presumably to make sure there was nothing that could link the house with his wife. That day, he took away the little fox terrier, saying he was going to take it to Mrs Bennett in Yorkshire. He paid Lilian Langman some money for the food she had bought for it. His update regarding his wife was more positive: he told the Langmans that Mary Jane was still ill but that she had started to improve and was now able to sit up in her bedroom. He also claimed that his wife had sent her love to Lilian's mother, Mrs Langman.

As arranged, Herbert met Allen at Glencoe Villas on Sunday, 14 October. Allen agreed to buy both the bicycle and the piano. After some bartering, the two men settled on a price of £23 for both. Allen paid a deposit of £6, agreeing to pay the balance on delivery. To prove authenticity of the goods, Herbert produced the 'original' receipt for the bicycle, which showed that

he had paid £15 and 15s. Naturally, the receipt was forged. Herbert told
Allen that he did not have a receipt for the piano but that he had purchased it from a man named 'Bartlett', who resided at 10 Woolwich Road,
Bexley Heath. 'Mr Bartlett' was in fact Herbert and the address was the
flat Mary Jane had occupied before she moved to Glencoe Villas. Whether
Herbert realised it or not, this was a smart move. The other occupants of
the building would no doubt have been able to tell Allen that 'Mr Bartlett'
had indeed owned a piano. Allen rode the bicycle home from Woolwich
that evening and arranged to collect the piano on Wednesday, 24 October.

Herbert returned to work at the Arsenal on Monday, 15 October. On
Wednesday that week, Alice left her situation, having worked a month's
notice. When she finished work that afternoon, she went straight to Woolwich, where she had arranged to meet Herbert. He was not at home when
she arrived. He eventually returned home at 9 p.m., explaining that he had
been at Bexley Heath, selling the piano. He was obviously lying, as he had
already settled the sale of the piano the previous weekend, but he may have
been at Bexley Heath packing up the house. The remark prompted Alice
to ask if Herbert had heard from his cousin. 'No,' he replied, 'I doubt I will
hear from them for a long time.' A few minutes later, he added, 'I shouldn't
be surprised if I never hear any more about them.' That was the last time
Herbert spoke about his 'cousin' in Alice's presence.

On Saturday, 20 October, Alice went with Herbert to Charlton to
view a house: 62 Heathwood Gardens. At the time, Charlton was a developing district to the east of Woolwich. New houses were springing up
everywhere. The small, terraced homes of Heathwood Gardens had been
designed for one or two families and were being bought up by landlords
for approximately £380 to rent out.[13] Despite its popularity, parts of the
district were dismal. The lower land to the north was being filled with
refuse to raise it in line with the other houses. The stench must have been
unbearable.

Among the new residents of Heathwood Gardens was Robert Allen
and his wife, Annie, who had moved to Charlton after they had married
in the summer. They rented three rooms at number 38, twelve doors down.
It may even have been Allen who recommended the street to Herbert.
At the time, it was the man's responsibility to rent and furnish a home.
Setting up home after marrying was the middle-class ideal and something
Alice would have dreamt of. She was pleased with the house and that
was enough for Herbert – he declared that they should live there and put
down a deposit straight away. Herbert paid £2 to the owner, Mrs Taylor,

in exchange for a five-month lease, that would start after their marriage in December.

On Wednesday, 24 October, Herbert met Allen and Parritt at Bexley Heath to oversee the removal of the piano. By then, all trace of Mary Jane and Ruby had either been removed from the house entirely or securely packed away in trunks. Nevertheless, Herbert was taking a significant risk that could allow Parritt to draw a connection between him and Bexley Heath. Perhaps he felt the damage had already been done. Lilian was at home that day and would later recall the piano being taken away.

Despite Herbert's pleas to Allen not to discuss his marital status, Herbert soon became one of the main topics of conversation between Allen, Parritt and John Cameron. Allen would later admit that his colleagues in the grocery store had told him the name of the girl Herbert was going to marry and much more besides. It would not have taken long for the three men to establish that Herbert had told them all different accounts of his life and the deceit soon caused Allen to develop misgivings about the deal he had made with Herbert. Allen spoke to Cameron, who suggested that he write to the bicycle manufacturer to establish whether the machine had been fairly represented. Allen did just that. The manufacturer wrote back to say that the receipt he had been supplied with was not genuine and that the bicycle would never have cost 15 guineas. With his misgivings about the bicycle confirmed, Allen began to question the authenticity of the piano. He sought the services of an expert, who examined the instrument and concluded that it was not worth what Allen had agreed to pay for it. Angry at being deceived, Allen confronted Herbert. Although he would later claim that he had not threatened to prosecute Herbert for fraud, Allen certainly made it clear that he thought he was being swindled. Allen's father-in-law, Walter Campion, was a police sergeant and his name would undoubtedly have figured in the conversation. Allen told Herbert that he knew the bicycle receipt had been forged and he now intended to find out if the piano was really his property.

The conversation caused Herbert a great deal of concern. He returned home in what Mrs Pankhurst later described as a 'very excited state'. He told his landlady that there had been some trouble over the sale of his bicycle and that he had to leave her house. He said that he was going to live at 18 William Street – 'but don't tell anyone where I am going', he added urgently. It was the last Monday in October, a date that Mrs Pankhurst would later recall as 'the day the CIVs came home'. The CIVs, or City of London Imperial Volunteers, were a British corps of volunteers supporting the war effort in South Africa. The CIVs' return was marked by a full day of celebrations on Monday, 29 October. 'London', declared *The Times*, had 'turned itself out for a holiday'.[14] By 9 a.m., the streets were 'full and festive', filled with people selling badges and flags, and an unprecedented crowd had lined the route from Paddington to St Paul's.[15] Woolwich, which was well known for its 'constant celebrations of British victories in South Africa',[16] would have been similarly turned-out. Herbert was in such a hurry to leave Mrs Pankhurst's house that day that he left behind several things, including Mary Jane's antique violin, a pair of 'opera glasses', a lady's umbrella and some sheet music.

Herbert's new residence, 18 William Street, was home to several people, including the Locks, a couple in their mid-twenties. At the time, Mrs Lock was pregnant with her first child, a boy. The house was opposite Woolwich police station and less than 300 yards from Mrs Pankhurst's front door. Unbeknown to Herbert, living two doors down at number 20 was Detective Sergeant Henry Holford of the Metropolitan Police. Herbert may have believed that William Street offered protection from discovery. If so, he had clearly underestimated Robert Allen. It was not long before Allen was made aware that Herbert had moved.

The rest of the week passed without incident. On Sunday, 4 November, Herbert joined the Meadows family for Sunday dinner at Mrs Meadows' house in Stepney. After dinner, Herbert and the Meadows siblings retired to the parlour for tea. Sunday afternoons in the Meadows house were usually spent playing cards, or – for the women – sewing. That afternoon, Alice's sister, May, was reading one of the Sunday newspapers. She came across a report on the inquest into the death of 'Mrs Hood' in Great Yarmouth. The inquest, the report stated, had closed the previous Monday, having recorded a verdict of 'murder against a person or persons unknown'.

'Oh,' said May. 'Isn't it odd that the Yarmouth killer has not yet been caught?' This was the first Alice had heard of the murder and she asked her sister to change the subject. Ignoring Alice's protests, May went on to say that it was strange that the police had never caught Jack the Ripper either. Alice would later claim that Herbert made no response to either statement. Various accounts survive to contradict Alice's recollection, including an extract from an interview with the Meadows family. One article claimed that one of Alice's brothers said, 'They had all felt rather pained and interested and wondered who it could be. May looked straight at

Bennett, expecting that he would join in the conversation, and say something; but instead, he made an unfeeling remark about women and the police, which caused them all to think he had very little feeling.'[17]

In a special report that was published in another newspaper, Herbert was reported to have made 'some commonplace remark about murderers not getting found out owing to the stupidity of the police'.[18] Other reports suggest that Herbert spoke only about the Whitechapel killings: 'Oh, I thought [Jack the Ripper] had been caught in America.'

The latter is widely considered to be the most accurate account, with no reference to the Yarmouth murder.

14

A VICTIM OF VANITY

'I have never been to Yarmouth!'

While Herbert was busy systematically dismantling his wife's house, police in London had been investigating Mrs Bennett's connection to Woolwich. Chief Inspector Alfred Leach, of Scotland Yard, had sought the assistance of local police officer Detective Sergeant Henry Holford. Their enquiries had eventually led them to the Woolwich branch of the Co-operative stores, where they encountered Robert Allen. It was Monday, 5 November – Guy Fawkes Day. The two detectives interviewed Allen extensively. He told them everything he knew about the Bennetts. Parritt and Cameron were also questioned and would certainly have told the police the story about the 'death' of Herbert's wife and child in South Africa. It would not have been at all surprising if the two detectives had left the stores that day feeling rather confused.

That evening, Herbert visited Union Street to pay Mrs Pankhurst 10s. in lieu of giving notice. She was pleasantly surprised to see him as she had not thought he would make good on his promise to pay her a week's rent for leaving so suddenly.

When Herbert left work on Tuesday, 6 November, Robert Allen was waiting for him outside Beresford Gate. Herbert had arranged to meet Alice and he had already changed out of his work clothes into a shirt, tie and pair of smart trousers. He was carrying his work overalls in a brown travelling bag. He was reluctant to talk to Allen and hurriedly walked past him. Allen rushed to keep up and eventually fell into step beside him. They had not got very far along the cobbled throughfare of Beresford Street when two men approached them from the opposite direction.

Allen stopped, as if he recognised them. 'Mr Bennett,' he said, motioning towards Herbert. He then pointed to the taller of the two men and added 'Mr Brown'. Before Herbert could react, the taller of the two men lurched forward and threw his arms around him. 'I am a police officer, and I arrest you for the murder of Mrs Hood on Yarmouth beach either on the night of the 22nd or the morning of 23rd September last,' he said. Herbert struggled against the detective's firm grip – 'I don't know what you mean!' he shouted. After two or three seconds, he asked, 'What for?' 'Mr Brown' – who was in fact CI Leach – repeated the charge. At that point, the second man – DS Holford – stepped in to assist his colleague. When the two detectives had secured their prisoner, they marched him the short distance to Woolwich police station.

During the course of their enquiries, the police had traced Herbert to Wickham Lane, in Plumstead, where they had come across Mrs Elliston. The Bennetts' old landlady was able to identify the woman in the beach photograph as her lodger, Mrs Bennett. Mrs Elliston's husband, PC Herman Elliston, was then called to identify Herbert. He was at the Woolwich police station on the afternoon Herbert was brought in. Chief Constable Parker was also present, as he had received word from Leach that morning that they were preparing to arrest their only suspect in the murder. Parker had caught the 2.20 p.m. train from Great Yarmouth to London Liverpool Street and rushed across the capital in time to see Herbert brought in.

When Leach and Holford arrived at the police station with their hand-cuffed prisoner, Herbert was in the throes of denying all knowledge of the murder – 'I don't know what you mean,' he protested, 'I have never been to Yarmouth. I have not lived with my wife since January last. I have found a lot of letters in her pocket from another man.' Leach produced the beach photograph and showed it to his prisoner – 'This is the photograph of the woman I have referred to,' he said. Herbert examined the picture closely. 'I don't clearly recognise it,' he said; 'is she dark?' Of the four police officers in attendance that day, Parker was the only one to have seen the body of the dead woman. He now recalled her lifeless form as she lay in the mortuary. 'No,' he interjected, 'she was exceptionally fair.' Herbert nodded, as if contemplating the remark, but made no further comment.

The beach photograph was later described by many as having a poor likeness to the woman it depicted. The common opinion was that Mary Jane appeared older in the photograph and her hair looked much darker. Mary Jane's neighbour, Lilian Langman, said the photograph was 'not very clear'. Poor likeness or not, if anyone could identify her from it, it was surely her husband.

Herbert had evidently been caught off-guard by his arrest and it had thrown him into a state of panic. When he had found himself in similar situations in the past, his first instinct had been to flee or to lie – or both.

Unable to do the former, he settled on the latter. Lying came so naturally to him that it is likely the words flowed from his mouth before he had a chance to consider the consequences. Claiming not to recognise his wife was a poor choice. PC Elliston confirmed that Leach's prisoner was the young man who had lodged with him in May and June of that year – the husband of the woman in the photograph. Herbert was then duly charged with the murder of the woman known until recently as 'Mrs Hood' and taken to a cell to be searched by Leach and Parker.

Among the articles the two officers recovered from their prisoner was a bunch of keys. Herbert was also found to be wearing a collar, shirt and tie, which all bore the 599 laundry mark. At the time, a collar carried clues to a person's class – a man's position within the social hierarchy was judged by how clean and stiff his collar was.[1] Since a well-starched collar was almost impossible to achieve at home, Herbert's pursuit of status had compelled him to continue sending his collars and shirts to Kingdom's to be professionally laundered after his wife had left Bexley Heath. It may also have been a clever ploy to fool the police into thinking that it was Mrs Bennett who was sending the washing in. If this was the case, it may have worked to begin with, but the police eventually traced the laundry back to Herbert.

Later that evening, Leach and Parker searched Herbert's room at 18 William Street. They used a key from the bunch they had recovered from Herbert to open the door to his bedroom. A second key unlocked a portmanteau that was located inside. The trunk was decorated with labels for the steamship *Avondale Castle*. When the officers opened it, they recovered several collars – all marked with the 599 laundry mark – two imitation pearl necklaces, fourteen letters from Herbert's sweetheart Alice Meadows, a male and female wig and a moustache made of real hair. The wigs appeared as if they had been in 'almost constant use' – perhaps worn regularly throughout the Bennetts' outward voyage to the Cape. The officers also found a revolver and cartridges. At the time, it was not illegal to own a gun and restrictions on the sale of firearms would not be introduced for a further two years. It is likely that the revolver found in Herbert's portmanteau was the one he had used to threaten his father-in-law, William Clark, when the two men had quarrelled over Mary Jane's piano. Finally, Parker retrieved a long gold chain and a small silver watch. The police officer would not realise the significance of this find until he returned to Great Yarmouth.

When the two officers examined the bundle of letters more closely, they found a receipt from the Crown and Anchor Hotel, Great Yarmouth, nestled among the envelopes. The bill was for a stay ending on Monday, 6 August, and was signed by 'William Reade'. The receipt connected Herbert to Great Yarmouth and immediately caught him in a lie – the two officers no doubt recalled Herbert's insistence that he had 'never been to Yarmouth' as he had entered the police station earlier that day. That was not the only receipt the two police chiefs found that would cast doubt over Herbert's innocence. Parker recovered 'either upon the prisoner or in his portmanteau' – there was later confusion – a receipt from the owners of Glencoe Villas, the Butler brothers, for a payment made releasing Herbert from the lease on the house.

Herbert assumed a 'sullen demeanour' that evening and lay on the floor of his cell for the rest of the night[2] – just as he had at the Ellistons' the night he had refused to get into bed with his wife. The following morning, Wednesday, 7 November, Parker visited him in his cell. 'I am the chief constable of Great Yarmouth and will be taking you to Great Yarmouth on the charge explained to you last night by Inspector Leach. I was present,' he said.

'Yes, I saw you,' replied Herbert. Parker had no intention of transporting Herbert to Norfolk that day – the papers were full of the news of his arrest and feelings in Great Yarmouth were running high. 'It is now my duty to caution you that anything you might say will be given in evidence against you,' Parker continued. 'Do you wish to say anything as regards your movements on the night of 22nd September?'

'I wish you to see Mrs Pankhurst,' Herbert replied unhesitatingly. 'She can prove where I was.' He paused for a moment, before adding: 'I should also like a wire sent to my sweetheart, Miss Meadows, in Stepney.'

The wire was duly sent. It read:

COME AND SEE ME AT ONCE.

Alice was already in Woolwich by the time the telegram was sent. When Herbert had failed to show up for their meeting the previous evening, she had assumed that he had taken ill and so she had gone to Woolwich on the Wednesday morning to check on him. Having learned from his landlady of her sweetheart's arrest, she went straight to the police station, where she encountered Leach. She was wearing the sealskin cape that Herbert claimed had belonged to his 'cousin'. It fell to Leach to convey the difficult news to poor Alice. When she later recounted the conversation, she recalled it being the first time that she had learned that Herbert had been married and that he and his wife had had a child. Three days later, she would give an interview to a newspaper reporter, in which she described the 'horrible' moment when she found out that her fiancé was accused of murder – 'I was horrified and dumbstricken.'[3] As Alice absorbed the news at the police station, she suddenly realised that the sealskin cape she was wearing must have belonged to her sweetheart's dead wife. She 'flung it off at once', before allowing the police to take it into evidence. She was then shepherded into an anteroom, where she was told to wait for Herbert to be brought in. Alice would later recall the meeting: 'I looked at him, and I read in his eyes what he did not say to me – "do you think I'm guilty?"'

'Bert, are you innocent of this?' asked Alice.

Herbert looked at her for a moment before saying, 'You, Alice, don't think I have done it?'

'No, I do not,' Alice replied firmly.

'Well, then I am innocent!' cried Herbert.

When Alice got up to leave, she turned to her sweetheart and said, 'I believe you, Bert. I will pray for you and you also pray for yourself.' Perhaps it was the shock of it all, but Alice's first instinct was to stand by her fiancé. When she left the police station that day, she went home to her mother's house in Stepney where she relayed the terrible news of Herbert's arrest to her family.

Later that day, Parker, Leach and Detective Inspector Gummer travelled to Bexley Heath to search Mary Jane's house. They entered the property through the main door at the side of the stout little terraced house, using the key that Lingwood had found in 'Mrs Hood's' purse at the Rudrums' house. The house was empty, save for a few sticks of furniture and several packed trunks. The blinds were tightly drawn and the rooms that were at one time alive with Ruby's childlike chatter were now cloaked in an eerie silence. In the downstairs rooms, the police officers found a used packet of hair dye and several collars marked H.J. Bennett and H. Bennett, which were all labelled with the 599 laundry mark.

Upstairs, in the back bedroom, Parker found a portmanteau, like the one recovered from Herbert's lodging house, which had also been decorated with Union-Castle Steamship Company labels. The chief constable unlocked it with one of the keys from Herbert. It was packed full of vases and empty photo frames. In the front bedroom, a chest of drawers was crammed full of women's clothes, all bearing the tell-tale 599 laundry mark. A spectacle case was lying empty on the mantelpiece and a second trunk was packed full of ladies' clothes and several papers relating to the SS *Avondale Castle*.

Earlier that day, after Parker had sent a wire to Detective Inspector Lingwood in Great Yarmouth to notify him of Herbert's arrest, Lingwood had, like Parker a day before, taken the 2.20 p.m. train from Great Yarmouth to Liverpool Street, where Parker was waiting to meet him. The two police officers went straight to Mrs Meadows' house, a journey that took approximately twenty minutes. Alice, in anticipation of their visit, had gathered some articles that she thought would be relevant to their inquiry. Among them were the eighteen letters that she had received from Herbert – she had kept every single one he had sent her – a gold shovel, pickaxe and bucket brooch that Herbert had given her, and her ruby and diamond engagement ring. Even with her supportive family by her side, the sense of betrayal that Alice felt must have been unbearable.

Owing to the confident predictions of several newspapers that the man arrested in connection with the 'Yarmouth Beach Murder' would be transported to Great Yarmouth that day, large crowds of people had begun to gather outside the South Town railway station and Great Yarmouth's town hall during the late afternoon and into the evening of Wednesday, 7 November. The great mass of people only dispersed when they were told that the last train had arrived from London without the prisoner aboard.

In order to avoid a repeat performance the following day, Parker ordered the police in Great Yarmouth to issue a statement saying that the prisoner would arrive on the mail train, which reached Great Yarmouth at three o'clock the following morning. As a result, the streets bordering the town hall and police station were thronged with people on the Thursday morning, all expecting to see the prisoner removed from the police station to the court to appear before the magistrates. In actuality, Herbert was still in London, and would not arrive in Great Yarmouth until just after 4 p.m., by which time most of the crowds had dispersed.

Accompanied by Parker and Lingwood, Herbert spent the whole of the journey to Great Yarmouth with his wrists securely shackled in front of him. He maintained a 'studied reserve', appearing sullen and only speaking when spoken to. His responses were blunt and brief. When the London train steamed into the South Town station that afternoon, the two officers were able to smuggle their prisoner swiftly into a waiting cab without attracting too much attention.

Herbert was taken straight to Middlegate Street police station, where a small crowd of diehard observers were still gathered outside. Among the crowd was a reporter for the *Yarmouth Advertiser and Gazette*, who described Herbert that day as 'devoid of any striking feature in his personal appearance, he belongs to the ordinarily intelligent artisan type, has short, dark hair and a tiny black moustache above a thick lipped mouth, and was quite simply and neatly dressed in dark clothes, with a black three-quarter length overcoat and hard bowler hat'.[4]

Before Herbert had left Woolwich police station, he had received a letter from Alice Meadows. In it, she asked him not to think of her if the dead woman was his wife: 'Think of your child instead. Pray to God who is the judge above us and put your trust in Him. And if you really committed this crime, ask God for forgiveness. I will pray for you.'

Not long after Herbert had been transferred from Woolwich by his captors, a middle-aged man called at the police station and asked to speak to the inspector in charge of the Bennett case. His name, he said, was William Clark, and he now revealed that he thought the woman who had been murdered on the beach in Great Yarmouth was his daughter. He explained to the officer on duty that his eldest son, William Charles, had been reading aloud an account of the arrest of the man Bennett in a newspaper that morning when it had suddenly occurred to him. William then produced a portrait of Mary Jane and Herbert Bennett together. It was a copy of the photograph that Herbert had sent to William Parritt. Mary Jane's father explained that the photograph had been taken three years previously. Herbert appeared slightly younger and was without a moustache, but the police officers immediately recognised him as the man they had in custody. When it became evident that the murdered woman really was his daughter, William broke down, and it was some time before he had recovered enough to accompany Holford to Scotland Yard to see Leach.

Like most people in Great Yarmouth, the Rudrums had learned of the arrest of Bennett from the newspapers. It was nigh on impossible to escape the reports – one journalist wrote that the affair was the topic of conversation not merely at street corners, but in 'every circle, all over Yarmouth'.[5] When Mrs Rudrum had heard the name 'Bennett', it had stuck a chord. She searched her correspondence until she came across the letter that Herbert had sent her that summer, asking for rooms. She 'immediately' recognised the handwriting as the same writing on the letter that had arrived from Woolwich on the Friday evening before her lodger's death. She handed Herbert's letter to her daughter, Alice, instructing her to take it straight to the police station.

When Alice arrived at Middlegate Street station, she found Parker sitting at his desk, processing the evidence that he had brought back with him from Woolwich. By now, it was Thursday evening, 8 November, and Herbert had been processed and placed in one of the police station's cells. Alice handed Parker the letter, explaining the connection to the letter 'Mrs Hood' had received. As she spoke, she looked down at the exhibits on the police officer's desk and spotted the long gold chain lying coiled up next to the small silver pocket watch that had been recovered from Herbert's lodgings. According to Alice, Parker asked her if she recognised the chain. 'I looked at it,' she would later recall, 'and said, "Why that is Mrs Hood's chain!"' Up until that moment, Parker had been unaware that a gold chain, and a small silver pocket watch, were missing from the dead woman's body. Picking up the watch, he then asked Alice if there was anything peculiar about it. 'If you open the back,' Alice replied, 'you will find the marks of the child's teeth there.' The chief constable duly opened the watch and, sure enough, there – just as Alice had described – were the tooth marks ...[6]

15

A SWARM OF SPECTATORS

'Sit down in front!'

O n the following day, Friday, 9 November, Herbert Bennett made his first appearance before the Great Yarmouth magistrates. Despite the proceedings being limited only to the formal evidence of arrest, a full bench of magistrates was in attendance. Herbert had been transferred to the cells in the basement of the town hall at nine o'clock that morning. At the time, there had only been a small number of people outside the building and the officers in charge of Herbert had been able to marshal him through a side door without attracting too much attention. As the expected hour of Herbert's appearance drew nearer, the narrow roadway from the police station to the town hall became thickly lined with spectators.

The hearing was due to be held in the town hall's large sessions court, which was positioned in the southeast corner on the first floor. The courtroom was accessed by an imperial staircase, which rose to the east. That morning, as the spectators climbed the staircase, light fell onto the steps from the painted glass windows above. The public gallery in the courthouse soon filled, but only a small number of the hundreds of people who had gathered outside were admitted. The two benches in front of the dock had been reserved for the wives of magistrates and prominent townspeople, and all the local dignitaries who could squeeze into the courtroom were there in all their glory.

All the sitting and standing room had been taken an hour before the proceedings commenced, with women outnumbering men by some margin. The court was still decked out in its original fittings from 1882, which included a panelled bench and dock. Behind the dock, an internal staircase led down to a secure room and side entrance on the ground floor. While the court filled, Herbert waited in the room below, no doubt contemplating what was to come.

Unsurprisingly, the press was well represented. When the mayor entered the courtroom, he spotted that one of the London journalists had brought a handheld camera into the press box. He immediately directed Parker to prevent the reporter from using it and the officer had the Kodak removed from the court. Although it would not be illegal to use a camera in a courtroom for a further twenty-five years, it was strongly disapproved of at the time.[1]

The proceedings began promptly at 11 a.m. It was the day of the Lord Mayor's Show in Great Yarmouth and the outgoing mayor, Benjamin Howard Press, presided. The customary vote of thanks to the retiring mayor occupied the first few minutes of the formal proceedings and then Lingwood and another officer descended the dock steps to fetch Herbert up from the cells. Herbert had taken some care over his appearance that morning and when he emerged from below court, he appeared well groomed. He wore a long coat and his slight moustache had been twisted and pointed upwards at the ends. 'Sit down in front!' cried several people from the back of the courtroom as the spectators vied for a better look at the prisoner. One reporter, apparently surprised by Herbert's appearance, described his 'general aspect' as 'one of an ordinary shopman'.[2] Another wrote that there was nothing repellent in his looks – 'vanity shows there, but not cruelty nor villainy'.[3]

Sketch of Herbert Bennett on the front cover of the *Illustrated Mail*, 24 November 1900.

Herbert stood between two policemen, placed both hands on the dock rail and looked out at the court. Perhaps he hoped to catch a glimpse of Alice Meadows. Sadly, he saw no one he recognised in the sea of faces that stared back at him. He appeared composed yet sullen. He paid close attention as the charge against him was read out by Parker. By this point, Herbert had admitted that the dead woman was his wife. As the officer read the words *'did murder his wife'*, Herbert's lips twitched nervously and his face flushed. He wrung his hands, clasping and unclasping his long fingers several times. The magistrate's clerk asked if anyone had been appointed to prosecute. Parker replied no, and then the clerk turned to Herbert.

'Are you defended?' he asked.

'No, sir,' replied the prisoner.

The clerk turned back to the bench. The chief constable, he said, would give a short summary of the evidence and then ask for a remand for seven days. The mayor agreed and Parker stepped forward. Herbert listened intently to the officer's testimony. When the time came for Parker to introduce the watch and chain into evidence, Herbert became visibly agitated. When the chief constable told the court that the watch and chain had been identified by the Rudrums as having been worn by the deceased woman while she lodged in their house, Herbert gripped the front of the dock. He shook his head, then, unable to contain himself for a moment longer, he exclaimed, 'She has not worn them for twelve months!' Herbert was instructed to be quiet, and Parker continued. When the officer had finished giving his evidence, the clerk asked Herbert if he would like to put any questions to the chief constable. 'No,' he replied, 'but I'd like to make a statement. Right through from the beginning, I swear I am not guilty.'

'You had better not,' cautioned the clerk, 'it may be used as evidence against you.'

'I only wish to tell the truth. I shall make a true statement from the beginning,' Herbert persisted.

The mayor, who was fully kitted out in his official dress, asked the prisoner if he intended to be represented – 'if it is your intention to be represented later on, then I advise you to reserve your defence'.

'I don't have the means to employ a solicitor,' Herbert replied, rather despairingly. It was true that Herbert was, by now, low on funds. Without Mary Jane, the violin trade had dried up and he had spared no expense in his pursuit of Alice's affections.

Eventually, the clerk managed to convince Herbert that it was not in his best interest to say any more than he already had: 'It will not prejudice you by not making a statement, but you might be prejudiced by doing so.'

The mayor then formally remanded the prisoner until the following Friday, 16 November, to give the police time to gather more evidence. As he was leaving the dock, Herbert turned once more to the bench: 'So you don't wish me to make any statement before that day?' he asked searchingly.

'It rests entirely with you,' the mayor responded, 'but if you take my advice, you will reserve your defence. You will have ample opportunity later.'

Herbert appeared to accept the advice and the court was adjourned.

Herbert was conveyed to Norwich's Thorpe station by the 3.14 p.m. train from Great Yarmouth. He arrived at just after 4 p.m. to a crowd of spectators. As he disembarked from the train, several guards surrounded him. The crowd surged towards the barriers the police had constructed, but they held in place. Herbert was quickly ushered into a waiting cab and was then hastily driven up to Norwich Prison where he would await his next appearance before the magistrates.

Among the spectators in the crowded courtroom that day was a local man named John Headley. Headley was a newsagent and newspaper correspondent who was attending court in his capacity as a reporter. When Herbert was brought into the dock, Headley recognised him immediately. He would later say that it was his 'honest belief' that he saw Herbert on the platform at the South Town railway station in the early morning of Sunday, 23 September: 'The likeness of the man standing outside that first-class carriage on that Sunday morning came suddenly to my mind as I gazed upon the prisoner. I was fascinated.'[4] The newsvendor picked Herbert out of an identity parade at the police station a few days later but would never swear absolutely to him being the man.

While the police were busily gathering further evidence against their prisoner, the press was conducting its own investigations into the man named Bennett. In the days following Herbert's arrest, 'special crime investigators' dashed to piece together a narrative of Herbert's life in what would later be referred to as a 'newspaper campaign of vilification'.[5]

Reporters – some posing as police detectives – hunted down witnesses and published key testimony before it was heard in court. Others were even accused of fabricating interviews in an attempt to further sensationalise their stories. Some articles were largely derived from hearsay and these more salacious stories were published alongside timelines with dates of key events and rumours about past criminal activity.

The crime continued to be the object of general conversation – '... residents of the seaside resort now hang breathless on every scrap of evidence likely to affect the case. In fact, the entire country has been electrified by the crime ...'⁶ The public's thirst for the latest details in the case encouraged reporters to dig deeper into Herbert's past. The *Yarmouth Advertiser and Gazette*, which only a week before Herbert's arrest had declared the murder to be a 'mystery for all time', now described events as having been 'revived and quickened to fever heat ...'⁷ Another newspaper declared that 'great excitement' had been caused in Yarmouth by the arrest.⁸

Not all newspapers joined the fray, and some even went so far as to condemn the action of the small number of 'outrageous gutter rags'⁹ that published reports that were prejudicial to Herbert's case. At the time, a new-fangled form of journalism dubbed 'Tabloid Journalism', or 'Yellow Journalism' (in North America), was taking hold in Britain. This new style was chiefly practised by reporters for the halfpenny evening and Sunday newspapers and was aimed at popular audiences. Characteristic of Tabloid Journalism was the use of bold headlines, emotive writing and sensationalist stories: 'For the new journalist, murder was attractive, not just because of the intrinsically sensational nature of the crime, but also because there was a strong human interest strand that could be exploited outside the formal criminal justice process, especially where there was a mystery about the perpetrator.'¹⁰

The 'mysterious' murder of 'Mrs Hood' was perfectly suited to this style of journalism and the Bennetts' story provided plenty of sensational durability that ensured pre-trial coverage that would last for weeks. Alice Meadows quickly became one of the most sought-after characters in the story. Three days after her ordeal at the police station, the London evening newspaper the *Echo* published an interview with her. The reporter described Alice as 'prostrated by grief'.¹¹ She was, claimed the reporter, 'so weak that she had to be led by her mother into the front parlour and placed in an easy chair'.¹² According to the journalist, Alice believed Herbert to be innocent from her 'very soul' and she was struggling to come to terms with his arrest. Despite accepting that she had been 'wronged and deceived' by him, Alice vowed to stand by her sweetheart. The marriage banns signalling Alice and Herbert's impending nuptials were due to be read for the first time that Sunday.

Two days after the interview with Alice appeared in the *Echo*, the *Daily*

Mail published an interview with the Bennetts' Plumstead landlady, Mrs Elliston. The story was published under the headline 'Was Bennett threatened by his wife?' In the report, Mrs Elliston allegedly claimed that when Mary Jane arrived at her house, she was 'richly dressed and wearing a profusion of jewellery'. She was reported to have recounted the Bennetts' argument on the evening before they had left, which had culminated in Mary Jane's threat to her husband that she could get him 'fifteen years'.[13]

In another account that appeared in the *Evening News* on the same day, Mrs Elliston was described as the woman to whom Mary Jane turned for sympathy and comfort. Referring to the Bennetts' visit to Cape Town, Mrs Elliston had apparently stated, 'I never quite believed that story, nor did I accept much else she told me.' It continued: 'Her stories of herself never agreed. This was not surprising. I don't think I ever saw a woman so completely under a man's control.'[14] In the same article, a detailed account of the fire at Westgate-on-Sea was published, alongside an interview with Mr Murton, the previous owner of the greengrocer's. Naturally, the press connected the fire with Mrs Bennett's threat to have Herbert arrested.

The following day, 13 November, the *Evening News* published an interview with Mrs Kato, the Bennetts' Rossiter Road landlady. Mrs Kato was in correspondence with the newspaper for three days. In that time, two articles were attributed to her. The newspaper man responsible for the reports would later be identified as Saqui Smith, a fiction writer turned journalist, who had been retained by the newspaper tycoon and co-founder of the *Daily Mail*, Alfred Harmsworth, in the 1890s, to carry the newspaper into the new era of reporting. In the first article, Mrs Kato was quoted as saying that 'if ever a woman was fond of a man, she was fond of him. As to him, he treated her in a way that would have crushed the life out of other women.'[15] Mrs Kato would later complain that her words had been misrepresented, particularly an account of a conversation that she had once had with Herbert on the subject of murder. 'One night,' began the account, 'Mr and Mrs Bennett were in her sitting room, when the conversation turned on different ways of murder. After some talk Bennett remarked, "There is only one way to do a job of that kind. Strangle them. It's quick and silent." Two days later, Mrs Kato was in contact with the newspaper again, this time to share her musings on bootlaces.

A casual remark about the bootlace, which was found tied around the neck of the murdered woman awakened a train of recollection in the mind of Mrs Susan Kato ... in a little safe which was used as a receptacle for food and odds and ends ... Mrs Bennett had stowed away some bootlaces brought with her from the little shop in Stockwood Street where they had sold them in conjunction with groceries. Some were for shoes, others for boots, narrow, made of inferior mohair – the kind you buy for halfpenny a pair. If a search were made of the house at Bexley, the police might find the safe or some bootlaces ...[16]

⪧16⪦

THE CHAIN OF
(CIRCUMSTANTIAL) EVIDENCE

'I saw him'

Meanwhile, police in Great Yarmouth and across London were working hard to strengthen what Chief Constable Parker described as the 'strong chain of circumstantial evidence' that they had already forged around their prisoner.

By now, Lingwood had become somewhat of a celebrity in Great Yarmouth and the surrounding areas. One reporter described the 'great credit' the public attributed to him for the 'Sherlock-Holmes-like-manner in which he had unearthed clues and remorselessly followed them up'.[1] Just after the murder, Lingwood had declared that he would not rest until he had solved the mystery and it was this dogged determination that had eventually led him back to the Crown and Anchor Hotel on Hall Quay. Here, he made further enquiries about the mysterious walk-in visitor that the 'boots', Edward Goodrum, had described to PC Platten on the morning following the murder. This time, Lingwood was armed with a portrait of Herbert Bennett. Without hesitation, the 'boots' identified Herbert as the man who had stayed at the hotel on the evening of Saturday, 22 September.

'He arrived just before midnight,' Goodrum recalled. 'He seemed out of breath, as if he had been running.' The 'boots' went on to say that the man had apologised for being so late, claiming that he had walked from the neighbouring town of Gorleston, having missed the last train. He remembered the man because 'he came in late and went away early'. Lingwood, who had in his possession the hotel receipt found in Herbert's lodgings, asked if Goodrum recalled seeing the same man over the August bank holiday weekend. 'No.' Goodrum shrugged. 'We were very busy bank holiday time.' He went on to say that he thought the Crown and Anchor's former waiter, William Reade, would be able to corroborate his story, but Reade had since left the hotel and he had no idea of where to find him.

It took a few days for the police to hunt down William Reade, but when they eventually traced him, his statement immediately strengthened the prosecution's case against Herbert. Reade was not only able to corroborate Goodrum's account, but he also claimed to recognise Herbert from two other visits. 'I was waiter [at the hotel] on Saturday, 4 August,' he said. 'I remember the prisoner coming to the hotel on that day with a lady. They stayed until the Monday afternoon following. I next saw the prisoner on the 15th September at the hotel. He stayed there the Saturday night, and I saw him the following morning, Sunday, 16th September.'

Referring to the evening of the murder, Reade said, 'He asked me for a bed, and boots asked me what room he should give him. I said number eight, and boots took him to that room.' Reade also recalled a short conversation that he had had with the man while serving him a breakfast of bacon and eggs on the morning of Sunday, 23 September.

'I suppose you are down on business?' Reade asked.

'Yes,' replied the man, 'I shall be down every Saturday night for the next three months.'

The man that Reade and Goodrum would later identify as Herbert Bennett had left at ten past seven that morning – 'I saw him go across the Quay in the direction of the South Town station,' Goodrum would later recall.

The hotel workers were asked to formally identify Herbert at a parade in the courtyard of the police station, under questionable circumstances that Reade reportedly referred to as being 'beastly unfair' – a comment that the waiter would later deny. 'There was Bennett and four or five others,' he recalled. 'I identified [Herbert] as the man who had been down on three occasions. Of the five men, I knew two. I did not say it was beastly unfair.'[2] William Borking, landlord of the Mariner's Compass, had also been there that day and would later claim, 'I walked straight over to the man they had in custody – viz., her husband – and touched him, only I felt bound to state that his moustache was much larger and fuller when he was in my bar. Then one of the detectives took from his pocket something that looked like a moustache, or what would make one, and said, "If that was on him, would it make any difference?" and I said, "Yes – why, that's the very way he wore his on that night."

'"You are quite right," said the detective; "we found this in his portmanteau at his lodgings when we searched them."'[3]

The false moustache referred to by Borking was likely to have been the one made by costumier Willy Clarkson according to Herbert's specification. The implication that Herbert wore the moustache over his own facial hair was later criticised, as its gauze backing would have made it difficult to attach.

In an attempt to uncover further evidence to connect Herbert to the Crown and Anchor Hotel on the dates in question, the police seized the hotel's counterfoils in search of bills that were paid over the weekend of 22 and 23 September. The hotel's books were scrutinised, but the crucial bills – along with several others – were found to be missing . . .

William Reade and Edward Goodrum would become key witnesses in the prosecution's case against Herbert Bennett. Unfortunately for Herbert, their evidence not only placed him in Great Yarmouth on the two key dates relating to the murder, but the timing of his alleged arrival at the hotel on the evening of Saturday, 22 September corresponded with the timing of the struggle Alfred Mason and Blanche Smith claimed to have witnessed on the South Beach. Furthermore, had the Crown and Anchor's walk-in guest left the hotel on the morning of Sunday, 23 September, at the time Goodrum claimed, he would have reached the South Town station just in time for John Headley to see him waiting on the platform for the 7.20 a.m. train to depart for London. That train arrived in London at 11.31 a.m., which would have allowed plenty of time for one of its occupants to travel the three miles from the railway station to Hyde Park, which was where Herbert Bennett was seen by Alice Meadows at approximately 12.50 p.m.

The local police appeared to be succeeding in their determined efforts to strengthen the 'strong chain' of circumstantial evidence against Herbert, which left their prisoner in a very precarious position as he again prepared to face the magistrates.

A CLOUD OF WITNESSES

'A great number of surprises'[1]

Herbert's second appearance before the Great Yarmouth magistrates took place on Friday, 16 November, a gloriously fine late autumn day.[2] A week had passed since he had first set foot in the ornate courtroom and, in the interlude, interest in the case had further intensified.

The doors of the town hall were opened at 9 a.m. and the public galleries of the spacious sessions court were filled to capacity by 10 a.m. Herbert's transfer from Norwich Prison had, once again, been shrewdly organised by the police. The prisoner was brought to town by an early train, which had steamed into the South Town station at 8 a.m. The blinds of the carriage that held him were kept tightly drawn until the cab that would transport him to the town hall arrived. He was then hastily removed and rapidly driven to the red-brick and terracotta building, where he was ushered through the side entrance and placed in confinement in one of the basement cells, pending the assemblage of the court.

Everyone was in a state of excitement that morning. Twenty to thirty London reporters had descended upon the courtroom and officials had been forced to open up the jury boxes to accommodate their number. As they awaited the prisoner, the reporters enthusiastically sharpened their pencils and shuffled the stacks of telegraph forms that awaited their feverish scribbles. Twenty-five magistrates sat on the bench alongside the new mayor, Mr Charles Somerville Orde. Mayor Orde was a local partner in the banking firm Barclays and Company. He was also a commissioner of the peace for both Great Yarmouth and Suffolk and was generally considered to be a well-meaning and charitable man.[3]

That day, the press had announced that a 'cloud of witnesses'[4] would be called, including fourteen locals and a number of Londoners. The police were remaining tight-lipped about the details of the case but had promised 'a great number of surprises'.[5] The London witnesses, who had arrived from the capital by train late the previous afternoon, were reportedly staying in one of the town's temperance hotels, which did not sell alcohol.

As the public gallery filled with well-dressed women and smartly attired men, the clacking and rumbling of the cumbersome engines along the quayside reverberated throughout the courtroom, reminding those inside how close they were to the River Yare. Female spectators occupied the majority of the public seating and were described by one newspaper reporter as taking the 'liveliest interest in the proceedings'.[6] A crowd of predominantly female spectators was not an uncommon sight in courtrooms at the time. 'It is a noteworthy fact,' commented a Victorian novelist, that, 'women who have been brought up in refined society ... who would faint at the sight of a cut finger ... can sit for hours listening to the details of a cold-blooded murder.'[7] Men marvelled at the phenomenon because it was so divorced from the stereotypical feminine 'norm'. The women who attended murder trials and sat through accounts of the most gruesome of crimes were – knowingly or not – challenging stereotypes.

The noises from the riverside were quickly drowned out by a buzz of chatter that erupted as Herbert's father and stepmother were ushered into the court. They were seated just behind the witness box. It had taken some days for news of his son's arrest to reach John Bennett. By the time it had, Herbert's first hearing had passed. Since then, John Bennett had instructed Mr Edward Elvy Robb, a solicitor from Tunbridge Wells, to defend his son. Robb was a well-known criminal advocate and one of the most successful lawyers in Kent.[8] The previous year, he had turned down the Tunbridge Wells mayorship but still took an active interest in the affairs of the town. The Crown had secured Mr Charles J. Wiltshire, one of the leading and most experienced solicitors in the Borough of Great Yarmouth.

When the court was brought to order at 11 a.m., the first few minutes of the formal proceedings were taken up by a presentation of two Royal Humane Society certificates for saving lives at sea. The applause for the two fishermen receiving the awards had hardly subsided before Chief Constable Parker boomed out the instruction to 'put Bennett up!' When Herbert appeared, he was looking 'very well'.[9] He walked briskly to the front of the dock and surveyed the court. He caught sight of his father and gave a small nod of recognition. From his position in the dock, Herbert could see the ships as they passed along the River Yare.

At the opening of the proceedings, Elvy Robb addressed the court. He wished to draw the bench's attention, he said, to a 'campaign of calumny brought against the prisoner by certain organs of the press'. In response,

Wiltshire said that, while he equally regretted the behaviour of some newspapers (reports in one newspaper in particular had been 'scandalous'), he wanted to assure the bench that the reporters had not had any assistance from himself or the police. Wiltshire did not name the offending newspaper, but Herbert's defence team would later be far more forthright in naming and shaming the rogues that were responsible for the prejudicial reports. 'I quite agree with the remarks,' said Mayor Orde. 'Speaking for myself, I can say I have not read any of those remarks in the press to which reference has been made.' He assured the court that the bench would approach the case with entirely unbiased minds.

When the time came for PC Manship to take the stand, the officer came under fire again, just as he had from the coroner at the inquest, but this time facing an exasperated Wiltshire.

'So, in your view, it is practically impossible for the dead woman to have done it herself?' Wiltshire asked.

'Yes, I should think it quite impossible,' PC Manship replied.

'Yet, you first stated the theory of suicide?'

'Yes, I told the doctor it was a case of either murder or suicide,' the constable responded, unperturbed. Mayor Orde then asked PC Manship to illustrate how the fatal knots were tied. A length of red tape was provided for the purpose, which promptly snapped when the witness pulled it tight around the forearm of another police officer. Laughter echoed throughout the court. Herbert, who had been watching keenly, joined in, before resuming his previous bored and sullen demeanour.

When the turn came for the medical men to give evidence, the mayor instructed that all women should be removed from the courtroom. Naturally, it was his attempt at protecting the women's 'delectate sensibilities', but the irony was not lost on one reporter, who commented that it seemed unfair that women should be removed, given that the crime involved the 'doing to death of one of their own sex'.[10] Exceptions were made for a small number of women with a special interest in the case, including Herbert's stepmother. The women were reluctant to go, so the process took several minutes. In fact, some women were so determined to remain in the courtroom that they attempted to hide behind the 'thick wall' of male spectators. They were soon found and ordered to leave. When the final female spectator had been ushered out of the courtroom, Dr Lettis took the stand. Throughout the doctor's testimony, Herbert sat back in the dock with his hands covering his eyes as his father and stepmother wept.

The court was adjourned for lunch at the close of the medical evidence.

As the men filled their bellies with bass, bread and cheese, the women re-entered the courtroom and claimed all the best seats in the public gallery.

Front cover of the *Illustrated Police News*, 1 December 1900.

That afternoon, Herbert seemed to shed his sullenness and assume an air of interest – he wrote notes that were passed down to his solicitor, which were chiefly ignored, and paid close attention to the evidence. When Mary Jane's father, William Clark, was asked to identify his daughter's watch and chain, he was unable to recognise the watch as the one he had given her when she was twelve years old, but at once recognised the chain as having belonged to his mother. On several occasions, the ordeal became too much for the poor man and his voice became choked with emotion. He carried with him a mass of his daughter's beautiful silky fair hair, which had fallen from her head during a severe illness that she had suffered at the age of sixteen.

Early the next morning, Saturday, 17 November, a group of men began walking up and down the quayside near the town hall with pink sandwich boards advertising: 'Town Hall. Popular entertainment'.[II] They were not far from the spot under the 'big clock' where Mary Jane had stood waiting to meet her mysterious companion eight weeks earlier. Further along Hall Quay, among a parade of hotels that faced the river, was the Crown and Anchor Hotel. It did not take long for Hall Plain, the broad square in front of the town hall, to become awash with people that morning. Herbert had spent the night in the Middlegate Street police cells and was said to be in good spirits. According to his warders, he constantly asserted his innocence and was certain of acquittal.

That morning, Alice Meadows was due to take the stand. By now, she was extremely fragile and susceptible to regular fainting fits. The general feeling towards her was one of sympathy and she was thought of with pity and compassion by most. According to one news reporter, she received hundreds of letters from well-wishers from across the country.[12] Alice was 'lovingly tended' by her sister, May, a 'pretty little lady' who was never far from her side.[13] That morning, May – who was still in mourning for her husband – was dressed from head to toe in black. Alice wore a similar costume of tailor-made dark clothes. She also wore a headdress of purple velvet with plumes of ostrich feathers and a black veil, which covered her pallid face. As Alice walked across the courtroom to take the witness stand, the women in the public galleries rose from their seats to get a better look at her. Before Mr Wiltshire, the solicitor for the prosecution, began his examination of the witness, he wished to say that while Alice had been indiscreet in 'going about with the prisoner', she was a respectable girl, and the prosecution did not suggest any 'improper conduct'.[14]

Despite her delicate appearance, Alice endured over two and a half hours of questioning. She spoke in a low tone and only looked at Herbert once – when she was asked to identify him. Herbert, meanwhile, sat in the dock with his eyes fixed on her. May sat directly behind the witness box, next to Herbert's father and stepmother, who appeared 'bowed with grief'. Alice fainted when she left the courtroom and remained in a semiconscious state until the late afternoon, when she had recovered enough to travel back to London. The composed nature in which she had given her evidence was praised by the press.

At the close of the day's proceedings, Elvy Robb made an application to the court on behalf of his client. He asked that Herbert's daughter, Ruby, who had remained in the care of the Rudrums, be taken into the custody of John and Selina Bennett. While Robb was speaking, Herbert signed a document, which was then read aloud in court.

'I, Herbert John Bennett, held prisoner in Her Majesty's gaol at

Norwich, do hereby nominate, constitute and appoint my father, John Jarvis Bennett, of Swanscombe, Kent, to be the sole guardian of my infant child, Ruby Elizabeth Bennett. As witness this hand and seal this 17th November 1900. – Herbert John Bennett.'

Mr Wiltshire objected to the request at once: 'It is only right that the mother's representatives should take charge of her. Mr Clark, the murdered woman's father, is very anxious to have the little one.'

'But surely the prisoner, the child's father, is the natural guardian?' Robb argued.

'He once referred to the child as a bastard!' Wiltshire retorted. 'That does not suggest that he cared very much for it.'

Mayor Orde observed that the child was in very good hands with the Rudrums and declined to take any further action on the matter. By now, the Rudrum family had become very fond of the little girl and they were quite determined to keep hold of her. Both sets of grandparents had been permitted to see Ruby – William Clark had visited her that very morning – and the Bennetts had seen her the Sunday before; but the Rudrums refused to hand her over permanently to either set of relatives. Fondness aside, the family were benefiting financially from having Ruby as part of their household. According to John Rudrum, the child brought as much into the house as a grown man.[15] At the close of her mother's inquest, the jury had donated their fees – a total of 13–14s. – to Mrs Rudrum for her care. The gesture was widely reported in the press and the family had since received a steady stream of money from across the country.

The Great Yarmouth police had also been deluged with offers to adopt the motherless little mite. That week, the Rudrums had given an interview to a London evening newspaper from their house in Row 104. At one point, Ruby was brought into the room. Mrs Rudrum had shown the little girl a photograph of her parents, which the reporter had acquired from the murdered woman's father, at which Ruby was alleged to have exclaimed, 'Oh! – Dadda – Dadda!'[16] In response to a question from the journalist as to whether the child answered to the name Ruby, Mrs Rudrum asked the little girl 'where Ruby was'. She immediately pointed to her own chubby cheek and replied, 'Ruby, me!' Mrs Rudrum explained that she had first learned the child's true name from one of the newspapers and and – from then onwards – she had been Ruby again.

Alice would have arrived back in London that evening to the sounds of newspaper boys hawking the news. One paper, the *Sun*, had published a sample of what it described as 'disgraceful verses', taken from a pamphlet that was being sold on the streets in Great Yarmouth. The pamphlet, which sold for a penny, was a popular form of street literature of the time, aimed at the working classes. The publications were a hangover from the broadside, which was infamously sold at public executions in the eighteenth and early nineteenth centuries. The broadside contained musical verses, songs and ballads that provided catchy, rhyming narratives. Penny pamphlets included similar content to the broadside, and some also included illustrations. The 'poetic atrocity' published in the *Sun* that day was an extract from one of a number of pamphlets that were sold throughout Herbert's incarceration. The verses read as follows:

> For they will while you live
> Much evidence they will give,
> That you will prove your darling you did slay …
> Herbert Bennett now look out,
> And mind what you're about,
> For with the girl you've had a tidy fling.
> And they found, upon my life,
> That dead woman was your wife.
> If you killed her now, my boy, you've got to swing.
>
> You are in a pretty mess,
> And, if I can guess,
> I think your courting days are nearly done;
> For they say, 'twixt you and me,
> With you it's all U.P.,
> And you'll very shortly go to Kingdom Come.
>
> For some unknown reason he decoyed her from her home.
> Then cruelly took her precious life away.
> Herbert Bennett has been arrested,
> His guilt will soon be tested.[17]

'Surely,' proclaimed the reporter for the *Sun*, 'no stories published by newspapers could prejudice the public more against Bennett than a publication like this.' Of course, by publishing the verses, the newspaper just further propagated the prejudice that had been whipped up by the publication. That fact was seemingly lost on the newspaper's editor.

Also published in the press that day were a series of crude sketches, depicting scenes relating to the murder and the arrest of Herbert,[18] and the *Yarmouth Independent* published a photographic reproduction of William Clark's photograph of the Bennetts.[19] A thick moustache had been added to Herbert's face, because it was known that several witnesses were saying that the man seen in Great Yarmouth on the night of the murder had one. The doctored version of the photograph was reproduced as a sketch and later published in the *Weekly Dispatch*.[20]

From the *Illustrated Police News*, 24 November 1900.

It was against this backdrop of prejudice and sensationalism that Herbert's magisterial trial concluded. His penultimate appearance at Great Yarmouth's police court took place on Friday, 23 November. He had spent the preceding week at the Norwich Prison. When he entered the dock that day, he looked a little paler than usual, but he still surveyed the court in the same indifferent manner that had become characteristic of his time there.

That day, the manager of the Mariner's Compass, William Borking, was the principal witness. He identified Herbert as the man he had seen in his bar on the evening of the murder. When asked how he had behaved on that evening, the landlord entertained the court by jauntily leaning against the edge of the witness box and twisting his moustache. He then caused quite the sensation when asked to describe the clothing the man in his bar had been wearing – 'prisoner was wearing a trilby hat, a steel-coloured coat and a peculiar clerical-cut vest[21] . . . I think I should know that waistcoat again,' he stated. Borking's description of the man's clothing was similar to that of newsagent John Headley, who described the man he had seen on the railway station platform early on the Sunday morning as wearing a 'light grey suit and a rather darker trilby hat'.

'What kind of waistcoat was it?' asked Robb.

'Well,' said Borking, 'his wasn't a common sort of waistcoat, like yours or mine.' The court roared with laughter. Herbert joined in heartily.

'I believe,' interjected Wiltshire, 'the prisoner is wearing the same coat and waistcoat at the moment.' The laughter disappeared from Herbert's face immediately. Then, in a peculiar turn of events, Mayor Orde ordered Herbert to stand up and unbutton his coat so that the witness could see his waistcoat. Hundreds of hungry eyes watched as Herbert, now ghostly pale, stood up and began to slowly unbutton his large overcoat. His long fingers trembled as he grappled with the buttons. When he eventually removed it – it was the only time he had taken it off, despite the oppressive heat in the courtroom – he was seen to be wearing a steel-grey coat and vest underneath. It was the same suit that Alice Meadows and Mrs Pankhurst had seen him wearing on the Sunday after the murder. The waistcoat was double-breasted, with a cut 'V' shape at the opening.

'That's the coat; that's the waistcoat!' Borking shouted dramatically, pointing a trembling arm across the courtroom towards the prisoner in the dock.

'This is not a square-cut waistcoat!' Herbert objected scornfully.

Robb at once instructed his client to be quiet: 'Don't speak another word,' he directed.

The landlord continued: 'It is the same waistcoat and the same blue tie, but not the same collar.' Robb requested that Borking's reply be taken down very carefully, namely: 'That's the coat; that's the waistcoat.'

'The colour of the coat and waistcoat,' Borking interjected.

Robb, turning to Borking, said, 'Now, Mr Borking.' The solicitor pointed to the waistcoat. 'Is that what you call a clerical-cut vest?' Borking looked ponderingly at Herbert for a moment and then, after a pause, said, 'Well, no doubt it is a peculiar cut.'

'Yes or no,' Robb persisted.

'No,' Borking replied sullenly.

In further evidence, Borking argued that Herbert's waistcoat would look very different without a tie. The exchange was widely considered a win for the defence and the thrilling scene left many of the court's spectators reeling with excitement.

AN ALIBI DISPROVED

'Have you anything to say?'

Among the other witnesses called to give evidence that Friday were Herbert's pals from the Woolwich Co-operative stores – John Cameron and William Parritt. The two men had been called at Herbert's request to provide an alibi for the night of the murder. Herbert's initial assertion that Mrs Pankhurst could provide him with an alibi had been duly followed up by the police. Mrs Pankhurst had, of course, immediately recognised the date as that of her grandmother-in-law's birthday party and had positively rejected the idea that Herbert had been in the house that evening. With his first alibi disproved, Herbert had confidently told Chief Constable Parker that he had been drinking in Rose's Distillery, Woolwich, with Cameron and Parritt on that fateful Saturday evening. Both men had been summoned to the court to provide evidence.

John Cameron nodded and smiled at Herbert as he passed the dock on his way to the witness box that day. Herbert returned the gesture. In evidence, both Cameron and then Parritt denied seeing the prisoner on the evening of the 22nd but stated that they had seen him in the Shakespeare public house on the following Saturday, 29 September. When it was Parritt's turn to take the stand, he became so overwhelmed by the whole ordeal that he fainted. He was caught by a nearby police constable and carried out of the witness box to a nearby chair, where he sat while restoratives were administered. When he eventually came around, he wept bitterly and was in no state to resume his testimony. The spectacle marked an end to the day's proceedings and the court was adjourned.

There was the usual rush for seats when the court reopened the following morning. When Herbert was brought up from the cells below, he made his customary survey of the courtroom, as he had done every morning. He spotted his pals from the Co-operative stores and smiled pleasantly at them, apparently unaffected by their damning evidence of the previous day. Parritt responded with a nod and a bright smile. He had recovered from his fainting spell and, when the court was brought to order, he was promptly recalled to conclude his testimony. The theatrics that had dominated a part of the previous day's proceedings were continued, thanks in part to young Blanche Smith, who – according to one reporter – gave the court a 'violent shock' when she entered the courtroom. She was wearing a bright-green coat and skirt and a hat of brown and light-blue velvet that was, in shape, 'first-cousin to a beef-eater's hat'.[1] A huge bunch of feathers protruded awkwardly from the side. Little pockets of laughter erupted as she walked across the courtroom towards the witness stand.

Just over an hour later, Mr Wiltshire announced that he had presented all of the evidence that he intended to tender on behalf of the Crown. He then asked the bench to commit the prisoner to trial at the Norwich Assizes.[2] Mr Wiltshire's statement appeared to shock Herbert, who looked over at his solicitor questioningly, as if seeking an explanation.

'Have you anything to say?' the clerk asked, addressing Herbert.

'No,' he said, standing up. His face had turned a deathly pale, but his voice was calm. 'I reserve my defence,' he added.

'And you call no witnesses?' asked the clerk.

'No,' replied Herbert.

Herbert's solicitor was then asked if he had anything to add. Mr Robb thanked the bench for the courtesy and fairness they had shown and then proceeded to thank Mr Wiltshire and the chief constable. When he had finished speaking, the mayor turned to Herbert and said sombrely: 'Herbert John Bennett, you are committed to take your trial at the next Norwich Assizes, on the charge of feloniously and of malice aforethought killing and murdering your wife on the beach in this town on the night of September 22nd, or the morning of September 23rd, 1900.'[3]

And so, exactly nine weeks after the death of Mary Jane Bennett, the man accused of her murder was removed from the police court and taken to the cells below to await trial. Among the ordinary spectators in the courtroom that day was the washerwoman Elizabeth Gibson. Despite William Borking having told the police that Elizabeth was in his bar on the evening of the murder, they had not formally interviewed her as a potential witness. Sitting in the public gallery that day, Elizabeth had recognised Herbert as the man she had seen in Borking's bar by the way he had twirled his moustache. She reported to the police station the following day and gave a statement to that effect. Gibson's statement provided the prosecution with much-needed corroboration of Borking's account, which was by now in question following his disastrous spell in the witness box.

Throughout the entire hearing, Herbert had shown little sign of emotion. He had not appeared nervous, save from the occasional pull at his short, straggly moustache. He recovered quickly from the shock of his committal and, later that evening, he was heard humming tunes while waiting to be transferred to Norwich. Alice Meadows was permitted to see him before he was taken away. According to an account of the visit that was published in the *Weekly Dispatch*,[4] Herbert 'seized Alice in his arms and kissed her passionately' before declaring that she was the only woman he had ever loved. The Meadows family were quick to dispute the accuracy of the report and – while Alice would later confirm that the visit had taken place – she denied giving the *Dispatch* reporter any details. In a letter published by the *Eastern Evening News* three days after the *Dispatch* report, Alice's sister, Fanny, wrote:

> I wish to call your attention on behalf of my sister, A. Meadows, to the alleged interview between her and H. Bennett appearing in last Sunday's *Weekly Dispatch*. I ask you to contradict the report, as it is a falsehood throughout, and it is likely to prejudice her. She had a short interview with him, but nothing approaching that made-up report published in the *Dispatch*.[5]

The Meadows family suspected that the account was strung together by what the newspaper man was able to coax out of the warder, who was the only other person in the room at the time. The heavily sensationalised account of Herbert's meeting with Alice gives an indication of the lengths to which some reporters were willing to go in order to get their story.[6]

The Rudrums finally gave Ruby up to Herbert's father and stepmother on 15 December, but only after Elvy Robb threatened High Court proceedings.

Mary Jane's words had no doubt been ringing in Selina Bennett's ears ever since she had first learned of her stepdaughter-in-law's death – 'If anything happens to me, Ma, you will look after my Ruby, won't you . . .?'

THE OLD BAILEY

'The wilful murder of Mary Jane Bennett'

O n 18 January 1901, Edward Elvy Robb applied to have Herbert's trial removed from the Norwich Assizes, quoting Palmer's Act,[1] an Act of Parliament that allowed crimes committed outside London to be tried at the Central Criminal Court if evidence suggested local prejudice would prevent a fair trial in the county where the offence had taken place. The request was granted on 24 January, two days after the death of Queen Victoria.

Four days later, a Grand Jury at Norwich reviewed Herbert's case and returned a true bill. The role of the Grand Jury was to review indictments and assess whether there was sufficient evidence to present the case before a trial jury. The cases they passed for trial were approved as 'true bills'; the cases they rejected were marked 'ignoramus' (or 'not found').

Preparations began.

The trial of Herbert John Bennett commenced on Monday, 25 February 1901.[2] It was the opening day of the Central Criminal Court's second sessions and the newly appointed Lord Chief Justice of England, Richard Everard Webster, 1st Viscount Alverstone, attended for the special purpose of trying Herbert's case.

Herbert had been transferred from Norwich Prison to Newgate Prison the previous week to await the start of his trial. Newgate, with its massive smoke-stained outer walls, had stood ominously on the corner of Newgate Street since 1188. The prison had closed to long-term inmates in the 1870s but was still being used as a holding prison for those awaiting trial at the Central Criminal Court, commonly known as the Old Bailey.[3]

By 1901, the Old Bailey was in a grim state of affairs. Its dirt-begrimed walls were unpleasant and its dingy and cramped interior was uncomfortable. In the main courtroom, where Herbert was to be tried, the interior windows faced the imposing granite walls of the prison. Natural light struggled to breach the thick layer of filth that coated the glass, and the gloominess that engulfed the courtroom was only slightly relieved by the artificial light of gas lamps. The only colour came from the dark crimson upholstery of the seats of the judges and civic authorities on the bench.

The atmosphere in the courtroom befitted the crimes that were tried there, and the trial that February was no exception. The second session opened with a particularly gloomy calendar, even for the Old Bailey. Fifty-five prisoners were listed in total and included an unusually high number of crimes of violence. Among these were three charges of murder, four of attempted murder, two of manslaughter, five of forgery, nine of house-breaking and three of wounding.

The murder cases that were to be tried alongside Herbert's were those of Maud Eddington, twenty-two, who was accused of shooting her sweet-heart in a shop in Fleet Road, Hampstead,⁴ and George Henry Parker, twenty-three, who was accused of murdering a man and wounding a woman on a train travelling from Southampton to Waterloo.

That morning, the Yarmouth witnesses – twenty-five in total – were brought down from Norfolk by the Mark Lane express, a fast train, which only ran on Mondays. They had departed from the South Town station at 7.20 a.m. under the stewardship of Lingwood, and when they arrived at Liverpool Street station, two horsed Great Eastern Railway omnibuses were waiting to transport them to the Old Bailey. The drive took fifteen minutes and, by the time they arrived at the Central Criminal Court, the narrow roadway of Old Bailey Street was flooded with people. A large number of police officers held strict cordons outside all entrances to the court, but the sensation-seekers continued to surge forward. The crowd got as far as the pavement outside the courthouse before the police drove them back. 'Passes only!' the officers cried above the hubbub. A small number of people broke away from the main swarm, defeated, but others reached inside their pockets for tickets and pushed forward towards the front of the crowd.

Despite an interval of five months since the discovery of the deceased woman on Great Yarmouth's sands and three months since Herbert's committal, the story of Mrs Bennett's murder and the arrest of her husband was still fresh in the minds of the public. Not for many years had an Old Bailey trial attracted so much attention and the intense interest surrounding the case had forced court officials to issue tickets to control admission into the court. Undersheriff Langton was responsible for ensuring that the process ran smoothly, and he had given strict orders that no one was to be admitted into the court without an official pass. There had been a large number of applications for seats from across the country, but particularly from Great Yarmouth. Most of the people who had gathered outside the courthouse that morning were left disappointed as the public gallery quickly filled to capacity. By special order of the Lord Chief Justice, all female spectators had been barred from the court. Despite receiving a 'letter-bag full of letters each day from distinguished ladies begging for a peep at the prisoner',[5] Alverstone held firm, citing the 'sensitive nature' of the case. Exceptions were made only for women who held a valid interest, notably Herbert's stepmother. Several women gained entrance to the courthouse regardless, in hopes of convincing Langton to grant them access to the courtroom. One newspaper reported that 'the corridor to [the Undersheriff's] office was like the vestibule to a theatre on the occasion of a fashionable matinee'.[6]

Undersheriff Langton was also responsible for managing the press. That morning, more than forty reporters were admitted to the court. Despite the large number of spectators, scenes inside the courtroom were much calmer than on the streets outside. The public accommodation consisted of a small gallery above the dock. By now, it was packed full to bursting and the spectators were 'wedged like rows of fish in a sardine tin'.[7] Among the sea of exclusively male faces were many well-known men, including actors and dramatists. Members of the press were seated in the well of the court, some spilling out into additional seating that had been provided in the area usually reserved for jurors in waiting. The case had also excited the interest of the white wigged junior counsel, who were now huddled together like a flock of sheep in the centre of the well.[8] Their number was so great that they overflowed and formed a line up the staircase to the entranceway.

Every inch of available space was occupied, save for the dock, which was framed on either side by glass. Before the introduction of gas lighting in the early nineteenth century, a mirrored reflector had been placed above the dock to reflect light from the windows onto the face of the accused so that the jury could 'read' their facial expressions. Sounding boards had also been hung from the ceiling of the courtroom in an attempt to amplify the voices of witnesses, but the boards had done little to improve the acoustics. The mirrored reflectors had by now been removed, but the sounding boards remained.

Just as the large gilt-framed clock above the dock began to chime, announcing the arrival of 11 a.m., the court usher called out a demand for 'silence!' and an expectant hush fell over the court. The whole audience rose from their seats just in time for the tall and impressive figure of the

Lord Chief Justice to appear. Alverstone had been appointed to the role of Lord Chief Justice of England four months earlier, following a lengthy career as a barrister, politician and judge. He was an even-tempered and kind-hearted man, which he would duly demonstrate through his gentle handling of witnesses. During his time in office, Lord Alverstone would oversee a number of notable trials, including that of Dr Hawley Harvey Crippen.[9]

That morning, when the Lord Chief Justice strode into the courtroom, he was accompanied by an imposing procession of civic officials. The Lord Mayor, who was also the chief commissioner of the Central Criminal Court, was among them. Despite taking no part in the court's procedure, the Lord Mayor sat in the most prominent seat on the bench, below the emblematic sword of justice. He was dressed in his full regalia, including a three-cornered hat of state. Lord Chief Justice Alverstone took the seat to the right of the Lord Mayor and the remaining seats were taken by sheriffs and aldermen, all clad in scarlet and fur. Their crimson robes were ablaze in the flickering light of the gas lamps. The bench, which occupied a whole length of one side of the court, faced the dock. The witness box was to the right of where the Lord Chief Justice sat and to the side of that was the elevated jury box. The foggy well of the court held the imposing array of bewigged and gowned counsel. The barristers wore white bands with double pleats down the middle as a sign of mourning for Queen Victoria.

Before the clock had ceased to chime, the clerk of arraigns, Mr Avory, gave the order to 'put Bennett up!' and all eyes turned towards the dock. A warder walked to the top of the black stone steps that led down to the holding cells below and gave a signal to indicate that the court was ready for the prisoner. A minute later, Herbert's footsteps could be heard ascending the spiral staircase. The captivated court watched in anticipation. Herbert appeared much the same as he had in the police court. He had lost a little weight and his time spent within the confines of Norwich Prison had left him with a rather pallid complexion. Despite this, however, he looked well groomed and was clean-shaven – save for his slight moustache, which was waxed firmly in place. His hair had been carefully brushed and he was well presented in a crisp white collar and blue tie. Several official-looking papers were protruding from the left-hand pocket of the fitted velvet-collared Newmarket overcoat that he was wearing. Among them was a copy of the Old Bailey calendar. In it, Herbert was described as a 'dealer', twenty-one, well educated. The indictment against him simply read 'wilful murder of Mary Jane Bennett'.

Herbert walked briskly to the front of the dock in two resounding strides. He looked boldly around the court and then up at the public gallery behind him. He then stood with his right arm resting on the narrow bench at the front of the dock. He placed his left arm behind his back, his long, bony fingers twitching nervously. The view from the dock in the Old Bailey was a far cry from the one he had had at the Yarmouth police courts. Instead of the peaceful scenes of the River Yare, he now looked upon the black, grimy walls of Newgate Prison – a clear sign of his worsening situation.

The sounds of crackling parchment signalled that the clerk of arraigns was ready to start the proceedings.

'Herbert John Bennett,' he announced in a loud, steady voice, before reading out the indictment. He then turned to the prisoner. 'How do you plead?' he asked.

'Not guilty, sir,' Herbert replied firmly.

Attention then turned to the jury, which comprised twelve men – all typical Londoners. Most were shopkeepers or owners of small businesses. At least three of the men appeared to be about the same age as Herbert. The prisoner was invited to challenge each of them before they were sworn in. Herbert keenly scanned the jury box, critically observing each man as he took his oath, but made no objections. The jury had been placed in the charge of an officer of the court, who was sworn to prevent them from discussing the case with anyone outside their number. The men would be housed in the Manchester Hotel for the duration of the trial at the expense of the sheriff of London.

While the members of the jury were being sworn in, Herbert's barrister, Edward Marshall Hall, entered the court from the robing room. He approached the dock, where he held a hushed conversation with his client. Marshall Hall was an impressively tall man who had no problem reaching the raised dock. He had left it until the last possible moment to enter the courtroom, perhaps due to his well-known disdain for the courthouse. Ten years earlier, the man responsible for the death of his estranged first wife, Ethel, had been tried in the very courtroom where he now stood. Since then, he had developed a strong hatred for the Old Bailey, often complaining of its grim and toxic environment.

THE GREAT DEFENDER

'Fighting a battle for himself'

The story of Ethel Marshall Hall's death was a horrific one. Just over a year after she and Marshall Hall had separated, she had become pregnant by army officer Count Raoul Guy Richard de Vismes et de Ponthieu.

The pregnancy had terrified Ethel and she was quickly crippled by anxiety at the thought that de Ponthieu would leave her. She desperately sought a termination. Since abortion was illegal under the 1861 Offences Against the Person Act and carried a life sentence for those who were found guilty, she attempted to end the pregnancy with medication that contained aloe (an abortifacient) prescribed to treat a so-called case of constipation. When that failed, Ethel sought the help of Dr Albert Laermann, who – after several failed attempts to end the pregnancy – injected acid nitrate of mercury into her vagina.[1] Ethel became morbidly ill and died six days later, after suffering horrific corrosive damage to her uterus. She was still pregnant.

Dr Laermann, who was found to have falsified his medical qualifications, was arrested and charged with Ethel's murder. Laermann was ultimately found guilty of a lesser charge of manslaughter and was subsequently sentenced to fifteen years in prison. De Ponthieu and a female associate, thought to have been complicit in Ethel's death, avoided prosecution. In the years that followed, Marshall Hall endured countless reminders of his first wife's death every time he defended a client in the courtroom where her killer had been tried.

The barrister had first attracted attention as a criminal advocate in 1894, when he had successfully defended a prostitute named Marie Hermann, who was accused of murdering a client. Marshall Hall convinced the jury to take pity on the woman and she was found guilty of manslaughter and sentenced to a mere six years in prison. Had she been found guilty of murder, she would have faced the death penalty. The barrister had been appointed Queen's Counsel (QC) in 1898[2] and had successfully defended two capital cases in his first year in silk, securing an acquittal in the first,[3] and a reduced sentence in the second.[4]

Unbeknown to Marshall Hall at the time, the 'Yarmouth Beach Murder' was the case that would really launch his career and he would go on to successfully defend a number of the era's most infamous murderers, eventually earning the title of 'The Great Defender'.

When the time came for Marshall Hall to defend Herbert's case, he was exhausted, having just fought – and won – a taxing election campaign in Southport. When the barrister had first taken Herbert's case, he, like many others, had been heavily influenced by the stories in the press and would later admit that he was 'satisfied' that his client was guilty.[5] As he delved further into the case, however, he became convinced of Herbert's innocence.

It was this belief that would compel Marshall Hall to defend Herbert with such passion that he appeared to be 'fighting a battle for himself and not the man he defended'.[6] Although by now known for his eloquent and impassioned speeches, Marshall Hall also had a reputation for being quick-tempered and high-handed.

Marshall Hall's fee was 50 guineas, which was funded by donations made by anonymous benefactors in support of Herbert's defence. According to Herbert's solicitor, Elvy Robb, who continued to work on the case, money had flooded in from all over the country: '... people that I never knew, never heard of, have written to me offering sympathy with the prisoner. And in some cases, it has been very practical sympathy. Two people have sent me large sums to be devoted to the cost of Bennett's defence, and I have received a number of smaller sums. The fact is, the newspapers had decided that the man was guilty at the very outset of the case, and that has created a revulsion of feeling among the public. That is why so many people have come forward to express a feeling that Bennett ought to be given the fair, clean chance anybody in an English Law Court has a right to expect.'[7] By the first day of the trial, Robb had accumulated between £300 and £400 in his client's name.[8, 9]

Marshall Hall was supported by junior counsel Mr George Thorn-Drury, Mr Forrest Fulton (the son of the Recorder of London, Sir James Forrest Fulton) and Mr Max Labouchere (Marshall Hall's nephew). The barrister's opponent was his good friend Charles Gill QC, who had been retained by the Crown for a fee of 100 guineas,[10] an almost unprecedented amount at the time. Gill was supported by junior counsel Mr Richard Muir and Mr A. Poyser and the prosecution's solicitor Mr Wiltshire. Gill was a well-respected criminal lawyer who was renowned for his calm and persistent questioning and strong command of the details of a case. He was described by one reporter as having a curious manner of impressing both judge and jury – 'he brings his facts out in short, jerky sentences which force you to rivet your attention at once'.[11]

When the jurors had been sworn in, Marshall Hall took up his position in the well of the court and Herbert, readily accepting the chair that was offered to him, sat down in the dock. A court official then placed a small pile of parchment and a quill pen on the narrow bench in front of him.

In a speech that occupied the entire morning, Gill detailed the evidence that would be called by the prosecution. The jury followed the barrister's steady stream of facts, dates and conversations closely, some diligently attempting to take notes. As the barrister's speech marched on, however, all notetaking was eventually abandoned. Herbert listened intently; his eyes fixed on Gill throughout. He sat with his right elbow resting on his knee, his long fingers stroking his chin. Now and again, he would seize the quill pen in front of him and make a note of some point he regarded as important. The Lord Chief Justice, who made very few notes at this point, sat reclined in his plush chair, with his arms folded on the table in front of him. Approximately two hours and twenty minutes later, the dim, muggy court was emptied for a thirty-minute lunch, before what would be a gruelling afternoon of testimony.

When the court resumed at 2 p.m., Marshall Hall took to his feet brandishing a small illustrated pamphlet. Before the evidence was called, he said, he wanted to draw the judge's attention to the publication, which claimed to offer the 'full story of the Yarmouth murder'. It had been produced by a London publisher and sold on the streets on Saturday. He handed the small pamphlet up to the judge. His lordship examined the publication, which was sprinkled with photos and pictures.

'If only your lordship would say a single word on it,' Marshall Hall continued.

'I certainly think it is highly improper that any publication of this kind should be issued during a trial,' the Lord Chief Justice said.

Marshall Hall's deviation from the official proceedings had clearly been designed to excite sympathy in the minds of the jury. The barrister, who was 'aflame with rage at the press and revving up for a fight',[12] was clearly determined to take any opportunity he could to demonstrate that his client was being mistreated by the press.

The pamphlet was quickly placed to one side and the first in what would be a long line of witnesses was permitted to take the stand. John Cockrill, Great Yarmouth's borough surveyor, produced various plans showing key locations and distances of places mentioned in the case. Next came young John Norton. The kindly Lord Chief Justice offered the boy a chair, which he gladly accepted, but when the young boy sat down, the swing bar in front of the witness box hid his face. Alverstone asked for it to be removed before John recounted his grim account of finding the body. He spoke in a fresh voice that had just a touch of the attractive 'sing' of the East Anglian dialect.[13]

Norton was closely followed by PC Manship, who was provided with a length of string before being asked to demonstrate a series of knots, including the deadly reef and granny knots that had been used to keep the lethal bootlace in place around the deceased woman's neck. Under the critical eye of the Lord Chief Justice, PC Manship avoided a repeat of the scenes in the police court when the tape he had been using to demonstrate the knots had snapped.

The medical evidence was then presented in detail by Dr Lettis and Mr O'Farrell. In cross-examination, Marshall Hall suggested that Mrs Bennett's injuries were consistent with her having been the victim of a botched sexual assault by an unknown assailant. It was the hypothesis by which the defence would proceed.

The medical witnesses were swiftly followed by beach photographer James Conyers. Conyers recounted the day that he had photographed Mary Jane on the beach with her baby, recalling in detail the clothes she had been wearing – a blue blouse, grey skirt and white hat with black band. He said that she was also wearing a gold chain round her neck and had had a satchel at her side. Conyers made a terrible witness – he contradicted himself and seemed happy to go along with whatever evidence he thought the examining counsel wanted to hear. This caused no end of confusion and a lot of amusement. Both prosecution and defence had made enlargements of his cheap little seaside tintype and one of these was now produced and handed to the witness.

'I have been in the trade thirty-five years,' Conyers exclaimed disdainfully, 'and I know that is a bad one.' Laughter rippled through the courtroom as Marshall Hall handed the witness a different copy of the enlargement. 'Ah, that is a good one,' said the photographer. 'It is a bromide print. I am speaking the truth, and that is a good one.' Renewed laughter prompted Marshall Hall to say rather sharply, 'Try to be serious if you can.'

'I am quite serious,' Conyers replied, 'and I will be serious.'

Marshall Hall then instructed the photographer to look at the chain on the woman's neck, which the witness said was a rope chain. The barrister produced the long chain that had been found in the prisoner's portmanteau. Handing it to Conyers, he said, triumphantly, 'This is a link chain, and not of the rope pattern.' Marshall Hall's statement caused a sensation in the courtroom. The significance of the point was not lost on Herbert, who looked up at the ceiling and smiled. Conyers suddenly appeared uncertain. 'I cannot say now that the chain is rope,' he said. 'It would be necessary to enlarge the photograph and examine the chain in it and the real chain side by side under glass.'

The Lord Chief Justice, who had been following the evidence with technical knowledge (he was a keen amateur photographer), interjected. 'The problem I have', he said, 'is that the chain is not in focus in the photograph.'

'Quite right!' said the witness.

Gill further questioned Conyers in an attempt to clarify his evidence, but the photographer then stated that the connecting links of the chain shown in the photograph were the same as in the chain found in the prisoner's possession. Marshall Hall was on his feet in a flash: 'Answer this question,' he said. 'Here is a strip of the ordinary chain – a few inches of plain links. This chain was found in the prisoner's portmanteau. Now is it possible that this piece of chain is identical with any pieces of the chain in the photograph?'

'No, it isn't possible,' replied Conyers, adding to the confusion.

The Lord Chief Justice examined the chain and photographs under a magnifying glass that he had borrowed from Marshall Hall, before turning to the photographer. 'You can stand down, Mr Conyers, unless somebody wants you,' he said. The jury were given the enlargements and magnifying glasses and were left to puzzle over the matter for themselves.

James Conyers was followed by another of Great Yarmouth's notable photographers, Frank Sayers. Sayers had photographed the deceased woman's body and several other locations and exhibits that were relevant to the case. Much like Conyers, the witness was extensively questioned by Marshall Hall over the design of the chain in the beach photograph, but he was far more uncertain: 'The chain between the beads might be either a rope chain or a link chain,' he said rather noncommittally.

Marshall Hall handed an enlargement of the beach photograph to the witness, along with an image of the chain that had been found in Herbert's portmanteau. The latter was one of the photographs that Sayers himself had taken. Marshall Hall asked the witness to compare the chain in the two images. Sayers explained that the chain shown in the beach photograph would have moved with the woman's breathing. This, he claimed, may have accounted for the difference in the appearance between the real chain and the chain in the photograph.

'Giving it a rope pattern effect?' asked Marshall Hall.

'It is difficult to say with such a small photo whether or not the rope pattern could be produced. But in the photograph, it appears like a rope pattern chain.' He then added hurriedly, 'Still, I could not swear to it.'

'Have you any doubt that the chain between the larger beads is that which is known as a rope pattern chain?' Marshall Hall persisted.

'The enlargement shows it has moved and it is not in focus. The appearance of the chain, in these circumstances, would be different to a photograph of a perfectly still chain,' Sayers replied.

The debate surrounding the famous gold chain was a fierce one, owing to the fact that the necklace and the small silver pocket watch were the only two items of physical evidence that the Crown had to link Herbert to the murder. Marshall Hall was convinced that the chain in the photograph was not the same chain that had been found among his client's possessions and he was determined to prove it.

The dead woman's father, William Clark, followed Sayers into the box. He was handed the watch and chain that were now in the court's possession.

'Are these the watch and chain that you gave to your daughter?' the Lord Chief Justice asked.

'Yes, my lord,' William replied without hesitation.

Objecting, Marshall Hall cried, 'You said at the police court that it was not the same watch!'

'No,' Clark replied firmly, 'I said if it was not the one, it was very much like it. It is difficult to speak with certainty when one has seen the watch only twice in eleven years.'

At this point, Marshall Hall rose and handed another photograph of Mrs Bennett to the Lord Chief Justice, which he claimed had been held back from the defence as the chain in that photograph also appeared to be of a 'twist' pattern.

'This has only just come into my hands from the Treasury solicitor,' he said. He claimed that it had been passed around the table in the well of the court until it had inadvertently been seen by a member of the defence's team. The Lord Chief Justice examined the image.

'Is this a photograph of your daughter?' he asked William.

'Yes, sir,' replied the witness, 'it was taken about four years ago.'

'The chain also appears out of focus in this photograph,' observed Alverstone.

'Your lordship is too much of an expert,' Marshall Hall responded. 'Will your lordship direct that it be enlarged?'

'Yes, I have no objection,' Alverstone replied.

William Clark was followed by Josef Hall, a pawnbroker and jeweller who kept a shop on East India Dock Road in Poplar. Hall explained that he had sold Clark the silver watch eleven years earlier. His order book was entered into evidence. The record of the transaction corresponded with the number on the watch, which also bore his private mark. Marshall Hall was unable to resist the opportunity to question the pawnbroker about the design of the chain in the beach photograph: 'Your substantial experience of jewellery must make you an expert,' he gushed. But the barrister's compliment failed to hit its target and the pawnbroker, who refused to be led on the subject, replied, 'I won't say if that is a rope chain.' He then added, rather firmly, 'I cannot say from a photograph.'

Next to be called was a cashier named Mr Barrow from the Westgate-on-Sea branch of Lloyds Bank. Barrow was called to prove that Herbert had deposited a cheque for £208 (the proceeds from the insurance claim on his burnt-out grocer's) in February 1900. When asked by Gill if he saw Herbert in the courtroom, Barrow looked all around the room, scanning the faces of the jury and counsel, and even that of the judge. Finally, he gazed at the prisoner in the dock before saying that he would not like to swear that he saw Bennett in the court.

The next witness was Henry Finch, the booking clerk for the Union-Castle Steamship Company. He gave evidence concerning the passages to South Africa that were booked under the name of Mr and Mrs Hood for the SS *Gaika*, at a cost of £48. 6s.

When asked by Marshall Hall in cross-examination whether he could identify the man who had purchased the tickets, Finch replied, 'I do not see the man in court who took those tickets.'

The final witness of the day was a man named Charles Wakefield, a cashier at the London & South Western Bank, who testified that Finch had deposited banknotes that matched those that had been dispensed by Barrow to Bennett at the Westgate branch of Lloyds Bank. This confirmed that the steamship tickets had been purchased with money from the insurance pay out. Herbert had watched the opening day's testimony unfold with interest, sitting for the most part with his chin resting in his right hand. Occasionally he would shift his position to look up at the large gilt-framed clock above the dock behind him or sit back in his chair with his arms crossed.

Those who observed him were struck by his lack of emotion. Had he not been sitting in the dock, his nonchalant air and indifferent manner would have given anyone watching the impression that he was just another ordinary spectator and not the man on trial for his life.

The officers assigned to the case had done an admirable job of investigating the crime.[1]

The role of the provisional police officer was to know their beats and the people who lived on them. The Yarmouth officers made local, foot-slogging enquiries, visited hotels and boarding houses, checked the railway station house and interviewed potential witnesses. They hunted down all possible leads and painstakingly investigated even the thinnest threads of evidence, building a picture of the victim and her life as they went. But this was not solely a 'local' crime, and when it had become apparent that it was not going to be solved by his department alone, Parker had eventually called for reinforcements.

Like provisional police officers, 'Yard' detectives were known for being observant and watchful. Their work pursuing criminals would regularly require them to disguise themselves, and it was wigmaker and costumier Willy Clarkson who would be called upon to provide this service. (Mr Clarkson would later claim to have disguised police officers and 'chosen civilians as females of the type that Jack the Ripper appeared to select for his knife: and these hung about in the shadowy courts and gloomy alley-ways in both the East and the West End in the hope of being accosted by the monster'.)[2] Some reports of the Yarmouth case claimed that a police officer had been inserted into the Woolwich Arsenal to work alongside and 'watch' Herbert Bennett prior to his arrest, but there is no formal evidence to support this. Leach, however, used this style of 'undercover' detective work when he arrested Herbert under the guise of 'Mr Brown'.

There was no mistaking Leach now. He was the officer who had finally collared Herbert Bennett, bringing a successful end to a six-week manhunt that had seen two forces work together to solve a complex crime.

⌒**21**⌒

SPOILING FOR A FIGHT

'That is not evidence!'

The next morning, Tuesday, 26 February, the streets outside the Old Bailey were alive with the cries of 'Yarmouth murder! Full account!' Verbatim reports of the previous day's witness testimony had flooded the newsstands and the newspaper-reading public were hungrily devouring them. One journalist commented that the scenes outside the courthouse resembled the opening night at the theatre.[1]

That morning, hundreds of people were turned away as the police once again struggled to regulate the traffic in the narrow thoroughfare of the Old Bailey. The arrival of the jury in a closed coach attracted the most attention, especially given that the crowd had no hope of seeing the prisoner, who had been smuggled into the courthouse via an underground passageway that connected the Old Bailey to Newgate Prison.

Overnight, the table in the well of the court had been removed by order of the Lord Chief Justice, after the rogue photograph of Mrs Bennett had been introduced into the case. A bench now separated the press from the counsel, cutting off all communication. The journalists in the well of the court were accompanied by artists from the illustrated papers, who prepared black-and-white sketches of the bench, bar and prisoner. The court was again crowded, almost to suffocation. The only witnesses excused from daily attendance were Dr Lettis and Mr O'Farrell and the borough surveyor, Cockrill, who had been discharged on the agreement that they would return if they were recalled.

At precisely 10.30 a.m., the customary three raps on the door at the rear of the court signalled that the Lord Chief Justice was ready to make his ceremonial entrance. The usher ordered silence and the court rose. When Herbert was called a minute later, he walked jauntily up the steps leading from the cells below and, upon reaching the dock, sat himself down comfortably in the chair that was offered to him. That day, Herbert was dressed in the same overcoat and spotlessly clean white collar that he had worn the previous day. His blue tie was fastened around his neck with a sailor knot.

From across the courtroom, Alverstone had been watching the prisoner's entrance with interest. Catching his eye, Herbert steadfastly returned the judge's gaze.

In an attempt to dispel any confusion that may have resulted from Barrow's testimony the previous day, the prosecution called George Hichen, the manager of the Westgate-on-Sea branch of Lloyds Bank. Hichen identified the prisoner as an account holder.

'Do you remember February 23rd, when Bennett came into the bank asking you to cash a cheque for £208?' asked Gill.

'Yes,' Hichen replied, 'I had a conversation with Bennett because he asked for cash for the cheque instead of passing it through his banking account in accordance with the usage of the bank.'

'Did you consent to let him have cash for it?'

'Yes, it was cashed by Mr Barrow, my assistant at the bank.'

Hichen was followed into the box by William Penton, an employee of the Union-Castle Steamship Company, who had identified the labels on Herbert's portmanteau. Penton explained that the labels were affixed to all pieces of cabin luggage and, when the 'Hoods' had taken their trip, he had noticed that one of the labels on Herbert's luggage had been torn to reveal part of the name Bennett written in pencil underneath. At this point, Herbert's portmanteau was brought into the court and the Lord Chief Justice examined the label carefully under a magnifying glass.

'The label does indeed bear the name Bennett,' he remarked.

'I am not contesting this point,' stated Marshall Hall. The barrister was not disputing the Bennetts' trip to South Africa and was keen to move swiftly past Penton's evidence, as he did not want the motives for his client's mysterious trip to the Cape to be questioned too deeply. Marshall Hall was convinced that Herbert's visit to South Africa, his employment at the Woolwich Arsenal and his tour of Ireland,[2] together with the revolver and cartridges found in his possession, were all consistent with Herbert having been a spy for the Boers.[3]

When Penton had left the witness box, the prosecution called the first in a long stream of witnesses who would provide insight into the Bennetts' domestic history. The first to tell their remarkable story was the Crown's primary witness, Mrs Emma Elliston. When she entered the courtroom that day, Mrs Elliston was wearing a lavish hat, trimmed with purple, which injected a flash of colour into the otherwise bleak and sombre court.

The landlady recalled Mrs Bennett coming to her house the previous May to rent rooms, before recounting the sad story of domestic unhappiness that had plagued the Bennetts' relationship during the short time they had lodged at her house. She recalled the threats she had heard Herbert use in all their pitiful detail. When she claimed that, on one occasion, Mrs Bennett had told her that her husband had smacked her in the face, Marshall Hall rose to his feet in objection.

'That is not evidence!' he cried, his voice booming out across the courtroom.

'No, it is not,' Alverstone agreed.

Shown the shovel, pickaxe and bucket brooch that Herbert had presented to Alice Meadows, Mrs Elliston said the brooch had been worn by the murdered woman while she lived at her house. The landlady then identified the small silver pocket watch, the case of which she had seen little Ruby biting. She was then handed the long gold chain. She identified it before explaining that the chain had been broken by the child and had been fixed back together again by thread. She pointed out the join where the chain had been mended. Herbert had listened to Mrs Elliston's testimony with a look of discomfort etched across his pale face. His barrister had also been following the landlady's testimony closely. Hers was the strongest evidence yet to be brought against his client, and Marshall Hall knew that he faced a challenge in weakening it.

When Marshall Hall had left the court the previous evening, he would have felt fairly positive. He considered the photographers' indecision over the chain to be a win for the defence, and the inability of Barrow and Finch to positively identify his client had only added to the uncertainty surrounding the case. It appeared that today's testimony, however, would be far more damaging for the defence. Perhaps it was this realisation that had put the barrister in a bad mood. Whatever the cause, by the time he took to his feet to cross-examine the modest landlady in the witness box, he was spoiling for a fight.

'Do you read the *Evening News* and the *Daily Mail*?' he asked, addressing Mrs Elliston.

'I have been worried too much to do so lately,' replied the witness.

Marshall Hall scoffed. 'Do you mean to say', he said, 'that you did not read your own statement of the case?'

'Yes,' Mrs Elliston replied, 'I saw it in some evening paper.'

'Were you much visited by people representing the evening newspapers?'

'There were only one or two.'

'Did you speak freely to them?'

'I did not say much to them.'

'We will see,' said Marshall Hall dramatically. Herbert settled back in his chair, the colour returning to his cheeks. The easing of his countenance signified the confidence he had in his counsel. His barrister did not let him down. In what was a long and strenuous cross-examination, Marshall Hall fired question after question at Mrs Elliston, in an attempt to prove that she had been overzealous in talking to the press. He produced a copy of the *Daily Mail*.

'Did you say this,' he said, reading aloud from the newspaper, 'that when Mrs Bennett arrived at your house, she was richly dressed and wearing a profusion of jewellery?'

'I did not say profusion of jewellery,' Mrs Elliston objected. 'She wore gold spectacles and two or three ornaments in her hair.'

'Did you say that her clothes were silk-lined dresses and that her underwear was covered with rich lace?' Marshall Hall persisted, still reading from the report.

'I said one of her bodices was lined with silk and that her underclothes were good and had lace on them,' replied Mrs Elliston.

'Did you say to a reporter that her purse was well filled with gold?'

'Yes; she had plenty of money.'

'Did you tell the press that you did not believe the story that the Bennetts had come from South Africa?'

'I did not say I did not believe it.'

'Did you say that they did not look like people who had come off a sea voyage?'[4]

'I do not remember!' exclaimed Mrs Elliston.

'That must have been an invention of the gentleman of the press then?' Marshall Hall continued.

'I suppose so.'

'Did you see it in the newspaper?'

'No,' the landlady replied adamantly, but Marshall Hall would not let the point drop.

'Did you see an article purporting to be an account you gave to a reporter in an evening paper?' he persisted.

'I read something in an evening paper,' Mrs Elliston admitted sheepishly, 'but I do not know when it was.'

Marshall Hall cast aside the copy of the *Daily Mail* that he had been flourishing in the poor woman's face and took up a copy of the *Evening News*, which had been loudly marked out in red ink.

'I suggest to you that this appeared on 12th November in the *Evening*

News,' he said. The journalists in court laughed when the barrister named the offending newspaper. Marshall Hall continued, quoting passages from the article: "'Her stories never agreed. This was not surprising. I do not think I ever saw a woman so completely under a man's control".'[5]

'She was very much under his control,' agreed the witness, 'but I don't think I ever spoke to a newspaper man like that.'

'Where did he get it then?' Marshall Hall asked, before adding sarcastically, 'Out of his head?'

'I did say that Mrs Bennett used to alter her tales sometimes,' Mrs Elliston replied miserably. 'Sometimes she would say one thing and then sometimes she would say another.' The landlady's responses had become fainter. 'But as true as God,' she said meekly, 'I did not say all that.'

In response to a further question from Marshall Hall, Mrs Elliston said that she had not mentioned anything about a fire at Westgate-on-Sea to the press. With hot indignation, the barrister read another statement from the *Evening News*.[6]

"'The plot of the Yarmouth murder deepens with the hours. Many weeks of patient investigation show that we have so far only skimmed the surface of this complex story ... Love of another woman was not the motive of the man. It became necessary to strangle the wife because in her hands she held the liberty of her husband. 'I can send you into penal servitude for fifteen years,' she said ... This was the danger ever before the eyes of Bennett.'"

'I never read that before,' cried Mrs Elliston.

'Then what paper did you read your account to the representative of the newspaper in?' Marshall Hall countered.

'I think it was the *Star* or the *Sun*,' replied the witness.

'Then don't you think that article in the *Evening News* was grossly unfair?' the barrister asked. Mrs Elliston quietly admitted that it was.

'There was a good deal of excitement at Woolwich, was there not?' enquired Marshall Hall.

'I do not know, I live at Plumstead and scarcely ever go to Woolwich. I have five children,' replied Mrs Elliston.

'I do not want to know about your children!' boomed Marshall Hall. The barrister refused to accept that the witness was unaware of what was happening in her neighbouring town, and demanded that she named the distance between Woolwich and Plumstead. He refused to let the point drop until she had done so and, upon confirming – 'about two miles' – Mrs Elliston promptly broke down in a flood of tears.

'Ah, yes,' Marshall Hall said contemptuously, 'the common refuge of your sex.' His remark, which was widely reported by the press in his Southport constituency, caused dismay among the 'Conservative women of the Primrose League who were stunned by their MP's lack of chivalry'.[7] The comment also earned the barrister a rebuke from the Lord Chief Justice.

'Please do not comment like that, Mr Marshall Hall,' he scolded.

'I must, my lord,' protested the barrister. 'I cannot help it.'

'Pass no comments, please,' Alverstone responded sharply. He then turned to Mrs Elliston. 'There is no necessity to cry,' he said kindly. 'Just try to pay attention to the questions and answer them as best you can.' When the witness had recovered her composure, Marshall Hall resumed his questioning. He asked Mrs Elliston if, at the time she gave her interview to the reporter, she had already given a statement to the police. At this point, Herbert rose from his chair, leaned over the dock and whispered something in his barrister's ear. Marshall Hall turned to the witness: 'Did your husband go and see Bennett the night he was arrested?'

'Yes,' replied the witness.

'So – you knew on the 6th November that this man was arrested and in the custody of the police, charged with murder. And yet, on the 11th and 12th November, you were gossiping about this case to a newspaper man?'

'I did not think it would do Bennett any harm,' sniffed Mrs Elliston.

Marshall Hall held up the copy of the *Evening News*, its highlighted red passages just visible under the glow of the gas lamps. 'And you as a woman,' he said, 'will say that you did not tell the man what appeared in that paper?'

Gill jumped to his feet. 'I must protest!' he shouted.

The Lord Chief Justice intervened. 'I do not think you are wrong to press it,' he said, addressing Marshall Hall; 'such articles are monstrous and wicked. But,' he cautioned, 'you ought not attribute more to this lady than she admits. I think, having read the article, there is a considerable amount that she could not possibly be responsible for.'

Marshall Hall took heed of the judge's warning and turned to the subject of the watch and chain. 'Had Mrs Bennett more than one chain?' he asked the witness.

'Only one watch and one chain that I ever saw,' Mrs Elliston stated confidently. Marshall Hall suggested that Mrs Bennett had owned an imitation gold chain, but Mrs Elliston immediately rejected the idea.

'And you swear the chain now put in is the same?'

'It looks very much like it.'

'You say that you tied the broken pieces with cotton, although you have previously said that Mrs Bennett tied them?'

'Mrs Bennett held the chain while I threaded the cotton,' the landlady explained. 'Then she tied the pieces and I helped her.'

Before the judge allowed Mrs Elliston to step down from the witness box, he asked her why she had spoken so freely to the press. She said that she had not made any statements to the press until she was asked to do so by a stranger who had come to her house. The man had told her that he was with the police, and it was not until later that she had realised that he was a reporter. A few days later, another man had come, but he had been honest and said that he was a representative of the press. She had given the longest statement to the man who had claimed to be a police officer. The judge's intervention had helped to demonstrate that Mrs Elliston had not knowingly shared harmful information with the press, but it had also helped the defence's case, as it proved the lengths to which some reporters were willing to go in order to obtain even the smallest detail. At the time, it was not unusual for reporters to pass themselves off as detectives. The journalistic interview was an emerging form of Tabloid Journalism and had taken firmer root in the last two decades of the nineteenth century. It served Marshall Hall's purpose that the case had been deeply compromised before it had come to trial, but the barrister would suffer repercussions as a result of his scathing attack on Alfred Harmsworth's newspapers in the years that followed.

Throughout Marshall Hall's fiery cross-examination of Mrs Elliston, Herbert had sat staring at the reporters in the well of the court, apparently transfixed by the spectacle of their flying pencils as they attempted to keep pace with the barrister's quick-fire questioning. As a shaken Mrs Elliston left the courtroom, the reporters returned their pencils to the narrow benches in front of them, where they would remain until the next fiery scene. Mary Jane's neighbours from Bexley were expected to be called next, but before they could take the stand, William Clark was unexpectedly recalled to answer questions relating to a number of irregularities on his daughter's marriage certificate.

William confirmed that he was aware that Herbert had overstated his age at the time of his marriage, explaining that there was a reason why the marriage needed to take place. In response to further probing, he quietly admitted that his daughter had been pregnant at the time. His statement caused a wave of sensation to sweep through the court. Marshall Hall apologised for the delicacy of his next question. 'The person who signs her name as a witness signs her name as "S. Clark",' he said. 'Her name was really something else, I need not tell you?' William gave no reply. Pressing the witness for a response, Marshall Hall asked, more directly this time, 'Was she your wife at the time of this wedding?'

'No,' admitted William.

'So, her name was not Clark?' continued Marshall Hall.

'No,' replied William quietly. His revelation caused a buzz of conversation to break out in the public gallery. Marshall Hall's questioning was clearly designed to throw doubt over the legality of the Bennetts' marriage, in hopes that it would be enough to cause the jury to doubt the Crown's suggestion that Herbert had killed his wife in order to marry Alice Meadows.

'Your daughter lived with her grandmother, why was that?' asked the Lord Chief Justice.

'She had two mothers,' William explained. 'Her own mother left us when she was a baby.' The witness went on to explain that he thought his daughter's birth mother had died, but it was almost impossible for him to know for certain. It is likely that William feared marrying again because there was a risk he would be committing bigamy. At the time, many women from broken marriages unofficially adopted the names of their new partners in an attempt to protect their reputations, which made them almost impossible to trace.

When the court had recovered from the shock of William's revelations, Mrs McDonald, who had lived in the Bexley Heath flat below the Bennetts with her husband the previous July, was called. She was dressed in a grey cape and black sailor hat that only added to the bleakness of the courtroom. Despite her drab clothing, her testimony threw a glimmer of light Herbert's way.

Contrary to Mrs Elliston's earlier testimony, which had portrayed Herbert as nothing short of brutish, Mrs McDonald now said that the Bennetts – whom she knew as the 'Bartletts' – seemed 'generally happy'. She recalled hearing them quarrel once but claimed that they mostly appeared to be on good terms. She added, however, that the prisoner only paid his wife and child short visits and had stayed overnight on only one occasion in the time that she had known him. Mrs McDonald duly identified Herbert as the man she knew as 'Mr Bartlett' and was then asked to identify pieces of jewellery, including the shovel, pickaxe and bucket brooch and the gold chain. By now, Herbert had grown tired of the repeated requests to stand up in the dock so that he could be identified and appeared greatly annoyed.

Under cross-examination, Mrs McDonald denied previously saying that she had never seen the chain, claiming that it was the watch she had not seen. She was then asked by Marshall Hall if she had ever seen Mary Jane wearing another chain. 'No,' replied Mrs McDonald – the only other necklaces Mrs Bennett had shown her were two made of pearl and a second, much shorter chain that belonged to the baby.

The scene then swiftly moved to the house at Glencoe Villas as Mrs Savage, one of Mary Jane's next-door neighbours, and wife to Mr Savage, the owner of Kingdom's Laundry, took to the stand. Described by one reporter as a 'bright looking vivacious woman',[8] Mrs Savage gave her answers in short, sharp sentences.

'Is there not considerable feeling about this case in Bexley Heath?' Marshall Hall asked the witness – 'The only answer is "yes" or "no",' he added.

Mrs Savage found a third option. 'I don't know,' she replied with irritating calmness that teetered on defiance. The court roared with laughter. Marshall Hall looked astonished.

'She is entitled to say that,' the Lord Chief Justice said hastily.

'Do you mean to tell me that on your oath?' Marshall Hall persisted disbelievingly.

'I do,' replied Mrs Savage.

'Why did you wait until January to volunteer a statement about Bennett wearing a trilby hat?' asked Marshall Hall.

'I did not want to be dragged into a murder trial, or a supposed murder case,' she replied. 'I wrote afterwards in the interests of justice.' Continuing, Mrs Savage recounted how she had noticed on the day the Bennetts had moved into Glencoe Villas that Herbert was wearing a black trilby hat.

'As to whether he wore brown boots or not, that, I suppose, is not relevant to this case,' Marshall Hall retorted sarcastically.

'If I could say,' Mrs Savage replied emphatically, 'then I would.' The witness went on to explain that she had been visited by Detective Bartle at the beginning of January – before she had written to the police – and he had asked her what Herbert had been wearing. 'I said at once a black trilby hat.[9] I'd also seen him wearing a dark bowler hat.' For a short time, the controversial trilby hat was one of the most hotly contested points in the case. Several of the Yarmouth witnesses claimed to have seen Herbert wearing the hat, as did Mrs McDonald, but Alice Meadows and Mrs

Pankhurst – the two people who saw Herbert the most often – claimed never to have seen him wear such a hat.

Mrs Savage continued to amuse the court with the prompt way she scored points off Marshall Hall during her cross-examination. By now, Herbert seemed to have recovered from his earlier annoyance and was smiling at the exchange that was taking place between his counsel and the witness. Mrs Savage's evidence was corroborated by her husband, John, who delighted the court when he announced that he himself wore a trilby because they were 'very comfortable hats'.

Following on from John's short testimony was Mary Jane's friend and one-time neighbour, Lilian Langman. In a soft voice that was no louder than a whisper, Lilian described in detail the visits Herbert had made to Glencoe Villas after his wife had left. Referring to Herbert's visit on 12 October, she said, 'On one occasion, the prisoner said he had come to take the dog to Mrs Bennett, who was in Yorkshire ill, although she was better and was sitting up in her bedroom. He said that she sent her love to my mother.'

'That is quite new!' Marshall Hall shouted. 'We have heard nothing of it!'

'It is not going beyond the proper limits,' Alverstone retorted.

In answer to a question about visitors to the house, Lilian stated that 'Mrs Bennett had no visitors while she was living at Glencoe Villas, except for Bennett'. She had never, she added firmly, seen any other man go into the house.

Lilian's testimony was particularly damaging to Herbert's defence, as it supported the prosecution's argument that Herbert's conduct *after* the murder was what truly revealed his guilt. In an effort to distract from Lilian's evidence, Marshall Hall took the opportunity to introduce another exhibit into the case. He handed Lilian a photograph and then a copy of the *Yarmouth Independent*. The judge, sensing that the barrister had some ulterior motive, intervened.

'What is the point of this, Mr Marshall Hall?' he asked. Marshall Hall replied that the point was an important one. 'A moustache has been painted into the photograph given in the newspaper.' Alverstone asked to see the photographs. He examined them, before remarking that, yes, it was apparent that there was a moustache on the one and not on the other. The exhibits were handed back to Lilian, and she was asked to identify the man as the prisoner. She did so and was then excused.

Lilian was followed into the box by her sister, Elizabeth 'Lizzie'

Langman, who, aged twelve, was the youngest witness in the case. As she peered out at the court that day, Lizzie faced a sea of men. Prominent among them was Marshall Hall, who was still reeling from Edith Savage's cross-examination. His stern features and imposing frame were enough to intimidate even the most robust of witnesses. For a young girl of Lizzie's age, it must have been a very overwhelming sight. This notion was clearly lost on Marshall Hall, however, and his sharp questioning quickly reduced the poor girl to tears. 'Do you recognise this veil?' he boomed, as the veil that had been found on the dead woman was passed up to Lizzie.

'Yes, the veil produced is the one Mrs Bennett purchased on the Friday before she left,' Lizzie replied confidently. Marshall Hall expressed surprise at how 'glibly' the young girl was able to identify it. The Lord Chief Justice quickly came to her defence, stating that he did not think she had said so 'glibly'.

'Well, it was put into her mouth,' Marshall Hall argued disdainfully. There was no kindness in the barrister's methods or his manners. By now, Lizzie had begun to sob. Alverstone turned to her. 'Come, child,' he said soothingly, 'there is no need to cry. You have answered fairly and properly. Can you say that this is the piece that was bought on that occasion?'

'I think it is,' Lizzie replied quietly. The young girl quickly regained her composure, and her evidence was concluded without further incident.

As the trial progressed, it would become apparent that, in addition to the constant references to his client's defence having been jeopardised by the press, Marshall Hall had another shrewd strategy to distract the jury from the evidence against his client: his criticism of the police. Before the court was permitted to rise for lunch, the barrister loudly complained that the three chief police witnesses – Leach, Parker and Lingwood – were 'constantly' in the court despite yet to give evidence themselves. Gill explained that Lingwood was overseeing the exhibits in the case and Parker and Leach were assisting his junior counsel. The barrister's objection was noted, however, and the Lord Chief Justice said that care would be given to ensure that witnesses were removed from court at the proper time. After it had been agreed that Lingwood would be barred from the court while the two witnesses from the Crown and Anchor Hotel – William Reade and Edward Goodrum – were testifying, the barrister quickly let the point drop. It was, undoubtedly, an attempt to distract the jury from the morning's damning testimony.

*

When the court reconvened after lunch, Mrs Pankhurst – who was described as a 'stylishly dressed Woolwich woman'[10] – was called. She presented a confident front when faced with Marshall Hall's probing cross-examination. When questioned about whether Herbert had stayed in her house on the evenings of 15 and 22 September, she was adamant that he had not. 'I never leave my beds,' she said with some indignation. 'I always make them up the next morning, and Bennett's had not been slept in.'

Henry Horton, the bookkeeper for the Woolwich Royal Arsenal, then provided a detailed account of the dates Herbert was absent from work. His insistence on tacking a resounding 'my lord' onto the end of every sentence he made in reply to Marshall Hall caused much amusement in the gallery. As a 'checker', Horton kept an attendance register of all the Arsenal workers. On Saturday, 15 September (the day Mary Jane travelled to Yarmouth), the record showed that Herbert was 'absent, sick'. He had been off work since 25 August and did not return until Monday, 17 September. He then worked every day from the 17th to the 22nd of September, including Friday, 21 September. On the 21st, he worked from 6 a.m. until 7 p.m. (meaning that he could not have been the man that Alice Rudrum heard Mary Jane talking to in the Row outside the Rudrums' house on that evening). Herbert attended work on Saturday, 22nd September, finishing at the usual time of 12.40 p.m. After that, he was not scheduled to work again until the following Tuesday, 25 September.

'And the book could not show that a man had been at work if he had not?' asked Gill.

'Certainly not,' the witness replied indignantly.

Horton was followed by John Cameron and then William Parritt. Cameron kept his gaze steadily averted from the dock as he recounted Herbert's story about his wife and child dying of fever in South Africa. As he spoke, Herbert leaned forward in his chair with a grave expression painted across his face. Asked about the mysterious golden-haired woman – thought to be Mary Jane – that Cameron had seen Herbert speaking to in the street, he recalled Herbert telling him that she was one of the 'good girls' he knew.

'The prisoner was of an immoral turn of mind,' he said. 'I understood what he meant by a "good girl . . ."'

Undoubtably, by that point, everyone in court did too.

Both men swore that they had met Herbert on the 29th and not on 22 September. Cameron, who was far more confident about the date, recalled having a new suit of clothes due to be delivered that day and he remembered going to enquire about them. Parritt appeared far less certain. It seemed that he had realised the consequence of his evidence and had perhaps vowed not to make things any worse for his friend than they already were. In an effort to refresh his memory, Gill read from the deposition he had given before the magistrates: "'I was in the stores in company of Cameron on 22 September, and I was with him the whole of the time until I left him just after 11 p.m. No one was with me at all except him that evening,'" he said. 'Is that right?'

'Yes, sir,' Parritt replied quietly.

It had been a fraught day in court, but there was no sign of the drama abating as the most hotly anticipated witness of the day prepared to take the stand.

Alice Meadows was under a considerable amount of pressure. It had been almost four months since the arrest of her fiancé, and in that time she had heard many a bad word said against him. Despite acknowledging the 'great many black incidents'[1] from his past, she still clung desperately to the hope that Herbert was innocent. One of the mysteries that left her most bewildered was the identity of the man who Alice Rudrum claimed to have heard kiss Mary Jane on the evening before her murder.[2]

The whole affair could have been ruinous to her reputation, but the reporters who hounded her, also – rather fortuitously – saved her. In what was, no doubt, an attempt to further vilify Herbert, the press had painted Alice as a living victim of Herbert's crimes. The narrative excited sympathy in the minds of the public, and Alice had soon found herself overwhelmed by well-wishers. As is often the case, a blessing can also be a curse, and this particular blessing meant that she was left with no choice but to endure the unceasing interest of a sensation-hungry public.

This was never so evident as on the occasions when she left the courtroom to take her lunch. The ABC tearoom[3] on Ludgate Hill was a two-minute walk from the Old Bailey and her passage to and from the courthouse attracted considerable attention. On one occasion, the tearoom had filled to the rafters with customers as soon as she had taken her seat at her lunch table. A large group of inquisitive onlookers then clustered outside the entranceway, jostling for a glance at Herbert Bennett's fiancée.[4]

ALICE MEADOWS.
(Sketched in Court this morning.)

Sketch of Alice Meadows, the *Sun*, 27 February 1901.

22

CROSS-EXAMINATION

'You trusted him?'

As the light faded on the second day of the trial, Alice Meadows' name was called. A buzz of whispered conversation immediately whirred around the public gallery.

When Alice appeared, she was dressed entirely in black with a straw hat and feathers. The juryman next to the witness box pushed forward a chair for her to sit on and she took her place, head bowed, her eyes firmly averted from the dock. Under the delicate guidance of Gill, the young woman recounted her painful story in all its harrowing detail. Without a trace of emotion, she explained how she had first made the prisoner's acquaintance, and how an attachment had sprung up between them. As she spoke, Herbert – who was now keenly alert – gave her a long and scrutinising glance. Alice seemed not to notice; her whole demeanour was marked by restraint and self-control. By the time Gill had concluded his examination in chief, the light had faded from the court. Marshall Hall's cross-examination was postponed until the following day and the court was adjourned.

The following morning, Wednesday, 27 February, was about as bleak outside as it was inside. Rain fell continuously, affecting attendance outside the courthouse. Ticket holders still arrived in great swathes, however, and by a few minutes past 10 a.m., many of them had taken their seats in the public gallery. In the well of the court, counsel was discussing the progress of the case.

As the Crown's case had begun to unfold, interest had increased among members of the junior bar, who again blocked up the gangways, making entrance into the court nigh on impossible.[1] Before the court rose that morning, the Lord Chief Justice enquired as to when the case for the prosecution was likely to be closed. Gill replied that he hoped to call his last witness that day. Marshall Hall added that he had a number of expert witnesses to call in regard to the watch and chain, and he feared they would not be finished until late on Saturday night.

*

The court was called to order and Alice Meadows was summoned to face Marshall Hall's rigorous cross-examination. As she entered the courtroom, Alice looked over at the dock and nodded and smiled to Herbert. She was wearing a black hat trimmed with royal purple and a short black jacket, and a lace handkerchief had been tied in a bow around her throat. Her face was hidden beneath a black veil, but her voice was unrestrained and perfectly clear. Marshall Hall was in a somewhat more conciliatory mood that morning. His fierce manner had given way to a slightly more sympathetic tone, which seemed to reassure Alice. Herbert had resumed his usual position with his elbow resting on his knee and was nervously stroking his face. He scanned Alice's features almost continuously, but she kept her attention firmly centred on the counsel. During the trial, Herbert's cheeks flushed in embarrassment in response to the evidence of only two witnesses. Alice Meadows, the woman to whom he had told so many lies, was one. The second was yet to take the stand . . .

Despite being a witness for the prosecution, Alice did little to harm the case for the defence. Throughout her testimony, she laid emphasis on the fact that Herbert had always treated her very well. She spoke of Herbert's good character and stated that he had never given her any cause for complaint. 'You found the accused kind, well behaved, affectionate and genial in every way?' asked Marshall Hall.

'Yes, everything I could wish for,' Alice replied quietly. It was the vital and positive view of his character that Herbert needed after Mrs Elliston's damning testimony of the previous day.

'And you trusted him so far as to go away with him on two occasions, once for a fortnight?'

'Yes.'

'During the fourteen days you were away in Ireland, he never took advantage of you?'

'No, he behaved like a gentleman.'

'Did he ever tell you he had been very immoral in his life?'

'No.'

'Did he speak to you of other girls he had known?'

'No, sir.'

'At Yarmouth, when you both stayed at the Crown and Anchor Hotel, there was no suggestion of immorality?'

'Not the slightest – he was perfect.'

Alice was subjected to thirty minutes of searching cross-examination before she was permitted to leave the witness box. At the close of his cross-examination, Marshall Hall asked if Herbert's moustache had grown since she had last seen him. Alice looked across at Herbert, whose face flushed.

'No,' she said. 'It is about the same. It was always a very slight moustache.'

'Never heavy?' asked the counsel.

'Never,' replied Alice. As Alice left the witness box, she threw one last, fleeting glance at the prisoner before sweeping out of the courtroom.

Alice was followed by a procession of witnesses from Great Yarmouth, the first of whom was John Rudrum. He recalled Mrs Hood's arrival on Saturday, 15 September, saying that he first saw her when she had turned into the Row at around midnight, in the company of a man. In answer to a question from Gill, the shoemaker said that he had last seen his lodger at about 6 p.m. on Saturday, 22 September. 'She was wearing a light dove-coloured coat and skirt,' he said. He next saw her the following morning when he identified her corpse in the mortuary. The stolid-looking man then became the subject of a vehement cross-examination at the hands of Marshall Hall.[2]

'On 27 September, you gave evidence before the coroner,' began the barrister. 'You said you did not see the woman on Saturday, 22 September.'

'It was taken down wrong,' the witness replied. Marshall Hall pulled out the depositions and located John Rudrum's in the pile of papers. 'Who told you to correct your statement?' asked the barrister.

'Nobody,' he replied.

The Lord Chief Justice objected to Marshall Hall's line of questioning. 'I wish to show the witness's evidence is unsatisfactory,' replied the barrister.

'You must abstain. Comment on the evidence, please,' Alverstone instructed.

Marshall Hall allowed the point to drop and turned back to the witness. 'Your photograph appeared in the newspapers as an important witness in this case?' he asked. Marshall Hall was referring to a piece that had appeared in the *Illustrated Mail*, the weekly edition of the *Daily Mail*, on 24 November. It had been published to mark the close in the Yarmouth proceedings and was the only newspaper to publish a full photographic account. The headline read: '*Complete Story of the Yarmouth Crime*' with John Rudrum's photograph appearing alongside a series of images of other prominent witnesses and locations relating to the crime. Sketches had been made from the photographs, which had then been published in the illustrated newspapers.

'Yes, but it was not my wish,' John Rudrum replied. 'I do not take in the London evening papers, and I have read little of what has appeared in them about this case.'

'Then why did you allow it?' Marshall Hall asked. John Rudrum made no reply. 'I suppose you thought you were an important personage in this case?' continued Marshall Hall. The question was again met with silence. 'Why, has this not been the event of your life?'

'Yes, it has,' Rudrum admitted, before saying that the murder was still the one topic of conversation in Great Yarmouth.

'Has there been *anything* else talked about since the 22nd of September?' Marshall Hall asked. The barrister continued with this line of questioning until the witness admitted that he had talked the case over with other people, including William Borking, the manager of the Mariner's Compass.

'Did you know Mr Borking has very strong views on supernatural powers?' the barrister asked. It was a bold statement coming from Marshall Hall, as he himself had been a secret follower of the spiritualist movement since the death of his first wife.[3]

'I do not know,' replied the witness.

Gill rose to his feet. 'My lord,' he said, 'I am loth to interrupt, but I cannot see how this bears on this gentleman's credit.'

Alverstone agreed with Gill. He turned to Marshall Hall. 'I think that you are entitled to ask him questions to suggest that the evidence he has given has been coloured,' he said. 'But I don't think you are entitled to ask him questions that throw discredit on another witness.' The damage had already been done, however, and Marshall Hall's statement would certainly have left the jury questioning Borking's character.

'I am going to suggest that Mr Borking's evidence is untrustworthy,' Marshall Hall stated, 'and I wish to show things that make his evidence unreliable.'

Mrs Rudrum, neatly dressed in black, followed her husband into the witness box. She was examined by Mr Muir, junior counsel for the Crown. The landlady described Mary Jane's daily life during her stay in Great Yarmouth, telling counsel that she was in the habit of taking the baby out during the day, and then went out alone in the evenings when the child was in bed. On the Friday evening before the murder, a letter had arrived addressed to 'Mrs Hood'.

The victim's clothing was now produced, and Mrs Rudrum was asked to identify it. She did so, and then Muir's questions turned to the woman's jewellery. 'She was wearing a long gold chain,' Mrs Rudrum said, 'five rings and a gold brooch.' At this point, the gold chain that had been found in Herbert's portmanteau was passed to the witness and she was asked to identify it. The landlady examined it carefully amid a breathless silence. 'I cannot identify the gold chain produced,' she said. Her statement caused a ripple of conversation to reverberate through the courtroom and, realising the impact that her words had had, she quickly added, 'I know she was wearing a link chain, but I took it to be a chain with longer links.'

'But it was not a rope twist chain that she wore?' Muir attempted to clarify.

'No, it was a link chain,' Mrs Rudrum said confidently.

'And you only saw one chain?'

'Yes.'

'Did you sit up on the Saturday night waiting for Mrs Hood?' Muir asked.

'Yes, but of course she did not return.'

'When you heard of the arrest of Bennett, what did you do?' enquired Muir.

'I looked for a letter that I had received from a Mr Bennett, asking for rooms, and I came to the conclusion that the handwriting was the same as that in the letter and on the envelope, which came addressed to Mrs Hood.'

At this point, the Lord Chief Justice, who had been examining the envelope that had accompanied the letter requesting rooms, remarked, 'The postmark is also—'

Marshall Hall interjected. 'Not "also", please,' he protested, obviously stunned. His objection was justified, as it had been Alice Rudrum, the witness's daughter, who had seen the postmark on the 'Hood' letter and not Mrs Rudrum. Alice Rudrum's evidence was yet to be given.

Nevertheless, Alverstone continued, glaring at Marshall Hall as he did so, 'The postmark is also Woolwich.'

Muir suggested that the part of the letter Mrs Rudrum had heard her lodger read aloud should be put into evidence and Marshall Hall was on his feet again, vehemently roaring his opposition. 'I really am astounded that the onus is put upon me to object. Even if it could be proved what was in this so-called document, my friend knows that this woman told lie after lie to this witness.'

'I do not think it is necessary to protest so hotly, Mr Marshall Hall,' Alverstone scolded, 'but I agree we cannot have the contents of the letter. I shall allow the question to be put as to whether the witness saw any of the contents of the letter herself.'

Muir duly rephrased his question and Mrs Rudrum recalled seeing the name 'Hood' at the foot of the letter – 'and I saw it was addressed to Mrs Hood, Number 3, Row 104',[4] she added.

When Marshall Hall rose to cross-examine the witness, he was still glowering. 'I suppose,' he began in a sarcastic tone, 'I should not exaggerate if I say that this is the most exciting thing that has ever happened in your life?'

'It is,' Mrs Rudrum agreed. 'I have taken great interest in it, but I have endeavoured to tell the truth about it.' The modest landlady was then subjected to a particularly searching cross-examination, which first challenged her recollection of the colour of the envelope that had carried the 'Hood' letter.

'Did you say before the magistrates that it was a blue envelope?' the barrister asked.

'Blue-grey,' Mrs Rudrum replied confidently.

'Dare you swear that you so described it before either the coroner or the magistrates?' Marshall Hall questioned sharply.

'I always speak the truth; there must be a mistake somewhere,' replied the witness.

Marshall Hall was vehement. 'Men's lives are lost through mistakes, madam!' he bellowed. 'No woman who knows anything about colour would call that envelope blue!'

'Oh!' Lord Chief Justice Alverstone exclaimed. Marshall Hall turned to face the judge.

'I hope, my lord, you will be patient with me,' he said.

'I do not think you have any reason to complain on that point,' Alverstone cautioned.

Marshall Hall, turning back to face the witness, continued. 'You said before the magistrate, and the coroner too, that the envelope was blue, did you not?'

'I said it was grey-blue. I am sure I did not say dark blue.'

'Madam, did I suggest you said dark blue?' Marshall Hall boomed. 'Don't you trifle with me! I pray you listen to my questions and give them every consideration.'

He pointed towards Herbert, who was sitting in the dock watching the spectacle unfold. 'This man's life is at stake!'

Mrs Rudrum was not to be swayed. 'I said grey-blue, I believe.'

'Madam, I suggest that is deliberately false. You know you said blue on both occasions.' By now, Marshall Hall had retrieved the poor woman's signed depositions and was waving them in front of her. He then read aloud from the depositions where it had been stated by the witness that the envelope was blue. 'Dare you now say you said "grey-blue"?' the barrister spat.

'When the magistrates asked if it was dark blue, I said "no",' she replied.

'Then the coroner and the magistrate's clerk both made a mistake?' Marshall Hall asked.

'There is a mistake somewhere,' agreed Mrs Rudrum. The barrister allowed the point to drop, turning instead to the topic of the watch and chain. His questions rained down on the poor woman for twenty solid minutes.

'As to the chain in the prisoner's possession, you positively identified that?' Marshall Hall asked.

'Yes,' she said, after failing to recognise it just minutes before.

'And the watch?'

'No', she said. Then, having realised by the reaction of the court that her statement about the chain had proved controversial, she attempted to explain her previous answer, saying that the chain was about the same length as the one the deceased woman had worn. 'I have had a great lesson on watch chains from Mr Robb. He couldn't pick this chain out of a great many,' she added. The Lord Chief Justice questioned the witness over Robb's involvement and Mrs Rudrum replied that Robb had been to see her about the chain and had told her that she might have made a mistake about it. The defence solicitor had visited her at home on the Thursday after Christmas, she recalled, to thank her for taking care of the prisoner's child, Ruby. While he was there, he had taken the opportunity to discuss with her the question of the chain. He had said that his wife had tried on some different chains as a test, and he had had trouble singling out any particular one.

It was not the first time, and would not be the last, that the ethics of the defence team were brought into question.

The chain was again produced and, looking at it alongside the enlargement of the beach portrait, Mrs Rudrum now said that she thought the chains were the same. In an attempt to prove the landlady wrong by demonstrating that the chains were of a different length, Marshall Hall counted the 'blobs' on the chain and the 'blobs' in the photograph, declaring when he had finished that there were thirty on the chain, and only twenty-one in the beach photograph.

'But the chain goes twice around the neck,' piped up one of the jurymen, 'so some of the blobs are hidden in the photograph.' The observant juror stood up and pointed to the area on the enlargement where the chain passed twice around the neck.

The Lord Chief Justice agreed. 'That is a perfectly right observation,' he said. He turned to Marshall Hall. 'You have been arguing that there was a fewer number of "blobs" by counting only once behind the neck,' he said. There was a collective intake of breath in the court, which left Marshall Hall seething. He refused to allow the subject to drop, calling for a jacket. A jacket was duly produced, and the barrister instructed a policeman to hold it in a convenient position so he could pass the chain (now temporarily pieced together for the purpose) twice around the neck. His lordship allowed Marshall Hall to finish his experiment before pointing out that Mrs Bennett was wearing the chain over a blouse in the beach photograph and not a jacket.

When the dramatic scenes had finally been brought to a conclusion, the court's attention was returned to Mrs Rudrum's evidence. The landlady was once again handed the chain and, having made further comparisons between it and the beach photograph, she now said, 'This chain is the chain in the photograph.'

'You have no doubt about it?' Marshall Hall asked.

'No,' the witness replied firmly. 'It is a link chain, and I said it was a little link chain from the first.'

'You have heard that the identity of the chain is in dispute?' asked Marshall Hall.

'One hears so much one hardly knows what to believe these days,' Mrs Rudrum replied.

'You are prepared to back your opinion against your honest doubt?'

'Yes, I think it is the chain,' she replied with conviction.

'Though you had doubts before, now that you have been cross-examined, you are positive?'

'Yes, I am.'

'What made you doubt when you first went into the box?'

'It was the light.' It was particularly dark in court that day; the gas lights had had to be lit earlier than usual.

'But the photograph has made you certain?' Marshall Hall persisted.

'Yes.'

The barrister explained that he intended to call expert evidence to show that the chain the woman had worn and the chain that was found in the prisoner's box – now produced – were not one and the same. His cross-examination then turned to the subject of Mrs Hood's mysterious brother-in-law. 'Did she say her brother-in-law was in love with her and jealous of her?' he asked Mrs Rudrum.

'Yes.'

'And she said she would not be surprised if he was following her about?'

'Yes, she said that.'

'You never saw this mysterious brother-in-law?'

'No.'

'But your daughter saw her with a strange man?'

'My daughter never said so!' Mrs Rudrum replied indignantly.

'Did she not?' Marshall Hall pondered. 'We shall see, madam!' Despite a determined effort by Marshall Hall to shake Mrs Rudrum's testimony, the modest landlady had held firm. Re-examined by Gill, she stated that no other letters had arrived for Mrs Hood after her death. The landlady braved the ordeal of giving evidence better than her daughter would. Now it was time for Alice to replace her mother in the witness box.

23

A VOICE IN THE DARK

'You are positive this is the man?'

When Alice Rudrum took the stand, she created renewed confusion.

At first, she positively identified the necklace found in Herbert's possession as the one worn by 'Mrs Hood' during the week of the murder. Later, during cross-examination, she agreed with Marshall Hall that the chain in the beach photograph looked more like a rope chain than a link chain. Finally, when a rope chain was handed up to her, she said it was not like the one in the portrait. Neither she nor her mother were able to identify the watch. 'All I can say is that Mrs Bennett wore a silver watch,' Mrs Rudrum had said, and Alice now described the watch as a 'small old silver one, *like* the one produced'.

Under Marshall Hall's searching cross-examination, Alice stuck firmly to her account of Mrs Hood's encounter with the mysterious man outside the Rudrums' house on the evening before the murder. 'On Friday night, September 21st,' she recalled, 'I saw Mrs Hood standing at the bottom of the row at the Quay end. As far as I could see, she was standing alone, but I heard a man's voice say, "You understand, don't you, I am placed in an awkward position just now."'

'Did you see the man?' Marshall Hall asked.

'No, I did not,' Alice replied firmly.

'Then why did you tell the magistrate you saw him?' Marshall Hall countered.

'I never said so,' Alice replied adamantly.

Marshall Hall picked up her deposition. 'You told the coroner that you saw the deceased standing talking to a man on Friday, September 21st, and that they were both standing sideways,' Marshall Hall said, referring to her statement. 'Why did you say "sideways"?'

'Because if the man had stood any other way I would have seen him,' Alice said. Pockets of laughter filtered down from the public gallery.

'Listen to this,' Marshall Hall continued, now reading aloud from Alice's deposition. '"He kissed her and bade her goodnight." If you didn't see him, how did you see him kiss her?'

'I didn't see it, but I heard it quite plain,' Alice replied. Alice's statement provoked another outburst of laughter – louder this time – and the Lord Chief Justice threw a disapproving glance towards the public gallery. Alice continued: 'I then heard the man walk away, and Mrs Hood came into the house.'

In response to further questioning, Marshall Hall established that the police had told Alice that she may have been mistaken in thinking the woman was Mrs Hood. 'But you are quite sure it was Mrs Hood?' Marshall Hall asked.

'Yes, I have no doubt,' Alice replied firmly. Like her mother, she was quite certain of her convictions and was not to be swayed.

'Do you know that the night this was taking place, Bennett was at work at the Woolwich Arsenal?' enquired Marshall Hall.

'Yes,' she said. Alice's evidence supported the defence's notion that another man was responsible for Mrs Bennett's death. Gill, keen to dispel the theory, asked if it was unusual for people to stand at the end of the Row. 'No, it's not unusual,' replied Alice.

Having given her evidence with 'great coolness', Alice Rudrum was permitted to leave the court. As she walked through the large glass doors at the back of the room, she screamed loudly and fell fainting into the arms of a nearby court official. Her loud cries filled the courtroom, and she caused quite the sensation as the crowd filed out for lunch.

When the court resumed after the break, William Borking was called. His name was already familiar to the jury, as Marshall Hall had announced earlier that morning that he would suggest that the landlord's evidence was untrustworthy. Borking stated that on the night of 22 September, a man and a woman entered the snug of his bar at around 9.45 p.m. He recognised the woman from the beach photograph, particularly recalling her jacket because of the pattern of the braiding. The prisoner in the dock was the man she was with, Borking claimed.

'He was wearing a grey suit and ordered a gin and a Johnnie Walker.'

'What?' piped up the judge. 'A gin and water?' Alverstone's confusion prompted renewed laughter, which had first arisen moments earlier when the witness had described the man in his bar as having worn a blue-front shirt 'like mine'. To which the Lord Chief Justice had commented, 'Like which? I do not see any front.' Borking had divided his ample beard to display his own shirt, as the court rejoiced with laughter.

In answer to a question from Poyser, the Crown's junior counsel, about whether he had noticed anything about the man, Borking replied, 'Yes, he was leaning against the rail of the bar, playing with his moustache.' In cross-examination, Marshall Hall drew attention to the prisoner's moustache. 'It is impossible to twirl an incipient moustache such as the prisoner has,' he said. 'He has not a heavy moustache. He is only twenty-one or twenty-two.'

'Why, I had a bigger moustache when I was twenty-one,' Borking countered jovially.

'Perhaps you had one before you were born!' Marshall Hall replied sarcastically. His statement caused yet another outburst of laughter. In response to further questioning by the barrister, Borking was forced to admit that he had consented to have his portrait taken for the *Illustrated Mail*.[1] Then, in scenes that were reminiscent of those that had unfolded during Herbert's magisterial trial, Marshall Hall ordered his client to stand. This time, Herbert was ready. He showed no indication of the nerves that had overcome him in the police court. As he sprang up from his chair, all eyes turned to him.

'Now undo your coat,' Marshall Hall directed.

Again, Herbert complied. He opened his overcoat to reveal the same double-breasted waistcoat with the 'V'-shape opening that he had been wearing in the police court.

Marshall Hall, who had been watching Herbert, now turned to Borking. 'Do you call that a clerical-cut waistcoat?'

'No,' replied the landlord. 'But he was not wearing a tie then.'

Turning back to Herbert, who was still holding his coat open, Marshall Hall instructed him to remove his tie. Herbert complied.

'Now, do you call that a clerical-cut waistcoat?' Marshall Hall repeated.

'No,' replied Borking. 'That was not the sort of waistcoat he wore on 22nd September. That was a peculiar-cut vest.'

Point made, Marshall Hall beckoned for his client to sit down and then glanced over at the jury with his eyebrows raised. Borking's evidence was corroborated by his washerwoman, Elizabeth Gibson. When she was asked to describe the man she had seen in Borking's bar on the night of the murder, she carried her hand to her mouth and imitated the action of twirling a moustache. Herbert watched with amusement.

'Does not every man with a moustache twirl it?' Marshall Hall asked in cross-examination.

'Not the way he did,' Gibson replied, quick as a shot. Despite Marshall Hall labouring the point that it had been eight weeks between the time she had first seen the man in the bar and the day of the last hearing at Yarmouth, Gibson would not be shaken on her identification of the prisoner. She did, however, admit that Herbert had a heavier moustache when she had seen him in the bar – just as Borking had said.

The young couple, Alfred Mason and Blanche Smith, told the story of what they had seen and heard on the beach on the night of the murder, but neither were able to identify the man or the woman they had seen that night. Herbert paid particularly close attention to Mason's story about the two young men that he and his brother, Walter, had seen on the beach the morning after the murder, but the court was unmoved by Alfred's statement. Blanche Smith, who was wearing a slightly more understated outfit than she had done for her previous spell in the witness box – a large picture hat, feather boa and three-quarter-length light jacket – confirmed Mason's tale.

Blanche was swiftly followed by the two Crown and Anchor witnesses, Edward Goodrum and William Reade. Goodrum, who was described as a 'smart young fellow of about Bennett's age',[2] was the first to take the stand. He recalled the man who had arrived at the hotel in an excited state on the night of the murder.

'Can you see the man now?' asked Gill. Goodrum glanced around the court. He looked first at the jury box, then at the bench, before finally resting his eyes on the dock. He pointed to the prisoner and said, 'It was the gentleman in the dock.' Cross-examined by Marshall Hall, Goodrum stated that he had not seen a portrait of Bennett in the Yarmouth papers on the day he identified him, and no, he had not read the accounts about the murder in the London papers.

'Do you expect the jury to believe that?' Marshall Hall said, in an accusatorial tone.

'They can if they like,' the young lad replied, 'it's the truth.'

'When did the police assist your memory as to the very mysterious stranger?' Marshall Hall asked.

'You can't say that!' the Lord Chief Justice interjected sharply. 'Put it in another form.' But Goodrum was already responding to the original question.

'I do not think the police assisted me at all,' he said. In answer to further questions, the witness said that he saw the police when they came to make enquiries on the Sunday following the murder, but he did not speak to them in detail about the stranger.

'Why not?' asked Marshall Hall.

'Because I did not think the man was connected to the murder.'

'Did you ever hear this man speak?' the barrister asked.

'Yes.'

'What sort of voice had he?'

'I can't say,' Goodrum replied uncertainly.

'Clothes?' continued Marshall Hall.

'I can't say.' By now, it was obvious where Marshall Hall's line of questioning was going.

'Boots?'

'I can't say.'

'Yet you are positive this' – Marshall Hall pointed dramatically to the prisoner in the dock – 'is the man?'

'Yes,' Goodrum replied simply. The 'boots' was then asked if he recognised Herbert from any previous visits, and he replied no – he had been told that Bennett was at the Crown and Anchor on the August bank holiday, but he did not remember seeing him.

William Reade, the 'typical figure of a hotel attendant',[3] came next and gave evidence that he recognised Bennett from each of his three alleged visits. Since he had stayed at the hotel on two occasions before the night of the murder, the waiter had not regarded him as a chance customer, such as the police were enquiring about. In cross-examination, Marshall Hall put it to the witness that he had only recognised Herbert after the press had 'taken up the case and sensational journalism had sent its lying filth broadcast through Yarmouth'. The witness replied that he had only glanced at the papers.

'But had the case not been a good deal talked about in Yarmouth?' Marshall Hall persisted.

'I wouldn't know,' replied the witness. 'I have been living fourteen miles out of Yarmouth since I left the hotel on 1st November.'

Marshall Hall had made a valiant attempt to shake the testimony of both men, but they held firm to their identification of Herbert, in what was a damning end to the day's testimony.

Despite being called to testify early on in the proceedings, Yarmouth photographer Frank Sayers continued to attend the trial as an observer. His part in the murder investigation had completely knocked the nerve out of him, and he would later recall being haunted by it for many months afterwards.[1]

Sayers watched the trial unfold alongside the other spectators in the public gallery – a cramped and suffocatingly stifling environment. When he escaped the confines of the raised gallery at the close of court each day, he would have welcomed the slightly fresher air of the lower court. The chatter of the spectators as they exited the court would always turn to an analysis of the day's evidence, and some believed the jury would return a verdict of not guilty.

On one particular day, Sayers heard a man behind him exclaim, 'He'll get off!'

Sayers, who had been following the case point by point, and watching Herbert carefully, cried, 'It's a million to one against it!'

He then turned to face the man who had spoken, and found himself staring into the 'terribly distressed' faces of Herbert's father and stepmother.[2]

24

DOUBT

'The counterfoil is not here, my lord. It should be!'

T here was only one topic of conversation at the Old Bailey as the trial reached its fourth day: whether the defence would put Herbert Bennett into the box. Just over two years earlier, the Criminal Evidence Act had come into force, which allowed the accused to take the stand to testify in their own defence. Since then, juries had come to expect the accused to take the stand and – when they did not – it was often seen as an admission of guilt. The consensus among the counsel gathered in the well of the court that morning was that Marshall Hall would not call his client. The truth was, the barrister was yet to make up his mind.

The rush outside the Old Bailey on that bright, early spring morning was more intense than it had been on any other day so far. The dramatic witness testimony of the previous day had caused renewed excitement, which was further added to by a rumour that a series of experts would be called later in the day to provide photographic evidence. These gentlemen had joined the other witnesses in the waiting room and were recognisable by their glossy silk hats, and the posies that protruded from the buttonholes of their fashionable jackets.¹ The prosecution had so far called thirty-seven witnesses, with fifteen to go.

The court opened with yet another protest by the counsel for the defence against statements made in the press. 'It has been suggested in the press, my lord,' Marshall Hall said, 'that during this case, there have been scenes between your lordship and myself. It is very painful for me to see such comments, as never during my whole experience of the bar have I received such courtesy and consideration at the hands of the judge.'

'Don't you think, Mr Marshall Hall,' Alverstone replied in his gentlest of tones, 'that you and I can afford to disregard such matters?'

'Perhaps you can, my lord, but I cannot,' Marshall Hall replied.

'Oh, I think you can,' the judge said, smiling. 'But I do think the press has a lot to answer for in this case.' Satisfied that he had achieved his purpose, Marshall Hall returned to his seat.

When the evidence commenced, the prosecution called Thomas Keats, the owner of the Crown and Anchor Hotel. On the weekend of the murder, Keats had been on holiday in the Sussex town of Hastings, in the south-east of England. He was therefore unable to provide any corroborative evidence regarding Herbert's identification and was instead questioned intensively over the hotel records. The hotelier stated that the Crown and Anchor kept a bill-book with counterfoils and that eighty of those counterfoils – including those relating to Herbert's alleged visits – had since been found to be missing. He could offer no explanation for this. When the receipts were made out, the bills were torn from the book, leaving the counterfoil. The counterfoils were then copied into a ledger. The ledger had an entry for 16 September for 11s. 6d. and an entry for 22 September, for 6s., but both corresponding counterfoils were missing, along with the counterfoils for transactions from 21 and 23 September.

'Have you showed this book to Mr Robb, the solicitor for the defence?' Gill asked.

'I'm not sure,' replied the witness uncertainly.

'Or his clerk?' persisted Gill.

'I do not know.'

'Did Mr Wood, a clerk to the solicitor for the defence, stay at your house one night recently?' Gill asked.

'Yes,' replied Keats.

Gill did not need to say any more – his implication was clear. The jury were left to draw their own conclusions as to whether they believed the defence had something to do with the missing counterfoils. Marshall Hall, however, would not allow an allegation such as this to pass without comment, and he attempted to snuff out any thought of wrongdoing during his lengthy cross-examination of the witness.

'What did he mean?' Marshall Hall bellowed in reference to Gill's question. Keats looked confused. 'Either my friend's question means something, or it means nothing,' continued Marshall Hall. 'He asked you if Mr Robb's clerk had stayed at your hotel. Have you any reason to believe that the clerk had the opportunity to tamper with that counterfoil bill-book?'

'I do not think so,' Keats replied, suddenly looking uncomfortable.

'I shall not,' Alverstone interjected, 'and I don't suppose the jury will, for a moment suppose that Mr Wood has touched the book.' Then, after a short pause, he added sternly, 'We don't try these cases on suspicion.'

Marshall Hall's attempt at a reply was cut off by the Lord Chief Justice, who said, now rather irritated, 'Let us get on, please.'

Marshall Hall turned back to the witness. 'And if the police had wanted to see these counterfoils on 23rd September, they would have been at their disposal?'

'Yes,' Keats replied.

'You were never asked to produce your books at the police court?'

'No.'

Further cross-examination established that the cost of staying at the hotel, including a breakfast of ham and eggs, was 4s. 6d. The waiter, Reade, who claimed to have given Herbert his bill on the morning following the murder, was recalled and handed the counterfoil book. Alverstone instructed Reade to find the counterfoil relating to the prisoner's stay. The court waited in anticipation as Reade sifted through the thin papers. When he had, unsurprisingly, failed to locate the counterfoil, the witness looked up at the judge. 'The counterfoil is not here, my lord,' he said, surprised. 'It should be.' The Lord Chief Justice directed the clerk of the court to 'carefully keep' the plain, ordinary-looking book and the trial was allowed to move on.

John Headley, journalist and Yarmouth newsagent, was next in the box. He stated that he had been at the South Town railway station on the morning of Sunday, 23 September, dispatching newspapers, when he had 'observed a man very much resembling the prisoner standing by a first-class carriage door in an excited and agitated manner'. Headley had assumed that the man was waiting for someone and was anxious that they would miss the train. 'I did not see him get into the carriage,' continued Headley, 'but he was not on the platform when the train had gone.'

Headley was asked how the man was dressed.

'In a light grey suit and a rather darker trilby hat,' the newsagent replied confidently. 'I also noticed that the man had a slight moustache.'

Marshall Hall, cross-examining the witness, pointed to the prisoner. 'Will you swear this is the man you saw?' he asked.

'I honestly believe it is,' replied Headley, 'but I would not like to swear positively to him.'

Marshall Hall picked up a copy of that morning's *Echo*. He turned to the witness. 'I have here a report of your evidence, before you were called,' he said. 'How do you explain that?' he demanded fiercely. Marshall Hall was livid that Headley had clearly given the press an account of his testimony before giving evidence in court. He turned to Alverstone. 'My lord,' he said, motioning to the newspaper. 'I must put this in.'

By now, the Lord Chief Justice was tiring of the barrister's constant complaints about the press. 'Do not think, Mr Marshall Hall, that I do not have an opinion about the conduct of newspapers in this case,' he replied. 'You will quite gather from what I have already said that I have. But you must remember that the jury have only to deal with the evidence.'

'Quite so, my lord,' Marshall Hall replied, 'but I am not putting this to the jury now. I am putting the matter before your lordship.' He handed the copy of the *Echo* to the judge. Marshall Hall had again forced Alverstone to denounce the actions of the press. The judge turned to the jury and said, 'Gentleman, I shall have to direct you in regard to how far any comments of newspapers – which were certainly very improper indeed last autumn – can have any value. But at present, we must deal with the evidence.' With the matter closed, Headley's testimony was allowed to resume.

In answer to a question from the jury, the newsagent said he did not remember whether the man at the station carried a parcel.

Headley was followed into the box by two Great Eastern Railway (GER) train guards – William Emms and James Ward – whose evidence concerned the arrival and departure of trains between London's Liverpool Street and Great Yarmouth's South Town stations. Acting-guard Emms had been in charge of the 5 p.m. train that had travelled from London to Great Yarmouth on the evening of the murder. Producing his record book, he stated that the train had arrived at its destination as scheduled at 8.28 p.m. The object of Emms's evidence was to show that Herbert could have travelled on that train and arrived in Great Yarmouth in time to meet his wife in front of the town hall at 9 p.m. Passenger-guard Ward, who was in charge of the first train to depart Great Yarmouth's South Town station on the morning of 23 September, stated that the train had departed on time at 7.20 and arrived in the capital a minute late, at 11.31 a.m. This would have given Herbert plenty of time to get to Hyde Park to meet Alice just before 1 p.m.

Next came Mrs Sarah Meadows, the mother of Alice Meadows. The witness recalled seeing Herbert at her house at around midday on Sunday, 16 September. Her daughter, May Lenson, who would be called as a witness for the defence during the fifth day of the trial, would provide corroborating evidence. May would recall the prisoner arriving at 'about 11.30 a.m.,' which would have made it impossible for Herbert to have been on the first train out of Great Yarmouth that same morning. May was, however, unable to swear to the exact timing, saying that it 'might have been sooner or later', and it was this uncertainty that would ultimately throw doubt over the Meadows family's account.

ONE 'T' OR TWO?

'You only knew this woman by the name of "Hood"?'

When the name of the next witness was called, Herbert's face flushed a deep crimson colour.

His cheeks were still aflame when the object of one of his most shameful lies took to the stand. Henry Simmons, the prisoner's sixty-two-year-old grandfather, had been tasked with the simple job of proving that he was still alive. According to one reporter, he had the appearance of a hale and hearty white-haired man.[1] Another described him as having 'plenty of white hair and a fringe of white beard beneath the chin, after the fashion so much in vogue with Yarmouth fishermen'.[2] Simmons's mere presence in the courtroom was enough to catch Herbert out in a lie, but when he had settled himself in the witness box, he added further fuel to the flame by stating that Herbert's paternal grandfather had died twenty years earlier. Simmons recalled being 'quite well' on 16 and 22 September and denied seeing his grandson on either day. He glared disapprovingly at Herbert as he left the witness box.

The next witness was Herbert's one-time friend and colleague at the Woolwich Co-op, Robert Allen. Allen, who had not been called to give evidence before the magistrates, was referred to by the press as a 'new and important witness'.[3] His evidence had been eagerly anticipated. The witness stated that he knew Mrs Bennett by sight and accordingly identified her from the beach photograph. During Gill's lengthy examination, Herbert appeared more fidgety than usual. Allen's testimony portrayed him as a man intent on making a bit of money from selling off his dead wife's possessions. It was far from the reformation of character that he undoubtedly wished to portray in court.

When Marshall Hall rose to question the witness, he looked like a man who had a great deal to say. 'You were assisting Leach to arrest this man?' he asked.

'Well – yes,' replied Allen mildly.

'A man with whom you had had a very serious quarrel?' Marshall Hall asked, surprised.

'I do not think so,' replied the witness. 'There was no serious quarrel between us.'

'Well, we will see!' countered Marshall Hall. 'You know the prisoner as Bennett?' he continued.

'Yes,' Allen replied.

'You owe him £17?'

'There is that to pay over the piano and bicycle transaction,' Allen agreed.

'How much have you paid for the piano and bicycle?' Marshall Hall persisted.

'A deposit of £6 out of £23.' Allen had started to become uneasy. 'Bennett has not asked me for the balance,' he added quickly.

'Have you said that if Bennett worried you for the money, you would prosecute him for fraud?' demanded Marshall Hall.

'No.'

'Did you say the cycle receipt was forged?' continued Marshall Hall.

'Yes,' admitted Allen.

'Why did you say that?'

'I was in doubt,' Allen replied. 'So I wrote to the manufacturer.'

'And the piano?'

'I said I would try and find out if the piano was really his property.'

'And you told him the bicycle receipt was forged?'

'Yes.'

'Do you suggest you were swindled over the bicycle?'

'Yes.'

'Did you want to have your revenge on this man who had swindled you over a bicycle by having him arrested in the street?'

'I do not want to be revenged at all!' protested Allen. He was then forced to deny that it was out of spite that he had taken the police to arrest Herbert out in the open instead of at his lodgings.

'Now what about the piano. Do you suggest that he swindled you over the piano?'

'Yes.'

'You've got the piano and bicycle and you propose to keep them?'

'I have them,' Allen said. 'But I don't know what I will do with them.'

'And are you willing to pay for them now?' Marshall Hall asked.

'I found some defect in the piano,' Allen said. 'It isn't worth the money.'

Herbert, who had been listening to the exchange with a broad smile across his face, suddenly jumped to his feet, leaned over the dock and whispered something in his counsel's ear. Marshall Hall turned back to the witness. 'Did you have a man from Broadwood's to value the piano before you bought it?' he asked.

'I had a man to examine the piano,' Allen replied. 'He told me it was not worth the money.'

'But yet you bought it!' scoffed Marshall Hall. 'Thank you – that will do.'

Marshall Hall had turned the tables on Allen, expertly representing him to the jury as a man who was willing to betray a friend over a petty quarrel. Re-examining the witness, Gill attempted to rescue matters. 'Did you know Bennett was wanted by the police on a charge of murder?' he asked.

'No,' said Allen, and Gill hoped that was enough to repair some of the damage that had been caused.

Mr Beasley, manager of the tailoring department of Arding & Hobbs in Clapham Junction, appeared next. He recognised Herbert as a regular customer, stating that the light-grey suit that Herbert now wore had been made by his staff the previous July. On 18 August, the prisoner had ordered a darker suit, which he had returned for remodelling on 29 September.

The court's attention then turned to the police evidence and there was a considerable flutter of interest when Detective Inspector Robert Lingwood was called. The red-faced man looked every inch the sturdy police officer that he was. During what was a very short examination, the dead woman's clothing was produced along with the mohair bootlace that had been cut from around her neck. Among the articles of clothing was a piece of baby linen marked with the tell-tale 599 laundry mark and a woman's white laced petticoat with 'Bennet' [sic] written on the waistband. When Gill had finished with the witness, Lingwood turned his rosy face to Marshall Hall for cross-examination.

The barrister questioned the detective inspector at great length. After a few preliminary questions, he returned to one of his favourite subjects: the newspapers. He read aloud from a report published by the *Evening News* on the Monday following the murder, which described the finding of the body and the woman who was missing from the Rudrums' boarding house.

'Now that is the sort of publicity that ought to be given by the newspapers,' chimed in Alverstone. 'That is quite proper.'

'What paper are you reading from, sir?' asked the detective.

'The *Evening News*,' replied the barrister.

'The London *Evening News*, sir?' asked Lingwood.

'Yes,' said Marshall Hall.

'Oh,' replied the detective, 'I don't know anything about that. We very seldom see the London *Evening News* at Yarmouth.' Asked what newspapers circulated in Great Yarmouth the day after Mrs Bennett's body was found, Lingwood named two local papers – the *Eastern Daily Press* and the *Eastern Evening News*. The barrister read a short extract from one of these newspapers in which the police appealed for help in identifying the body. Lingwood confirmed that the details had been provided by the police. In an attempt to trace the source of the controversial photographs that had appeared in the London evening papers and the Yarmouth weeklies, Marshall Hall then asked Lingwood if he had given the press the photograph of Herbert and his wife.

'No,' Lingwood replied. 'But I saw a portrait in the hands of some press representatives.'

'Can you tell me who gave the photograph to the press?' Marshall Hall continued.

'No, I cannot,' replied Lingwood, before assuring him that the police had had nothing to do with it.

'Did it occur to you that the identity of the woman as Mrs Bennett depended entirely on photographs?' Marshall Hall asked.

'That, and the mark 599 on the linen,' Lingwood replied. 'There was also the mark on the petticoat,' said the detective, indicating the garment.

'Ah!' cried Marshall Hall. 'Ah! The petticoat. Now just look at the half-blotted name on the waistband of that garment. Do you notice anything peculiar about it?'

Lingwood separated the petticoat from the other linen and examined it closely. While he was scrutinising it, the barrister said, rather sarcastically, 'Yes, see if your police ingenuity will enable you to discover anything.'

'Do you mean, sir,' said Lingwood, 'that the name Bennett is spelt with only one "t"?'

'Ah!' exclaimed Marshall Hall. 'I thought you would detect that! People who write their own name don't spell it wrongly, do they?'

'I should think not, sir,' replied the detective.

'Do you recognise that handwriting?'

'No.'

Marshall Hall remarked that it was a curious thing that Mrs Rudrum had in her possession a petticoat marked with the name 'Bennet' while the police were scouring the country for evidence as to the identity of the woman. 'And yet,' he exclaimed, 'it was not handed in to the police until 16th January!' He looked at Lingwood. 'How was that?' he demanded.

'Mrs Rudrum was responsible for that, sir,' was all the detective would say.

Lingwood was then questioned about the deceased woman's chain. The detective had first heard that it was missing from Mrs Rudrum on the Sunday after the murder. He knew that finding it would uncover a valuable piece of evidence. Shown an enlargement of the beach photograph, Lingwood refused to give an opinion about whether the chain was of a rope or link design. The picture was just too indistinct, he stated adamantly.

While Marshall Hall was attempting to coax a response from the detective by telling him to use his intelligence as a police officer, the judge had been closely examining the enlargement. He now called Marshall Hall's attention to three areas of the photograph that he considered important. He marked the areas of interest and handed the enlargement down to Marshall Hall, saying that he would have to call the jury's attention to those parts. Marshall Hall took up a watchmaker's glass and studied the photographs. At this point, Lingwood stated that he had supplied the prisoner's solicitor, Robb, with a copy of the beach photograph. The Lord Chief Justice asked where that copy was and Marshall Hall was forced to admit that it had been stolen, along with one other document of 'great importance'.

'What!' cried the judge. 'Is there a suggestion that the prosecution—'

'Oh no, my lord!' interrupted Marshall Hall.

Gill was on his feet in a flash. 'I hope we are not quite so bad as that,' he said, smiling. Introducing yet another mystery into the case, Marshall Hall intimated that he would have more to say about the missing papers at a later date.

When he had finished with Lingwood, the barrister ordered Mrs Rudrum back to question her over the mysterious petticoat. As soon as the poor woman had taken her position in the witness box, Marshall Hall fired his first question at her. 'How did Mrs Bennett spell her name?'

Mrs Rudrum looked confused. 'How would I know, sir?' she said. 'Her name was "Hood".'

'How would you spell it yourself, then?' Marshall Hall asked.

'I don't know, sir,' replied the landlady.

'Oh, try,' coaxed the barrister.

'B-e-n – I can't, sir. I'm such a bad speller.'

'You are asked to spell Bennett,' the judge said sternly. 'Please make an effort.'

Mrs Rudrum looked pained. 'B-e-n-n-e-t,' she said, before pausing and then adding another 't'.

'You said one "t" first, and then two; which is it?' Marshall Hall snapped.

'I meant two "ts",' the witness insisted.

'Ah, but you said one "t" at first. Write it down,' instructed Marshall Hall.

'I cannot, sir,' Mrs Rudrum protested. 'I am such a bad scholar.'

'Very well,' the barrister replied, apparently satisfied. 'But you mean to tell me that this petticoat was hanging up in the woman's room when Lingwood came on 23rd September?'

'Yes; he saw it, I think,' the landlady replied.

'Did you not see that he was searching for all the clothes he could find?'

'You must remember that I was terribly upset that morning,' Mrs Rudrum replied.

During further questioning, the landlady was unable to express an opinion as to the type of ink that had been used to mark the petticoat. 'All I can say is that it was not marked in my house.' In answer to the judge, the witness said she could not imagine how the police had missed the petticoat, which had been hanging up on a peg behind the door to the woman's room on the morning the search was made.

'I understand you only knew this woman by the name of "Hood", and did not know her name was Bennett until after the prisoner was arrested?' Alverstone asked.

'That is so, my lord,' replied the witness.

Quite what Marshall Hall was trying to prove at this point was never made clear. The deceased woman's identity was no longer in dispute by the time the petticoat was found, and there was no question over whether the deceased was the prisoner's wife. The petticoat did, however, throw the Rudrums' testimony into doubt. If one of them had indeed marked the petticoat, was there anything else that they had been less than honest about? This was, undoubtedly, the question that Marshall Hall was hoping the twelve men in the jury box would be asking themselves. After what was her second severe round of questioning at the hands of Marshall Hall, Mrs Rudrum was allowed to leave and the chief constable of Great Yarmouth, William Parker, took his place in the witness box.

ON YOUR OATH?

'You lying scoundrel! The poor woman was your wife'

T he stalwart officer, dressed in plain clothes, reported that the police had made extensive enquiries about a woman named 'Hood' after the deceased's body had been recovered from the beach. It had not been until 6 November that he had heard the name Bennett in connection with the case. As he spoke, Chief Constable Parker's voice boomed across the courtroom. The reporters in the remotest corners of the crowded court who had had to strain to hear many of the other witnesses, notably Alice Meadows, were grateful for the reprieve.

In cross-examination, Marshall Hall established that Parker had not known that Mrs Hood's watch and chain were missing when he went to London to search Herbert's box. 'Of course, the chain was shown in the photograph, but nothing was said about it,' Parker stated. It was a long time before he saw the Rudrums and he did not remember Lingwood or PC Platten telling him that the woman's chain was missing.

'Do I understand that up to 6th November, you did not know the importance of this watch and chain?' Marshall Hall asked.

'I knew the importance of it but did not know where to look for it,' replied Parker.

'When before the magistrates the watch and chain were produced, did the prisoner say, "My wife has not worn that chain for some months"?'

'No,' replied Parker. 'He said she had not worn it for twelve months.'

'Are you quite sure he said for twelve months?' Marshall Hall persisted.

'I am quite sure he said that she had not worn it for twelve months or a twelvemonth,' Parker said firmly.

'I suggest the prisoner used the expression "for a few months",' Marshall Hall countered. Parker would not be swayed. 'No,' he replied resolutely.[1] Marshall Hall was probably acutely aware that a number of witnesses could be called to testify that they had seen Mary Jane wearing a long gold chain in recent months. In reply to a question about the circumstances that led to Alice Rudrum's identification of the chain, Parker insisted that he had not held the chain up and asked Alice if she recognised it. 'She recognised it at once as it lay coiled up on the desk. I made no reference to it at all.'

Attention then turned to the watch. During Parker's initial examination, the barrister had objected to a statement the chief constable had made in reference to the teeth marks that were visible on the watch. As a result, the watch had been passed up to the jury, who were examining it critically. 'If the deceased had two watches,' Marshall Hall mused, 'it is quite likely the child would have bitten both?'

'Yes,' admitted Parker.

'Now,' said Marshall Hall, 'I am very bold this morning. I will take your impression on this point. What is your impression – as a man and not as a police officer – of the similarity of the chain in the photograph and the chain I produce?'

The chief constable insisted that he really could not say – 'I am not an expert in photography,' he said lightly.

Marshall Hall's final round of questions were concerned with Herbert's arrest. 'When the prisoner was arrested, did he say he had never been to Yarmouth?'

'Yes,' replied the chief constable.

'Did he not afterwards correct himself and say that he had been there for a bank holiday?'

'No,' replied Parker. 'He never said that from first to last in my presence.'

When the court resumed that afternoon, the last of the three principal police witnesses, Chief Inspector Alfred Leach, took the stand. Leach, a 'man of good height',[2] briefly recounted the police investigation in London, recalling the events that had led to his team establishing the deceased woman's true identity.

Just as Marshall Hall rose to cross-examine the witness, a barrister entered the court and said in a stage whisper, 'Botha surrendered. Official.' The news from South Africa caused a flutter of excitement. That day, Field Marshal Kitchener of the British Army had opened peace negotiations with General Botha, the commander in chief of the Transvaal Boers. The reported surrender of General Botha quickly gained traction in London but was discredited in the press the following day.

The judge called for silence and Marshall Hall began his questioning. 'When you arrested the prisoner,' he asked Leach, 'why did you not say, "I arrest you for the murder of your wife?"' Leach could not say. 'But did Bennett not then say, "I don't know what you mean?"' continued the barrister.

'Yes,' replied the detective.

'And then didn't you say, "You lying scoundrel! The poor woman was your wife!"?' Marshall Hall asked.

'No, I did not,' Leach replied.

'Did you say anything of the kind?' Marshall Hall persisted.

'No, I did not,' Leach repeated, more firmly this time.

'On your oath?'

'Yes, on my oath.'

'Did the prisoner not reply – impertinently, if you like – "It is wonderful how soon persons of the same family get to know each other"?'

'No, certainly not,' Leach replied. He appeared altogether perplexed and Marshall Hall failed to clarify the matter.

Before evidence for the Crown was brought to a close, Gill called Albert Eardley, the man with whom Herbert had shared a room at the Pankhursts' house and his colleague at the Woolwich Arsenal. Asked about the events of Saturday, 22 September, Eardley stated that he remembered the day clearly because it was the anniversary of his mother's death. He recalled leaving work at 12.30 p.m. (shortly ahead of Herbert) before spending the afternoon at the Crystal Palace, Sydenham Hill, in Southeast London. That evening, he returned home sometime between 10 p.m. and 11 p.m. and went to bed just after 11 p.m. He did not see Bennett that evening or the following morning. Confusion swirled during Eardley's cross-examination, when Marshall Hall asked if he had spoken to Herbert about his visit to the Crystal Palace on the Sunday morning. 'No,' Eardley replied.

'Did you not tell him you had ordered a rubber stamp [as a souvenir] at the Crystal Palace and showed him some views [postcards] you had bought?' the barrister asked.

'I don't think so,' replied the witness.

'Then how did he know?' asked Marshall Hall. Before Eardley could answer, the barrister added, 'You remember, though, that you talked about Stevens having left [Union Street] the night before?'

'Yes,' replied the witness. The spectators, who had been following the conversation closely, burst out laughing. Clearly confused by Marshall Hall's questioning, Eardley had contradicted himself. Marshall Hall dropped to his seat at once, triumphant. With the laughter still ringing in the background, Gill rose to his feet. 'Who was it to whom you spoke about Stevens leaving?' he asked.

'Mrs Pankhurst,' Eardley replied. His answer sparked another round of laughter.

Walter Pankhurst Sr and his grandmother, Elizabeth, were called to further corroborate Eardley's and Mrs Pankhurst's evidence that Herbert had not slept at the Union Street address on 22 September. By this point, the assertion had become difficult to contest.

Mrs Comfort Pankhurst was then recalled to answer questions relating to the layout of various rooms in her house. Following a request from the jury the previous morning, architectural plans had been drawn up of 41 Union Street by Benjamin Spencer of the Woolwich police. When the plans were introduced into evidence, Marshall Hall muttered a comment about the police.

'You don't suggest the plan is incorrect?' asked Alverstone loudly.

'No, I do not,' Marshall Hall replied, before adding – rather sarcastically – 'but I do suggest there are surveyors. But I suppose they want to keep it in the family.'

Marshall Hall then turned to Mrs Pankhurst and suggested to her that Herbert had slept in Stevens's room on the night of 22 September. 'What I put to you is this,' he began. 'When you went into Stevens's room on the Monday morning, you found the bed had been disturbed.'

'It had not,' Mrs Pankhurst replied firmly.

'Now, Mrs Pankhurst?' Marshall Hall said incredulously.

'I am on my oath, and I am telling the truth,' the witness replied hotly. Mrs Pankhurst had been a strong witness and was very firm in her assertions – similarly to Mrs Rudrum – but she was now beginning to buckle under Marshall Hall's severe questioning. Alverstone, sensing her change in temperament, attempted to reassure her. 'You must not mind the way the questions are put by Mr Marshall Hall,' he said. 'I will see that you have the proper protection.'

'Thank you, my lord,' the landlady replied.

'I do not wish to take the least advantage of you,' Marshall Hall objected, feigning surprise. In further questioning, Mrs Pankhurst stated that she had made both Stevens's and Bennett's beds up on the Saturday morning. Bennett's had not been slept in on the Saturday night and Stevens's had not been touched when she went in to thoroughly turn out the room on the Monday. Bennett had slept in his own bed on the Sunday night, which made the idea that he had spent one night sleeping in Stevens's bed before returning to his own quite absurd. At this point, Herbert rose from his seat and appeared as though he was about to speak. He thought better of it, sat back down and, instead, scribbled a note to his counsel. He then buried his head in his hands and sat quite still for several minutes.

When Marshall Hall had finished questioning the witness, the Lord Chief Justice turned to the witness box and said, 'Mrs Pankhurst, you know the solemnity of it. Are you quite sure of all you have said?'

'Yes, my lord,' she replied adamantly. 'I am quite sure.'

The landlady was trembling and ashen pale as she stepped down from the witness box.

EXPERT TESTIMONY

'That is my honest and candid opinion'

T he chain, by now, had become the most contested point in the case.

Towards the end of the fourth day, the court's attention turned to the expert testimony of a series of specialists in the fields of photography and jewellery. Fierce debate raged amid a backdrop of learned discourse on the scientific points in the dispute. The Lord Chief Justice, with his amateur knowledge of photography, followed with interest. When the counsel had finished with the experts, the judge took each of them in hand and interrogated them further. As the witnesses took turns speculating, judge and jury scribbled down voluminous notes and carefully scanned the photographs.

A second enlargement had been introduced into evidence, which provided another point of comparison. This almost life-sized portrait of Mary Jane had been made from the negative of a photograph originally taken in July 1899 by the firm A & G Taylor Photographers, Regent Street, London. It was aptly referred to as the 'Taylor photograph' and was entered into evidence by its creator, Alfred Strivens. The original print, which had come into the possession of the defence on the first day of the trial, had been vignetted – a technique that was used in portraiture to soften the edges of the subject. This process had also affected the appearance of the chain. The enlargement made from the negative had resulted in a 'clean' copy, but the chain still appeared slightly out of focus even in this reproduction.

The Crown's principal expert witness was a photographer named Mr W.H. Kaye. Kaye's firm – the London Stereoscopic and Photographic Company – had led the stereo-view[1] craze that swept across the UK in the 1850s.[2] The witness had been appointed by the public prosecutor to photograph the chain under a series of different conditions in an attempt to establish whether its appearance in the beach photograph could be replicated. Kaye had been tasked with identifying the effect vibration had, as one point that everyone agreed upon was that breathing had some effect on the appearance of the chain.

Kaye had produced several experimental images the previous evening with the aid of an electric light. The chain had been removed from the custody of the court by Leach. When an announcement to this effect was made in court, Marshall Hall immediately protested, hotly arguing that a representative of the defence should have been present when the chain was photographed. Leach was recalled and ordered to confirm that he had been present at all times when the chain was removed and photographed. When the court had heard Leach's testimony, the Lord Chief Justice said, 'I think it a perfectly right thing to have been done.'

'The prisoner should have been represented,' Marshall Hall argued.

'I do not wish to justify what I have said,' replied Alverstone firmly. 'Considering the questions most properly put in cross-examination with regard to what the photograph is supposed to show, it would have been very wrong if further investigation had not been made.' The judge intimated that his word was final, and Kaye was permitted to continue with his evidence.

Gill's examination of the photographer had barely restarted, however, before Marshall Hall interrupted for a second time. 'The atmosphere in here is very bad,' he protested. 'I can scarcely breathe.' It was yet another of Marshall Hall's clever ploys to distract the jury's attention from the evidence. Alverstone issued an order for additional windows to be opened (a request that Marshall Hall could have quietly made for himself) and Kaye continued.

'I took several photographs,' he said, 'and in all except one – in which the chain was fixed, and the plate exposed for four seconds – the link-chain appears in places as of a rope pattern.' Kaye went on to explain that any slight movement of the chain shifted the light between the links and caused the highlights to run into each other. This, he said, resulted in a rope-like appearance when the chain was photographed. Referring to the enlargement of the beach photograph, the witness explained that the chain was out of focus and the conditions under which the photograph was taken would also have affected how it appeared in the image. He went on to compare the appearance of the chain in the photographs he had taken with the Taylor photograph and stated that the chain appeared to take on the appearance of a rope chain in certain areas in both photographs. The photographer would say no more in conclusion, other than that he did not think anyone could say for certain what sort of chain it was in the beach photograph. It was under that air of uncertainty that the prosecution rested. Marshall Hall's relief was, undoubtedly, palpable.

In the dying hour of the day, Marshall Hall opened the case for the defence. He chose not to proceed with his opening speech, instead opting to move swiftly to his own expert testimony. The first came in the form of Howard Welby. Welby was the proprietor of a firm of jewellers based in Garrick Street, Covent Garden, and a personal friend of Marshall Hall's. The barrister had discussed the question of the chain with Welby and the jeweller shared his opinion that the chain in the beach photograph was of a rope pattern. When he took to the stand, Welby stated that he believed that the chain in the photograph was, more specifically, a 'Prince of Wales' pattern. This view was upheld by the next witness, another jeweller named Wordley. At the close of Wordley's evidence, the court rose and the jury were permitted to retire after what had been yet another long day of evidence.

Earlier, it had been announced that the jurymen would be allowed to attend the theatre the following evening – under the strict supervision of Undersheriff Langton – if the trial had not yet reached a conclusion. The twelve men no doubt viewed the prospect as a welcome departure from their standard evening routine, which had been limited to playing cards, billiards, dominoes, chess and draughts in their rooms at the Manchester Hotel. The twelve men were not the only people to welcome the close of court that day – Herbert looked particularly weary when he stepped down from the dock.

When the court reconvened the following morning, a further hour and a half of expert testimony was heard. For a time, the court was abuzz with technical terms and points of scientific interest that the spectators wearily attempted to follow. The evidence had to be paused on a number of occasions so that the more technical terms could be explained to the jury. During the examination in chief of the defence's final expert witness – a photographer named Percy Lankester – Marshall Hall asked the witness to describe the effects of 'halation' on a photograph. The term was unknown even to Alverstone, who asked for it to be spelt. 'Hell-' – began Marshall Hall, provoking a titter of laughter in which even Bennett joined – 'a-tion'.

Lankester politely interrupted the barrister in order to provide the correct spelling – which led to renewed laughter in the court – before proceeding to describe the phenomenon. 'Halation is the reflection of light from the back of the plate onto the film.' It was possible, he explained, that in making the enlargement of the beach photograph, the effect of halation could have made the 'blobs' on the chain appear larger and could also have produced the effect of oscillation or vibration. 'I do not think it possible that this link chain could be the same chain as is shown in the beach photograph,' Lankester concluded. 'That is my honest and candid opinion.'

'Well,' the Lord Chief Justice replied, 'we may not agree about the chain, but we all now thoroughly understand the photographs!' Alverstone's comment perfectly summed up the nature of the expert evidence – it had been dominated by contradictions and conflicting opinions. The in-depth examination over the chain also distracted from the question of where the chain that Mary Jane had been wearing was, if this was not it...

Before he stepped down, Lankester was asked to identify two photographs that he had taken so that they could be entered into evidence. They were carefully shielded from view and all Marshall Hall would say was that the photographs showed 'localities' connected to the case.

By now, any anxiety Marshall Hall had felt over Kaye's testimony had passed. Frustrated though he was that more people did not share his certainty over the chain, he was confident that he had done enough to place the identity of it in doubt.

Before the court rose on the morning of Friday, 1 March, the barrister held a long conference with his client alone in his cell.

'If only you will go into the box and admit everything except the actual murder,' he said, 'then I can get a verdict, but of course, you must admit that when you saw the papers the day after the murder, you knew it was your wife, but that you were afraid to communicate for fear of losing Alice Meadows.'

'I cannot say that,' replied Herbert, 'because I was not at Yarmouth on the 22nd, and I never knew that the murdered woman was my wife till I was arrested.'

Despite his strong belief that his client was innocent of the murder, Marshall Hall had no doubt that Herbert had been in Yarmouth – as the prosecution claimed – on the nights of 15 and 22 September.

Exasperated, Marshall Hall told Herbert his attitude was hopeless. Defiant, Herbert refused to go into the box at all.[1]

28

EVIDENCE OF AN ALIBI

'I have not a shadow of doubt about the man'

When Marshall Hall rose to give his opening speech on day five of the trial, he began with another fierce attack on the press.

The defence, he claimed, had been forced to conduct their enquiries in secret, out of fear that anything discovered would be disseminated to aid sensation-mongering. Marshall Hall was gearing up to deliver one of his most sensational surprises yet and the court was poised to receive it.

'It has been a disgrace and a scandal – nothing less ... no other words can express the way in which the newspapers have tried, condemned, and everything short of executed the man Bennett within twenty-four hours of his arrest. But', he said, which a tinge of excitement in his voice, 'if the press has done irreparable harm, it has also done good ...' A murmur reverberated throughout the courtroom. Marshall Hall allowed his words to hang in the air for a few moments before continuing. 'It has brought to light an absolutely independent witness who might not otherwise have come forward.' Surprised gasps erupted as the announcement sent a thrill through the crowded court. 'That witness', declared the barrister, 'is Douglas Sholto Douglas, and he will testify that Bennett was in London with him on the night of the murder ...'

The barrister's statement was a surprise even to the prosecution, but Gill retained his composure.[1] One reporter would later compare Marshall Hall's announcement to the act of 'dropping a bombshell into a highly expectant court'.[2] The barrister claimed that the defence had kept the alibi a closely guarded secret in order to shield their witness from the press. The fact that it would also have caught the prosecution on the backfoot and given Gill limited time to prepare for cross-examination would, of course, never have occurred to him ...

The decision of whether to call Sholto Douglas had been an impossible one for Marshall Hall. He had grappled with the choice of whether to stop at what he considered to be a good negative defence, or to attempt to establish Bennett's innocence positively by calling Sholto Douglas.[3] It was possibly the most important decision in the case, and ultimately one he had left to Herbert to make. That morning, when the barrister had met with Herbert in his cell, he had attempted to impress upon him how vital a decision to call an alibi witness was. He asked him honestly if he had been in the company of Sholto Douglas that day and Herbert replied confidently that he had.

'Now, Bennett,' Marshall Hall had said gravely. 'I am going to leave you for two hours with this piece of paper.' He handed Herbert a scrap of parchment that was blank save for two short sentences: 'I wish Douglas called' and 'I do not wish Douglas called'.

'After that time has passed,' he continued, 'strike one statement out and send me this piece of paper via the warder. Remember that you never said a word to suggest this alibi before Douglas turned up, and you have declined to go into the witness box to corroborate.'[4]

As instructed, Herbert had returned the paper two hours later. The words 'I do not wish Douglas to be called' were struck out.

Marshall Hall's choice to leave such an important decision up to his client was unprecedented, but the die had been cast, and after lunch on the fifth day of the trial that had gripped the nation, one of the most sensational developments in the sorry saga began to unfold ...

Undoubtedly, spectators and reporters alike had spent the intermission theorising over the surprise witness's testimony, while the prosecution had hurriedly fumbled to prepare for cross-examination.

When Sholto Douglas stepped into the witness box that afternoon, he made a dramatic bow to the bench, before placing his silk hat on the stand in front of him. He was described by one reporter as a 'spruce and alert, middle-aged London merchant, with the neatest gloves, smartest umbrella and the glossiest of silk hats'.[5] At just twenty-nine years old, Sholto Douglas would undoubtedly have taken offence to at least part of that description. Amid an atmosphere of simmering expectation, the witness recalled his meeting with Herbert in fine detail. His evidence was faultless.

On the morning of Saturday, 22 September, Sholto Douglas had gone to work as usual. He was a manufacturer of fancy goods at the London Fancy Box Company, 131 City Road, in the East End of London.[6] That morning, he had received a letter from a former customer, a company called Langdale, with an order for a special design. 'You will see the entry in my order book,' Sholto Douglas said. The book was produced and the entry

– dated 22 September – was pointed out to the jury. That morning, continued Sholto Douglas, he had reopened the company's old account and had then put the letter into his pocket. He recalled taking it out again during the afternoon to study its requirements. As a rule, Douglas left the office at 1 p.m. on Saturdays and usually spent the rest of the day in his garden or out walking in the countryside near to his home. It was a fine day, so he decided to go for a walk. He left the house at around 4 p.m., with the intention of walking to King John's Palace, Eltham, which was approximately three miles away. Having spent some time exploring, Sholto Douglas decided to walk home via Lee Green. As he passed through the village of Eltham, he lit his pipe. He was heading towards the Eltham Road when he was 'overtaken' by a young man, who asked him for a light for his cigarette. Sholto Douglas obliged, handing the man his box of matches.

'Do you recall what the man was wearing?' Marshall Hall interjected.

'Yes, a light grey suit and a black bowler hat.'

Marshall Hall then produced the two large photographs that he had put into evidence under a veil of secrecy earlier in the day. The court now learned that they showed the spot where the witness claimed the prisoner had accosted him. Sholto Douglas identified the photographs before continuing with his narrative.

The young man thanked Sholto Douglas for the matches and then remarked that the days were drawing short. 'We must expect it,' replied Sholto Douglas. 'This day week is quarter day, 29th September.' The witness had hoped that would be an end to the conversation, but the young man fell into step beside him and walked with him towards Lee Green. By this time, it was around 6 p.m., and the last train from Liverpool Street to Great Yarmouth had left the station almost an hour earlier.[7] As the two men walked, the stranger spoke about working at the Woolwich Arsenal as a draughtsman and said that he had travelled a great deal, most recently to Ireland. He also mentioned Bexley Heath, either saying that he had just come from the village, or that he lived there. The two men walked side by side until they reached the Lee Green crossroads. Here stood the Tiger Inn, Lee's oldest pub. Sholto Douglas had visited the pub maybe half a dozen times before, but not recently. He was thirsty after a long walk, so he asked the young man if he would like to join him for a drink. 'He was a respectable man,' Sholto Douglas said, 'but not the sort of man I wanted to associate with, so I hoped it would be a polite way of shaking him off.'

The witness paid 5*d*. for the drinks – a glass of bitter for him and spirits for the younger man. When he had finished his drink, Sholto Douglas rose from his seat, saying that he ought to be getting home. The young man followed him out of the pub and, when they were outside, he pointed to a sign above the shop next door to the Tiger Inn.

'Oh,' he said. 'A namesake of mine apparently lives there.' Sholto Douglas looked up at the sign. It read: *F.K. Bennett, shaving saloon.*

'He then said, "You have not told me your name,"' Sholto Douglas recalled, 'but I did not tell him my name.' At that moment, the driver of an omnibus about to start off for Peckham called out to the conductor, asking for the time – 'Seven o'clock,' came the reply. Seeing this as his opportunity to leave, Sholto Douglas shook the young man's hand and they parted. The witness made off in the direction of Hither Green while his companion headed north, towards Blackheath. Marshall Hall, who had allowed the witness to tell his tale with few interruptions, now rose, poised to examine him further. 'About the middle of November,' he asked, 'you saw the reports of the Yarmouth murder trial. What occurred?'

'Well,' replied Sholto Douglas, 'when I found that the name of the man charged with the murder was Bennett, when I read of the light grey suit and that the man worked at Woolwich, I took him for the same man I saw when I was out for a walk on that Saturday, 22nd September. I thought I was justified in making further investigation. I learned afterwards that the prisoner had been in Ireland. All this made me think it was my duty to communicate with the police. I telegraphed to Mr Robb at Tunbridge Wells.'

Robb, certain that Herbert would be committed for trial by the Yarmouth magistrates regardless of Douglas's testimony, had held back the evidence to give the defence time to test the alibi.

'Do you have any doubt as to the man's identity?' asked Marshall Hall.

Standing in the courtroom that day, Sholto Douglas was as sure as ever that the mysterious man he had met on that fateful evening was the prisoner. 'No, none whatever,' he replied certainly. 'I have not a shadow of doubt about the man or the date.' Sholto Douglas was one of the most assured witnesses in the entire case, despite claiming to have been in Herbert's company for only an hour. He claimed to have recognised Herbert 'instantly' when he had gone to identify him at Norwich Prison almost four months after their initial meeting.

'I had a good look at him, both full face and profile.'

'And what was your opinion?' asked Marshall Hall.

'The prisoner was the man I met in the lane on 22nd September,' the witness replied firmly.

Sholto Douglas's ability to recall dates and specific details made him the perfect alibi witness, but his story concerned the defence because it was almost *too* perfect. To quote a famous (albeit fictional) detective of the time, George Grodman, 'the suspiciously precise recollection of dates and events possessed by ordinary witnesses in important trials ... is one of the most amazing things in the curiosities of modern jurisprudence'.[8] Perhaps it was for this reason that the atmosphere in the courtroom that afternoon was one of 'eager expectation' when Gill rose to cross-examine the witness. The fervent crowd had been awaiting Gill, who had a reputation for being one of the deadliest cross-examiners at the bar.

'Did you meet anybody else to speak to on this particular Saturday, 22nd September?' Gill began.

'No,' replied the witness.

'Did he speak to you at once?'

'Yes.'

'What did you do to get rid of him?'

'I could not get rid of him,' Sholto Douglas replied, 'that was the worst of it. I quickened my pace, and so did he. He forced his attentions upon me and was with me for about an hour.'

'A man you had never met before, and whose company you did not desire, was with you for one hour?' Gill asked, surprised.

'Yes.'

'Has such a thing occurred before in your experience?' Gill asked doubtfully.

'I cannot say that it has,' Sholto Douglas replied.

'How long were you in the public house?'

'About half an hour, but I did not time it,' replied the witness. 'I did not meet anyone that I knew in the course of the walk, nor while I was in the public house.'

'You say he told you he was a draughtsman in Woolwich Arsenal; are you sure you did not read that in the papers?'

'Certainly not,' Sholto Douglas replied adamantly, 'he told me that. Of course, I read in the newspapers that he had been employed at Woolwich.'

'Did you tell him anything about yourself and your family?' Rather conveniently, Sholto Douglas had told him nothing.

'He forced all this information on you?' continued Gill in a doubtful tone.

'Well,' replied the witness, 'we were conversing, and I could not be rude.'

'What did you think of him?' asked Gill.

'I thought he was a man beating up for a drink,' Sholto Douglas replied. A ripple of laughter erupted while Herbert chuckled quietly to himself. 'And I thought a drink would get rid of him.' In reply to further questions by Gill, the witness said that there were two or three people in the bar at the time, but no one he knew. The prisoner did not speak about himself in the presence of these people. While they were in the bar, the two men discussed the new line of trams running to Eltham and how, by cutting down trees, it would spoil the neighbourhood.

'Did you leave the inn together?' asked Gill.

'Certainly,' Douglas replied.

'Having told you where he lived, where he worked, and where he had been, the only thing left for you to know was his name?' Gill asked sarcastically.

'Yes,' Sholto Douglas replied.

'You say he had a light grey suit on?' Gill asked.

'Yes, and a bowler hat.'

'Did you notice what shirt he was wearing?'

'No.'

'Anything about his tie?'

'I believe it was a blue tie, but I couldn't swear to it,' replied Sholto Douglas.[9]

'You were in touch with Mr Robb while the case was proceeding before the magistrates?' Gill asked.

'Yes,' replied the witness.

'Had you any desire to conceal your identity?'

'Yes,' Sholto Douglas said, 'at that particular time I did not wish to figure too prominently in a murder trial.'

'Why not?' Gill asked curiously.

'I was negotiating a partnership, and I did not want anything to crop up to stop it. I said I should not like my name or my private or business address to appear in the newspapers. Now, of course, it is another matter, as the deed of partnership is signed.'

'You knew that if you were correct, your evidence would be very important?' asked Gill.

'Undoubtedly,' Sholto Douglas replied.

'When did you make your statement?'

'I dictated it sometime in January and signed it then. That was after I had seen the prisoner in Norwich [Gaol].'

'Was the prisoner alone when you saw him?'

'Yes, he was quite alone,' Sholto Douglas replied, before hurriedly adding, 'but I could have picked him out from any number of men.'

'You say you can fix the Saturday because you took a certain order on that day?'

'Yes, also by the dates on my flower-pots. On Saturdays, September 15th and 29th I was potting, and I know this, as I date the pots when I put shoots in. There are none bearing the date September 22nd.'

'When did you look up the dates on your flower-pots?'

'I came across them accidentally,' Sholto Douglas claimed. 'It was while repotting some shoots early this year, after I had been to Norwich.'

In re-examining the witness, Marshall Hall finally revealed the mystery of the 'missing documents' that he had alluded to during Lingwood's examination the previous day. It also presented him with yet another opportunity to vilify the press. 'I believe your private address was contained in one of the documents which went to Mr Robb?' he asked.

'Yes,' Sholto Douglas replied.

'Do you know that document has been lost? I say "lost",' the barrister said scathingly.

'I have been told so.'

'Did you lately receive a visit from a representative of a paper known as "the *Morning Leader*"?'

'Yes, he came to interview me – on 5th February.'

'Was that almost immediately after you heard that this paper had been lost with your address on it?'

'Almost immediately.' Hushed murmurs arose from the press box as the journalists considered Marshall Hall's implication.

Although Gill's careful cross-examination had failed to catch Sholto Douglas out, the barrister had managed to establish that every detail of his evidence could have been picked up from the newspapers. He had also cleverly highlighted the fact that Sholto Douglas's version of events relied solely on his word and recollection alone. Not one element of it could be corroborated. This was in stark contrast to the prosecution's evidence, which benefited from a mass of corroboration.

As Sholto Douglas stepped down from the witness box, silk hat and lavender gloves in hand, Herbert glanced around the court with a smile. Marshall Hall was less impressed. He was already regretting putting

Sholto Douglas into the witness box. The barrister could not shake the feeling that Sholto Douglas was mistaken – either about the man or the date. Despite this, he believed Sholto Douglas to be an entirely honest man – an assertion that he would be forced to reassess some years later.

29

A STORY FOR HALF A SOVEREIGN

'She was not a good wife'

I f the court was left reeling by Sholto Douglas's testimony, the atmosphere was only set to intensify further when the next witness took the stand. Mrs Kato, the Bennetts' Rossiter Road landlady, would provide an entirely different account of the Bennetts' lives together from any of the other witnesses so far.

In his opening speech, Marshall Hall had referred to the landlady as an 'absolutely responsible witness'.

'This woman', he now declared, 'has said nothing to the newspapers, although one of them put a scandalous statement into her mouth.' The spectators were already anticipating a controversial cross-examination.

Mrs Kato's story disagreed entirely with that of the prosecution's star witness, Mrs Elliston. When asked to describe Herbert, Mrs Kato claimed that he was 'very kind to his wife and child and never complained'. Herbert flashed a smile across to his old landlady.

'What were the habits of Mrs Bennett?' asked Marshall Hall.

'She was not a good wife,' replied Mrs Kato. 'She seemed fond of dress and jewellery and she neglected the child.'

'What was the colour of her hair?'

'Fair like mine,' the witness replied, removing her hat to demonstrate the lightness of her hair.

'Oh, very nice,' observed Marshall Hall shrewdly. 'Perhaps the witness might be allowed to keep her hat off, it's very hot in the court.'

'Oh, it doesn't matter,' Mrs Kato said, before replacing her light-brown Alpine hat.

'Did you hear Mrs Bennett talk about money?' Marshall Hall continued.

'Yes, sometimes,' replied Mrs Kato. 'She often asked Mr Bennett for money.' In response to a question about Mrs Bennett's jewellery, the land-lady stated that the deceased woman had had two long chains and a smaller one. One of the long chains, she said, was an imitation and the other was real gold. Gasps were heard in the public gallery and the reporters in the press box scribbled frantically.

'Do you know', continued Marshall Hall, 'if she ever pawned the gold chain?'

'Yes, once, when she wanted to make money on it. Then she bought the imitation chain. I have seen the imitation chain quite close. It had no links. It was a more snaky-looking chain. There were blobs on it. The snakiness was between the blobs.' Mrs Kato went on to describe an occasion when Mrs Bennett had asked her if she could tell the difference between the two chains – she said that in the new chain the links were closer together.

'Did you ever see the two chains together?' asked Marshall Hall.

'Yes, one Wednesday. Mrs Bennett was wearing the gold chain and was talking about it. Just then my baker came to the door and I went upstairs.'

'What did you see?' Marshall Hall asked.

'The baby was playing with the imitation chain.'

Marshall Hall then produced the silver watch that had been recovered from Bennett's lodgings. 'Do you recognise this watch?'

'It is similar to one of the two I have seen her with,' replied Mrs Kato, to renewed sensation. 'I remember a day when one of the watches was returned from the repairers, and the other was broken in a fall from the mantelpiece. We had some conversation about it at the time.'

By the time Gill rose to cross-examine the witness, a deep silence had engulfed the court. No one dared make a sound for fear of losing part of the narrative. The barrister's initial questions were directed at Mrs Kato's account of the watches and chains.

'You were seen by the police but did not disclose the story of the two watches and the two chains. Is that correct?'

'Yes,' Mrs Kato replied.

'Why?' Gill asked.

'Because I was not asked,' replied the witness. A series of gasps arose from the gallery. Further questioning established that the witness had told no one that there were two chains until the previous December, when she had first mentioned it to a gentleman from Mr Robb's office. Despite claiming to have then realised the importance of the evidence, Mrs Kato had failed to disclose the information to the police.

'The police saw you on February 11th, and you did not mention it to them?' enquired Gill.

'No.'

'You say Bennett was a kind-hearted husband, loving and affectionate?' Gill asked.

'Yes, he was,' replied the witness adamantly.

'I want you to do yourself justice, Mrs Kato. Do you say that he was a fond father, devoted to his child?'

'Yes.'

'Passionately devoted to this, his only child?'

'Yes.'

Gill picked up a press cutting from a pile of papers in front of him. He raised it above his head so it was clearly visible. His mannerisms were far less dramatic than Marshall Hall's, but the scene was, nevertheless, reminiscent of Marshall Hall's cross-examination of Mrs Elliston.

'You are the lady who gave the "life of Bennett" to the London *Evening News* on the 13th November?' he asked.

Mrs Kato suddenly looked uncomfortable. She shot a nervous glance at Elvy Robb before answering 'yes' in a much less confident way.

Gill nodded his head. 'Listen to this,' he said, before quoting: '"With all her faults, Mrs Bennett was a lovable little creature, and if ever a woman was fond of a man, she was fond of him. As for him, he treated her in a way that would have crushed the life out of any woman."' Gill looked up at Mrs Kato. 'Did you say that?' he asked, looking directly into her eyes.

'That was put wrong, sir,' Mrs Kato objected. 'I wrote correcting it.' After pausing for a moment, she hurriedly added, 'What I said was, "A woman of finer feelings would not have lived the life Mrs Bennett did."'

'The *Evening News* also contains a conversation on "murder" between you and Bennett,' continued Gill. 'When Bennett said the best way to commit murder would be by strangulation as it is quick and much quieter.'

'That is not right!' cried Mrs Kato. 'The conversation had nothing to do with murder. It was about the slaughterhouse and the killing of pigs.'

Gill looked doubtful – he had never heard of a slaughterhouse using strangulation as a method to kill pigs.

'Did you write to the paper to correct these important mistakes?' Gill asked.

'I was in communication with the *Evening News*.'

'For how long were you in communication with the papers?' he asked.

'About three days,' the witness replied meekly.

'How late in the year was this?' asked Gill.

'December or January, I think.'

'To the same paper?'

'No, but to the same gentleman.'

Gill then had a surprise of his own. 'I have a letter in my hand,' he declared, with a touch of Marshall Hall's exaggerated pizzazz, 'written by you on the same night this statement appeared in the *Evening News*.' He handed Mrs Kato the letter. She looked at it and the colour drained from her face.

'Really, my lord,' protested Marshall Hall, 'I did not think the Treasury were in communication with the press!'

The one letter was followed by several others, which showed that Mrs Kato had been in frequent communication with the press. Mrs Kato had, by now, grown quite faint. She was given a seat and a glass of water. The Lord Chief Justice recommended she take her hat off, which she finally did.

> "'Dear Sir – I am thinking deeply about Bennett and the motive for the murder. As you know, the motive is almost clear. But if I could see you again, I would like to offer you in detail a little of Bennett's personal history ..."

'Is this one of your letters?' Gill asked.

'Yes – I wanted the public to understand what an unhappy life his had been,' Mrs Kato replied quietly.

Returning to the letter, Gill continued:

> "'... so you can put it before the public and show by what means a man can be driven to desperate acts. I should like to be guided by you in this matter. It may also afford one little solace to Miss Meadows to know this. Do your best, for you might find much that will lighten the chain which is drawn round Bennett and Alice Meadows. The quality of mercy is not strained, it falleth as a gentle dew from heaven. You know the rest.'"

'The chain of evidence, I meant,' interjected Mrs Kato. 'I wanted people to know the facts.'

Gill ignored the witness and continued reading. "'P.S. – I am writing a few of the facts and shall not let any of the papers have them unless you refuse them.'" I also have here a postcard, in which you say, "I have called to mind the occasion on which the expression hanging, or strangling was used, and will be glad to explain fully if you will again call. Wire me in case you wish for any further information, as I may be going out." And in the letter following that postcard,' Gill continued, 'you say – "Other circumstances coupled with the details you gave me, have enabled us to very nearly, if not actually, hit upon the true motive of the crime." Was the *Evening News* the only paper to which you wrote?' asked Gill.

'No, sir,' the witness replied quietly.

'Did a representative of any other newspaper call on you?'

'Yes, sir, one or two,' admitted the witness.

'Did any of them pay you money?'

'I had a New Year's Eve present from the *Evening News*,' Mrs Kato admitted sheepishly.

'What was it?' Gill persisted.

'Half a sovereign,' Mrs Kato replied. Her admission provoked a wave of hostile mutterings in the public gallery.

'When the deceased woman came to your house, which chain was she wearing?' he asked.

'The snaky one – not the one now produced.' She pointed to the chain that had been found in Herbert's lodgings, which had been handed up to her to identify. 'I only saw her wearing this one once.'

'What!' Gill exclaimed, surprised. 'This woman who was so fond of dress and jewellery, and of spending money, wore the imitation chain?!'

'Yes, sir,' the witness replied firmly.

'Why did you not mention the chains to the police?'

'I don't know, sir,' Mrs Kato replied. By now, she was cowering in the box and she would barely meet the barrister's searching gaze. 'I thought I'd done wrong in speaking to the gentleman from the *Evening News*. When I suggested to him that there were two chains and two watches, he said, "That is all bosh." So, I thought it would be better if I did not speak until the proper time.'

'Your desire was to make things as pleasant for Bennett and Alice Meadows as you could?' asked Gill.

'Yes, as good as I could for Bennett. I only felt sympathy for Miss Meadows. I was not asked about the chains by the police.'

'But why keep such an important fact back?'

'I might not have been believed if I had spoken.'

'That was the reason?' persisted Gill.

'That was the chief reason. When things are misconstrued, it is best to leave them in more competent hands.'

'These more competent hands being the *Evening News*!' Gill retorted scathingly. Further questioning revealed that Mrs Kato had failed to mention the two chains even to the *Evening News* representative – despite offering to furnish him with 'further particulars' – right up until December.

'But you spoke about the two watches?' Gill asked, feigning confusion.

'Yes, sir,' she replied.

'What was the other watch like?' Gill enquired.

'They were both very similar – lady's small silver watches.'

'Did both have teeth marks upon them?'

'The baby played with both,' she replied, as if in confirmation. At this point, Mrs Kato was handed the small silver pocket watch that had been found among Herbert's possessions. 'Is this one of them?' asked Gill.

'I believe so,' replied the witness.

Marshall Hall had been watching the exchange with disdain. He now rose and set about attempting to repair some of the damage done by Gill's cross-examination.

'Have you spoken the truth today, Mrs Kato?' he began.

'Yes, sir, everything I have said today is the truth.'

'Did the police tell you that no one had spoken of either Bennett or his wife as you had?'

'Yes, I was told that no one had said a kind word about Bennett but myself.'

'Now, what was the name of this reporter?' Marshall Hall muttered. He took up the press cutting that Gill had quoted from earlier, before setting it down again and then dramatically rummaging around in his papers. 'Ah!' he cried, apparently locating the paper he needed. 'Mr Saqui Smith, 12 Whitefriars Street, Fleet Street. I wonder if he is in court.' He turned back to Mrs Kato. 'Could you recognise this Mr Saqui Smith, Mrs Kato?'

'Yes, sir,' she replied.

'Do you see him?' Marshall Hall asked, turning to glare out at the press seats. 'Is he in court? I'm told he is a man with a heavy, dark moustache.' The barrister began scanning the faces of every reporter in the well. 'Do you see him?' he asked again. A nervous energy consumed the press box, as its occupants looked about their number for any sign of the man singled out. After a few moments spent studying the faces of the men, Mrs Kato replied, 'No, sir; I don't see him.' Marshall Hall continued to glare at the reporters, his piercing gaze making many of them look visibly uncomfortable. 'Would you know him again?' he asked, turning back to Mrs Kato.

'Oh, yes, sir,' replied the witness.

Marshall Hall's dramatics were, of course, designed to distract the jury from Mrs Kato's indiscretion and were an attempt to transfer all blame for her scandalous communication with the press to the *Evening News* reporter. 'Did Mr Saqui Smith tell you when he came to you on behalf of the *Evening News* that there was not a particle of doubt about Bennett's guilt?'

'Yes, sir, he said Bennett was undoubtedly guilty,' replied Mrs Kato.

'And he persuaded you into believing it too?'

'Yes, sir. He did at the time.'

'Did he say anything about chance?'

'Yes, he said Bennett had no manner of chance of getting off.'

'And this was how the newspaper reporter broached the subject with you?'

'Yes.' Marshall Hall returned his gaze to the reporters, before slamming the press cutting down hard on the table in front of him. 'I wonder if there is any law that could reach this man!' he demanded angrily.

When Marshall Hall had concluded his re-examination of the witness, Gill rose for a second time. He produced another letter from the witness to the reporter Marshall Hall had identified as Saqui Smith. It was an appeal for money. After saying that she had a debt to meet and was in great distress, Mrs Kato asked if a small sum could be lent to her. 'I did write saying that I was in considerable trouble,' Mrs Kato admitted. 'I had one or two bills owing, and that, perhaps, he could lend me a little till the winter was over.'

'You wrote to Mr Robb, the solicitor for the defence, shortly afterwards?' Gill asked.

'Yes,' replied Mrs Kato.

Satisfied, Gill sat down. As soon as he had returned to his seat, Marshall Hall jumped up and – with great indignation – strongly refuted the suggestion that Mrs Kato had come forward in the hope of getting money, prompting the witness to confirm that her rail fare was all the money she had received. Mrs Kato's testimony concluded the evidence for the defence.

The gilt-framed clock above the dock had just struck 4 p.m. when Marshall Hall rose to address the jury. His speech was described by one reporter as 'the most sensational incident in the week's proceedings',[1] and was listened to with breathless attention by everyone in the court, including the prisoner, who leaned forward on the dock rail, face flushed and eager.

In a fine, powerful voice, Marshall Hall dramatically led the jury through his story, dismissing with a 'contemptuous laugh of bitter scorn'[2] the thesis of the prosecution in one breath and then, in the next, pleading in soft tones on behalf of the man who stood in the dock.

'Never in the history of the law', he declared, 'has a prisoner been so handicapped by the most outrageous gutter rags which have circulated at night under the guise of halfpenny papers. This sensational journalism, imported from America – and a disgrace to America – seems as if it will deprive England of its proudest boast, that it is the one country in the world where one could get absolute justice.' He dared not speak of the man, Mr Saqui Smith, of the *Evening News* (but speak of him, he did). 'A man who, when another fellow creature stood arrested, and was absolutely remanded on the charge of murder, could go to a witness like the poor, kind-hearted Mrs Kato and bully her into the conviction that this man, Bennett, was already convicted of the crime. I cannot trust myself to speak of the man in the terms in which I should like to describe him. The only word that occurs to me is the word ghoul. G-h-o-u-l! – I spell it to you, so that you may not mistake it. He seems like an animal that would revel in the lifeblood of his own species. I only pray that he is in court today to hear what I have said of him.'

Marshall Hall's speech continued in a similarly dramatic fashion. 'Probably never in the history of criminal cases has there ever been a case more surrounded by mystery than this,' he claimed. The barrister referenced the fire at Westgate-on-Sea, the Bennetts' trip to South Africa and their subsequent living apart in London. He pondered for a long time about the mysterious man who Alice Rudrum claimed Mrs Bennett had been with on the night before the murder. The jury knew that this could not have been the accused, he stated, as he was at work.

Then there was the mystery of the murder itself. Were the jury satisfied that this was the man who was seen on the beach at Yarmouth at eleven o'clock at night? 'Was not the murderer more likely some seafaring man, who, seeing this golden-haired woman with jewellery and a satchel by her side, thought these things more valuable than they were; who, having an old bootlace in his pocket, strangled her with that, and cleared off without leaving any trace?' The idea that Herbert had gone to stay at the Crown and Anchor having murdered his wife was 'preposterous', he said, and it was 'inconceivable' to think that his client would use a bootlace as a murder weapon in a premeditated crime. 'The prosecution would claim that it was a premeditated, planned murder. With a broken bootlace!' Marshall Hall exclaimed mockingly.

When Marshall Hall eventually made it to the topic of the watch and chain, he said he was 'astounded that the prosecution had endeavoured to prove the watch and chain the prisoner had was the property of the deceased woman, [as] no man other than a madman would have torn the watch and chain from the woman's neck and carried it away to preserve it as damning evidence of guilt which would lead him to his doom'. He labelled the police 'violent partisans' in the case – 'they were almost as keen as a pack of hounds on the trail of a fox' and directed the jury to reject the evidence of any witnesses that they thought might have been 'got at' by the police.

At 5.15 p.m., Marshall Hall brought his speech to a temporary conclusion. 'The crime was full of mystery,' he declared, before promising the jury that he would deal in detail with the evidence of the witnesses the next day. He then turned to the Lord Chief Justice. 'This, I think, would be a convenient moment to break off,' he said.

It was hoped that the jury would reach their verdict by the evening of the following day.

When Marshall Hall left the courthouse that evening, he was informed that a telegram had been received by Elvy Robb with an urgent message from a stationer at Lowestoft.

Have Lowestoft police made report? If not communicate at once: most important.

When the telegram had arrived earlier in the day, Robb's clerk, Mr Wood, had immediately investigated it, and found that the stationer, John Rochford O'Driscoll, had made a report to the police identifying a potential suspect four days after the murder.

Marshall Hall instructed Robb to send for the man at once.

30

A PECULIAR CUSTOMER

A desperate defence

When the court reassembled the following morning, Saturday, 2 March, the atmosphere was one of marked relief.

Counsel had indicated that the protracted trial might at last be brought to a close that day. The previous five days had been gruelling and physically draining, particularly for Marshall Hall who had been acutely affected by the toxic environment of the Old Bailey. The public galleries were especially crowded that morning and if the spectators were expecting more dramatic scenes, they were not to be disappointed.

Marshall Hall's countenance bore no sign that he had yet another surprise to throw before the jury when he took his place in the courtroom that morning, but he certainly had one.

'I have a reputable tradesman, carrying on business at Lowestoft as a newsagent,' he said, 'who will tell you that on September 26th, a tall dark man with a moustache entered his shop in an agitated condition, and asked for a paper that contained the best account of the Yarmouth murder. The newsagent observed that one of the man's boots had no lace. He communicated with the Lowestoft police and understood that his testimony was forwarded to the police at Yarmouth, but apparently no notice was taken of it.' Marshall Hall asked leave to call the man and the Lord Chief Justice agreed.

Mr John Rochford O'Driscoll then entered the witness box to recount his story of the suspicious stranger with the scratched face who had come into his shop a few days after the murder. His story was corroborated on all accounts – except for the bootlace – by his shop assistant, William Overy.

Chief Constable Parker was recalled and admitted receiving the report from Mr O'Driscoll within a week of the murder. When asked what action he had taken, he replied, 'I received many reports at the time and investigated them all as well as I could.'

Despite being caught on the backfoot yet again, Gill expertly refuted O'Driscoll's and Overy's evidence by recalling Dr Lettis, who stated that he had found no trace of blood or epidermis under the deceased's finger-nails, which made it unlikely, argued Gill, that the murdered woman had scratched anyone. Marshall Hall deftly countered Gill by suggesting to the doctor that traces of epidermis could have been removed as the deceased clutched at the sand in the final struggle before death. O'Driscoll's story fitted perfectly with Marshall Hall's theory that the murderer was a seafaring man, and the court was swept up by the drama of it all.

31

IS HE OUR MAN?

*'You will go down to your deathbeds remembering this as one of
the most sensational murder trials ever tried in this court'*

hen the morning's excitement had come to an end, Marshall
Hall continued his address to the jury and utterly transfixed
the court.

His speech was described by one reporter as a 'stirring attack on the evidence for the Crown'.[1] Bennett, he spat, had been 'tried and found guilty of murder by the newspapers'. Marshall Hall treated Saqui Smith – the unfortunate reporter the barrister had plucked from a bunch of rotten apples in order to parade him before the jury as a convenient scapegoat – like one of the heartless rogues who skulked across the pages of the once-popular penny dreadfuls that had captivated the country. During a particularly enlivened few minutes, Marshall Hall declared that the evidence put forward that the prisoner was in Yarmouth on 15 and 16 September was 'not sufficient upon which to even hang a cat'.

'But there remains the question of the chain,' Marshall Hall continued, 'before which the other things pale into insignificance. I see now why the Crown has clung to the identity of this watch and chain. I should have thought that [if] this man [pointing to Herbert], was the murderer, and had kept them in his possession, that fact alone is enough to intern him in any lunatic asylum.'

At this point, the foreman of the jury rose from his seat. 'We are satisfied as to this part of the case,' he said. This was not about to stop Marshall Hall on his favourite topic, however, and he forged on regardless.

Referring to the evidence from Lowestoft, the barrister declared that 'in Mr O'Driscoll there has come the hand of Providence at the last moment to protect this man, tried as he has been by his journalistic peers and found guilty – to protect him by giving them a faithful clue which proves two things – that the prosecution theory was utterly unsound, and that the evidence of Sholto Douglas was absolutely true. Upon this point, I think you will agree, and you will go down to your deathbeds remembering this as one of the most sensational murder trials ever tried in this court, when you recall the extraordinary way in which these two witnesses have come to life.'

The prosecution's case was 'untenable', and even the questioning of 'probably the ablest cross-examiner at the bar' had failed to shake the evidence of two key defence witnesses: O'Driscoll and Sholto Douglas. He regretted, however, that the prosecution had made use of 'journalist information' for the purposes of cross-examining Mrs Kato. 'She might have been poor,' he said, 'and she might have written a letter to this venomous beast who had sidled himself into her confidence to gain information for the rag he represented. She was just the weak, kindly sort of woman that this Saqui Smith would prey upon.'

As his speech drew to its conclusion, Marshall Hall reflected on his handling of the case. 'I have done this case very imperfectly,' he said, 'but the physical strain of doing a case in the atmosphere of this court is very great. Seven years ago, I complained that the atmosphere of the court was a scandal, and I say the same today. In these circumstances it is almost impossible that I should not have missed some point. I only wish a man like Sir Edward Clarke had had the chance of doing what I have so imperfectly done . . .'[2] The barrister ended with a powerful appeal to the jury to 'wipe from their minds all prejudice and prejudgment' and consider the evidence given before them. They must find a unanimous verdict, he declared gravely, and there should not be a single doubt among them. 'I pray that the jury might honestly come to a righteous decision; and whatever your conclusion is, I and the prisoner will accept it as a righteous verdict, because we know that the decision would have been arrived at by the most careful consideration of the evidence.'[3]

Marshall Hall's speech had lasted for two and a half hours. Herbert listened intently to parts of it, craned forward in the dock so he could catch every word. He betrayed little emotion, except when the barrister referred to his character – '. . . this utterly worthless man – immoral and a forger with more than a suspicion of arson against him. This man had been utterly worthless in the past . . .' At this point, he had hung his head and covered his face with his hands. During the less eventful parts, Herbert appeared bored. At one point, he suddenly leaned over the dock and tapped Marshall Hall on the shoulder as if he had something quite urgent to say.

'May I have the window shut?' he asked. 'I feel a draught.'[4]

*

Charles Gill had not intended to address the jury, but owing to Marshall Hall's speech, he said, 'it appeared to be necessary to bring the jury's minds back to the case'.

There was no great mystery about the 'Yarmouth murder', he said. Things were tolerably clear now that they had all the facts. The prisoner's wife was 'long suffering but she would not have submitted to having a rival, and she was always a danger to the prisoner,' he continued.

Herbert appeared anxious on only two occasions during Gill's reply. 'Absolutely no answer', said Gill calmly, 'has been given regarding the most important questions of the case: where was the prisoner on the 15th September? Where was he on the 22nd? How did he get possession of the watch and chain? If the prisoner was not the man who committed the murder . . . when did he learn that his wife had been murdered?' During these parts of Gill's speech, Herbert sat somewhat more uneasily in his chair, resting his head in his hands, or wiping the perspiration from his forehead with a handkerchief.[5] 'A great deal has been heard about the conduct of certain evening papers,' continued Gill. 'That matter was introduced in order to influence the mind of the jury and excite their sympathy for the prisoner. However reprehensible the conduct of the papers might be, it had nothing to do with the question the jury has to decide and should be absolutely ignored by them.'

Gill dispensed with several of the key points made by the defence in a few sentences.

'Mrs Bennett constantly wore her watch and chain and there was nothing to show why on that night she should not have done so . . . The identity of the watch and chain as the property of the dead woman and its possession by the prisoner were matters proved beyond the possibility of doubt [photographic evidence aside].[6] Was it conceivable that Mrs Bennett had a second chain and no human being ever saw it except Mrs Kato, the "poor, honest, simple-minded creature", as counsel for the defence has described her? I submit that it is not . . . The press had given the utmost publicity to the case. Was there only one man – the prisoner – who did not know of it? Or did the prisoner know that his wife was murdered and that he had murdered her?

'The answer to that question is in the prisoner's conduct. How quickly after the murder had Bennett disposed of his ailing grandfather! Having no longer to fear his wife, he made arrangements to get rid of Glencoe Villas and had hastened his marriage with Alice Meadows . . . It was strange that the prisoner had not mentioned the incident of his meeting with Mr

Douglas, which was of the greatest importance to him. That story was one without a shred of corroboration. It was also strange that the man who was suffering at that time from a bad toe, as he had told Alice Meadows, and who had a bicycle, should be taking a long country walk. No person ever saw Mr Sholto Douglas in the company of the prisoner, and every statement he made was matter that could have come to his knowledge through reading the particulars published in the papers.'

The barrister then reminded the jury that 'the strength of the case did not depend upon one witness, or any one fact, but lay in the cumulative force of all the facts'.[7] In response to Marshall Hall's comment that Herbert would have been 'mad' to have kept the watch and chain had he been the murderer, Gill said: 'If no criminal ever made a mistake, no criminal would ever stand in the dock.' The court listened with bated breath. Turning to the jury, Gill said, 'Gentlemen, if you are not satisfied with the facts we have placed before you, we shall, of course, be happy to acquit the prisoner, but if you are irresistibly forced to the conclusion from the cumulative evidence that the prisoner murdered his wife you must not shrink from discharging your duty in bringing in a verdict of guilty.'

The court had barely had any time to recover from Gill's speech before the Lord Chief Justice began his summary. By now it was 4.30 p.m. and the proceedings marched on in hope that a verdict might be reached by the evening.

Marshall Hall would later refer to the judge's speech as a 'deadly summing up'. Alverstone spoke in the clearest of tones, which reverberated like a bell through the court. It was his duty, he stated, to direct the jury in the evidence, and he implored them to make a judgment on the case based on the evidence alone. Alverstone proceeded to carefully weigh up the points both for and against the prisoner. He left nothing out which told in Herbert's favour, but the cumulative force of the facts left the impression of a damning indictment against the prisoner. The Lord Chief Justice concluded his summing-up at 6.35 p.m., after speaking for two hours.

Shortly after, the jury retired. When the judge had left the court, Herbert was taken down the staircase to the cells below. In his wake he left an excited court, which resounded with discussion. On the bench, the aldermen leaned over each other's shoulders to examine the enlarged photographs, which had played so prominent a part in the case, and the spectators in the public galleries were heard speculating on the result. They did not have long to wait.

The jury took just thirty-five minutes to reach their verdict. This signalled that there had been very little debate or disagreement among the jurors, which – given the weight of evidence against the prisoner – would have left the defence uneasy.

At 7.10 p.m., as night fell, after a trial lasting six days, the usher demanded silence and the jury slowly filed back into the box. The Lord Chief Justice strode to his seat. Herbert stepped lightly into the dock as the foreman of the jury rose to his feet. He looked deathly pale. The excitement that had been at fever pitch just minutes before was still bubbling away under the surface.

A hush descended over the enthralled court as the curtain went up on the final scene in what was one of the most sensational and eagerly anticipated trials of the early twentieth century . . .

THE VERDICT

'I say I am not guilty, sir'

The clerk of arraigns rose. 'Gentlemen,' he said, addressing the jury, 'have you agreed upon your verdict?'

In a clear, firm voice, the foreman replied, 'Yes, we have.'

'Do you find Herbert John Bennett guilty or not guilty?'

'Guilty!' replied the foreman in a steady voice. A quiver of emotion ran through the court.

'You say he is guilty of wilful murder?'

'Yes.'

'And that is the verdict of you all?' The foreman threw a glance at Marshall Hall, whose concluding remark had undoubtedly weighed heavily on the jury's deliberations. 'Yes,' he replied starkly. There was a short pause as the foreman returned to his seat. The clerk of arraigns then turned to address Herbert.

'Herbert John Bennett, you stand convicted of the crime of wilful murder. Have you anything to say for yourself why the court should not give you judgment according to law?'

Herbert, now standing, placed his hands on the front of the dock and said, firmly, unwaveringly, 'I say I am not guilty, sir.' His voice had not been heard in the court since his plea on the first day of the trial. It was described as a rough, deep bass voice with a certain gruffness, which was distinctly harsh and displeasing.[1] As the marshal opened out the square of cloth known as the black cap, Herbert leaned on the front of the dock, apparently unperturbed by the solemnity of the occasion. The black cap, which one reporter remarked was like a large black silk hanky,[2] was placed on the crown of his lordship's wig, the four corners falling low over his face. The court fell silent again. Herbert was breathing hard, but he was unflinching. Everyone knew what was coming.

'Oyez, oyez, oyez.' The voice of the usher filled the court, strictly commanding silence while sentence was passed. 'God save the king!' There was a touch of emotion in the Lord Chief Justice's voice as he pronounced the death sentence.[3]

Herbert listened to Alverstone's address with perfect self-control. 'Herbert John Bennett,' Alverstone said, in a low and solemn voice, 'after a protracted trial, in which the jury has paid the closest attention to the evidence, and in which you have been most ably defended, and every point that could have been taken for your defence has been taken, the jury have found you guilty of the murder of your wife ... the sentence of the law is that you be taken from this place to the place whence you came, and from there to the place of execution, and that you be hanged by the neck until you be dead; and that your body be buried within the precincts of the prison in which you are confined last after your conviction. And may the Lord have mercy on your soul!' Following a hushed reminder from the clerk of arraigns, Alverstone added, 'I have also to direct that you be committed to the Sheriff of Norfolk for execution.'

The Lord Chief Justice then left the courtroom. The case had taken its toll and he looked pale and haggard. When the officials had disbanded, Herbert was removed from the dock for the final time. He walked away with a firm step. And so ended the sensational trial of *King vs Bennett*.

Herbert John Bennett had shown the greatest coolness throughout the six days of his trial. A minute after the bootlace, with the death knots still intact, had been passed in front of him, he was laughing merrily at a remark made by a witness, as if he had not a care in the world. He showed no emotion when his deceased wife's bloodstained clothes were laid out in front of him, nor when he was presented with the enlarged photographs. Herbert was exactly the type of man, summarised one reporter, 'who would murder his wife, go to bed in a hotel, eat a hearty breakfast the next morning and then rush off to catch a train to meet his sweetheart'.[4]

It did not take long for the news of the verdict and sentencing to reach the large, expectant crowd that had gathered outside the Old Bailey. The general opinion was that the jury would disagree. When the news finally trickled out of the courthouse and into the crowd, a loud cheer arose, which was immediately punctuated by loud cries of 'Shame!' As the verdict penetrated further into the dense throng of people, the noisy demonstrations grew as the sounds of hissing and hooting intermingled with bursts of cheering. The hardiest of the spectators lingered for some time outside the courthouse, in the hope of catching a glimpse of Herbert as he was removed to Norwich, but they were to be disappointed. Arrangements had been made for Herbert to remain the night in Newgate Prison, where he was housed in a cell adjoining the one that had been occupied by George Parker, a man who had been sentenced to death for his crimes the previous day. Herbert had made no comment whatsoever since the verdict had been passed – this was in stark contrast to his past behaviour. Reports suggest that, throughout his trial, he had spoken freely to the prison warders about his certain acquittal.

The news of Herbert's conviction spread like wildfire across the country. The verdict was most eagerly anticipated by those in Norfolk. Evening newspapers with 'special editions' sold in record time, with the verdict appearing in the 'stop press' column.[5] One reporter claimed that for every one person who wanted to know the result of that day's by-election in Maidstone,[6] a hundred desired to know the result of the jury in the Bennett case.[7] The *Norfolk Daily Standard*, which had achieved what it described as 'phenomenal' sales during the week of the trial, released their evening edition within five minutes of the newspaper receiving the telegram from the court.

Front cover of the *Illustrated Police News*, 9 March, 1901.

33

TRIAL BY PRESS

'Bennett is the victim of a miscarriage of justice'

In the northeastern town of Lowestoft, a crowd had gathered outside the local office of the *Eastern Evening News* to await reports from London. A telegram recording the verdict had just arrived from the newspaper's London correspondent and was immediately placed in the front window of the office. The news that the 'Yarmouth murderer' would be put to death was met with enthusiasm from the baying crowd, but they refused to disperse until they had the full story.

An announcement that the 'extra special' edition of the newspaper would be brought out at 10.20 p.m. encouraged the crowd to disband, but only temporarily. A short time later, the townspeople had gathered again, this time with renewed vigour. The road outside the newspaper's office was soon impassable due to the sheer mass of people, and vehicles attempting to gain access had to be diverted. Men, women and children alike scrabbled to be at the head of the crowd so that they would be the first to get their hands on the final instalment of the murder story that had enthralled the country. As the throng edged ever forward, 'swaying to and fro like waves on a shore', there was a cry of 'Here come the papers!' The great mass of people surged forward. The sound of glass cracking pierced the noise of the crowd and – suddenly – there was a loud smash as one of the newspaper office's plate-glass windows gave way, sending those who had been pressed up against it moments before tumbling inside. With another loud crack, a second windowpane broke.

Bodies fell in all directions, arms outstretched, reaching out for a copy of the special edition, which sold out within half an hour. One reporter would later describe the chaos the crowd left behind – 'the office floor was an assortment of pocket handkerchiefs, feathers, bits of ribbon, one great coat in shreds, and various other trifles ... outside, the pavement was strewn with broken plate glass and fragments of hats'.[1]

The event demonstrated just how insatiable the public's appetite for sensational crime news really was.

*

Alice Meadows fainted when she heard the verdict.

The 'mental anguish' she had suffered over the preceding weeks had, concluded one reporter, left her 'in a weak state of health'.[2] The poor woman neither wrote to nor visited Herbert after his sentence was passed, but she did express disbelief over the verdict. 'I shall always have a doubt about Bennett having murdered his wife. Sometimes everything seems so plain and so straightforward that I almost feel half inclined to believe him guilty, and then I get so bewildered and puzzled that I don't know what to think . . .'

Alice was not the only person to cast doubt over the verdict. In an article headlined 'BENNETT'S SENTENCE: Mr Sholto Douglas Speaks Out',[3] the fancy box manufacturer was quoted as saying, 'I am still convinced that the man I had a conversation . . . with on that fateful Saturday night was Bennett. Nothing but a confession of the murder from the lips of the condemned man himself will make me believe that it was some man other than Bennett whom I saw that evening. I shall go down to my grave', he added, with considerable emotion, 'believing in the innocence of Bennett . . . [He] is the victim of a miscarriage of justice.'

Meanwhile, the police detectives investigating Sholto Douglas's story ascertained from the governor of Norwich Prison that certain statements reported in the *Weekly Dispatch*,[4] relating to Sholto Douglas's visit in January when he positively identified Bennett, were 'absolutely untrue'. On 4 March, Governor Bell wrote a note to the Home Office, refuting the claim that the 'Witness asked warder to ask Bennett to turn to the side'. A statement from the chief warder confirmed the governor's recollections and further claimed that Sholto Douglas had been admitted to the prison as an 'ordinary visitor' and not for the purposes of identification, despite the visit having been arranged by Herbert's defence team.[5] Naturally, this led the police to suspect that Sholto Douglas was not being as honest as he had led the defence to believe . . .

Despite uncertainty expressed by a small number of people, the verdict in the Bennett case was met with approval by the press at large. The *Telegraph* proclaimed that 'no one who had followed the course of the trial . . . can doubt that the verdict was a just and right one'. In an article that criticised Bennett for not exercising his right to take the stand, the *Morning Post*'s headline screamed 'WHY DIDN'T HE GO IN THE BOX?' – '. . . he was unable to say where he was, he could not face cross examination – the inference to his guilt was overwhelming'.[6] The day after the trial concluded, *The Times* reported that 'the defence, if weak, abounded in surprise . . .' and boldly declared that the verdict was 'society's retribution visited upon a heartless crime with no circumstances of extenuation'.[7]

The case had been a big money-spinner for the press, with one local newspaper declaring that its machinery was 'kept running until close on to 11 at night'.[8]

In an attempt to keep the narrative flowing between the verdict and execution, the newspapers set about picking at the scraps that had been left behind in the aftermath of the trial. The *Yarmouth Mercury* declared that it had 'tracked down' O'Driscoll's mysterious customer to Lowestoft's neighbouring town of Gorleston.[9] A man named Mr Sellars, who was an engineer on a ship that sailed from Lowestoft, was interviewed but ultimately found to have been at sea on the night of the murder. The *Illustrated Police News* ran a story headlined 'Strange Meeting of Four Notorious Murderers',[10] in which they discussed Herbert's incarceration alongside three infamous felons of the era.

Much had been said during the trial about the conduct of the press, with Marshall Hall's unceasing barrage of remarks never failing to go uncommented upon. At one point, the *Referee*, a weekly sports newspaper, had mockingly remarked: 'In view of the case having been taken out of the hands of the police by the Press, the Treasury is of the opinion that there is no necessity to bother a judge and jury with it. The Home Secretary has, however, suggested to the Crime Investigators of the Fourth Estate, that, just as a matter of form, they might in future carry the New Testament with them and administer the oath to the witnesses whose evidence against an accused person still innocent in the eyes of the law they propose to publish.'[11]

It was not until after the trial had ended that the prejudicial actions of certain newspapers attracted the condemnation of their profession. On 5 March, the London District of the Institute of Journalists released a statement emphatically condemning the behaviour of 'certain London halfpenny newspapers in interviewing probable witnesses in connection with the Yarmouth murder case and publishing the interviews in a highly objectionable form'.[12] A few days later, the *Law Journal* expressed disappointment that contempt of court proceedings had not been brought against certain newspapers.[13]

At the time, contempt of court was a particularly broad and ill-defined misdemeanour, dependent wholly on the decisions of each court and presiding judge as to procedure, punishment and even scope.[14] One case referred to by the *Law Journal* had been brought against the owner of the Surrey Theatre on London's South Bank – a Mr Williams – in 1823, in what is widely considered to be the first example of 'trial by press'. The previous year, John Thurtell had been arrested on suspicion of the murder of a Mr Weare and, by 1823, he was awaiting trial. At the same time, the Surrey Theatre was gearing up to open a play called *The Gamblers*, which had clearly been based on accounts of the murder that had been published in the newspapers. The playbill promised 'THE IDENTICAL HORSE AND GIG *Alluded to by the Daily Press*',[15] and the scenery was based on key locations in the case. Thurtell's lawyers applied for an injunction and an action was brought against the theatre owner, Mr Williams, and J. Romney, a printer, whose name appeared at the foot of the playbill. Thurtell's lawyers claimed that the performance greatly prejudiced the prisoner at the time of his trial. The judge ruled that 'any attempt whatever to prejudice a criminal case, whether by a detail of the evidence, or by a comment, or by a theatrical exhibition, is an offence against public justice, and a serious misdemeanour'.[16] Mr Williams was ultimately found guilty of the offence.[17]

Throughout the 1890s, there had been a growing frequency of applications for contempt, which quickly developed into a concern that contempt cases were being brought as a means of gagging newspapers. This prompted a ruling in 1896 by the then Lord Chief Justice – Lord Russell – and Mr Justice Wright, which stated that proceedings should only be exercised in 'extreme and serious cases ... to be administered with the very greatest caution'.[18] It bolstered the confidence of some reporters, who saw it as a chance to push the boundaries between fair and honest reporting and sensationalism. There was a marked reluctance from politicians to regulate the press for fear of prejudicing themselves. The result was that rogue reporters regularly escaped the rule of law.

Following the Bennett trial, Marshall Hall vowed to take the issue of press interference in criminal trials to the House of Commons, with the intention of advocating for the introduction of a bill 'making it a misdemeanour, punishable on conviction by fine or imprisonment, or both, for any person to publish in the press, or in any public manner whatsoever any comment upon any criminal charge or accusation made against any individual whilst the hearing ... was pending either before a court of summary jurisdiction or before a court of record'.[19] Marshall Hall's desire for the law to be extended stemmed from the defence's abandoned attempt to take steps to prevent the reappearance of a series of scandalous articles and publications that had been circulated during Bennett's magisterial hearing, having learned that the High Court had no power to punish the press for articles calculated to impede the course of justice, if at that time the course of justice had not reached the Superior Court.[20] Thorn-Drury, acting for the defence during the High Court application to remove Bennett's trial to the Central Criminal Court in early 1901, had discussed the issue before two High Court judges, Mr Justice Bruce and Mr Justice Phillimore. Justice Phillimore had reminded Thorn-Drury that 'every person doing anything to impede the cause of justice is liable to indictment' but expressed his regret that 'the High Court has no power to prevent acts which might interfere with the administration of justice in the lower courts'.

The debate was duly brought before the House of Commons at the end of March 1901. The home secretary, Charles Ritchie, strongly condemned the subject of press interference in criminal proceedings and promised a review of the law. In response to further questions, the attorney general, Robert Finlay, 1st Viscount Finlay, stated that the 'whole subject' was under consideration and the comments of both the home secretary and the attorney general were met with approval from the house.

In the summer of 1901, legal proceedings would be brought against the special crime reporter Charles Windhurst, and the editor, Charles Tibbits, of the *Weekly Dispatch*, in a case that indicated that newspapers would be subjected to increased scrutiny. The men stood accused of attempting to pervert the course of justice in connection with a child-neglect case that had been heard earlier that year.[21] The Crown claimed that reports attributed to the two men had been designed to create an atmosphere of prejudice against the accused and jeopardised the defendants' right to a fair trial.[22] Many of the statements related to matters that would not have been admissible in court. Tibbits and Windhurst were found guilty of perverting the course of justice, but sentencing was deferred in order to obtain a decision from a higher court as to whether there was enough evidence to support the conviction. The deferred trial was presided over by no less than Lord Chief Justice Alverstone and, in a case that spanned several months, the defendants' guilty conviction was upheld in a landmark victory for the Crown, which demonstrated that newspaper journalism could – and would be – subjected to the full force of the law.

APPEAL

'I do not and cannot believe that he murdered his wife'

While the newspapers were busily fumbling around for scraps in the wake of Herbert's conviction, letters were being dispatched to and from Whitehall, as the defence launched one final, desperate bid for their client's liberty.

Despite Marshall Hall's bold claim that he (and his client) would accept the jury's verdict as righteous 'whatever their conclusion',[1] he now vowed not to let his client go to the gallows without doing everything in his power to secure an exoneration.

At the time, the Court of Appeal only heard civil cases,[2] so appeals to reprieve criminal judgments had to be made directly to the home secretary. The home secretary had the power to commute sentences, but the king was the only person in the land with the authority to overturn a capital sentence.[3] Plagued with guilt over Bennett's conviction, Marshall Hall made several feverish attempts to appeal for clemency on behalf of his client. He wrote first to the Recorder of London, Sir James Forrest Fulton:

The more I think of it the more convinced I am that [Bennett] never murdered that woman. That he got her down to Yarmouth meaning to take all her goods & chattels from Bexley Heath I have no manner of doubt, but I cannot believe he murdered her . . . I am not the sort of man to worry unnecessarily about anything least of all about a worthless life like that, but honestly and solemnly I do not and cannot believe that he murdered his wife. My own theory of it is that he did go to Yarmouth, that he did write the Hood letter, and that he did take his wife out that night and gave her drink and that then leaving her about 10.30 or 10.45 he went to the hotel leaving her near the Rudrum's [sic] house and that some prowling scoundrel saw her golden hair and golden chain, &c., and beguiling her to the beach, for sexual purposes, and she resisting there was a struggle, an attempted rape, and murder . . . And now I will not bother you further, but I want you to see Ritchie, & tell him that, tho' as an advocate I am

debarred from expressing an opinion in Court, yet as a <u>man</u>, after the
Trial is over, I say this that I would not personally knowing all I do know
take the responsibility of hanging this man . . . though it may be a matter
of great merit to make such a fine defence on behalf of a guilty man, it is
discreditable to have been unable to convince the Jury of the innocence of a
man you yourself believe to be innocent.[4]

Fulton duly forwarded Marshall Hall's letter to the home secretary,
Charles Ritchie, who, having also received a letter from Elvy Robb, agreed
to review Herbert's case.

Sir –
<u>Re Herbert John Bennett</u>
    . . . Bennett has written to me and has instructed me to communicate
with you and to ask if you will be good enough to consider the facts of
the case with a view to seeing whether you can recommend His Most
Gracious Majesty the King to repute the capital sentence with a view of its
commutation to penal servitude for life or such other punishment as may
be deemed fitting . . .
    I am Sir, your obedient servant,
    E. Elvy Robb.[5]

Marshall Hall's letter was also forwarded to the Lord Chief Justice for
comment, and – on the same day that Robb's letter was received by the
Home Office – Alverstone wrote a damning reply, refusing to endorse
Marshall Hall's plea for clemency: 'I wish I could bring myself to feel any
doubt about the case. I am unable to do so. In my opinion, the conduct of
Bennett subsequently to the 14th Sept is absolutely inconsistent with the
theory of the defence to his innocence.'[6]

On 14 March, in what was his first and only account of events, Herbert wrote to the home secretary, requesting clemency. He claimed to have
been 'tried on suspicion, and <u>not</u> evidence', by a jury who had entered the
box with their 'mind made up' on account of the prosecution colouring his
past life, which he admitted had been an 'immoral one'. Despite it being
Herbert's one opportunity to make a case for his innocence, the petition
lacked both new insight and fresh evidence. He maintained the assertion
that he had not been in Great Yarmouth on 16 or 22 September. 'On Sept
22nd, I intended to pay a visit to Gravesend to tell my people there that
my wife had left me & that I was going to get married again at Christmas,

but on second thought I changed my intentions, thinking it would upset them, & so I went to Bexley by Bus & then went for a walk through Lea Green [sic] to Blackheath where I picked up with Mr Sholto Douglas in the manner he has described before the jury, & of which I swear every word is Gospel Truth …' (The most notable point in his petition is the discrepancy over the location of the meeting with Sholto Douglas – '… went for a walk through Lea Green *to Blackheath where I picked up with Mr Sholto Douglas*…' Sholto Douglas, whose evidence was extremely precise on all points, claimed that he had met Herbert on the Eltham Road.) Herbert's petition ended with an appeal. 'The judge stated that if there was the least doubt in the case I was entitled to the benefit of the doubt, & I consider there is a great doubt in the case, & that I have been most unjustly convicted & on these grounds I am taking the liberty of appealing to you for justice & I trust you will give me your kind & careful consideration …'[7]

That day, Herbert also wrote a letter to the editor of the *Sun*, which was passed to the newspaper by a member of Herbert's defence team.

Dear Sir –
I wish to inform you that I am not allowed to write to the Editor of the 'Sun,' but as it is my desire that something should be done for my child, I shall be glad if you will let the Editor know that I shall be thankful if he will open a subscription list for her benefit.
I must again thank you for all you have done for me & my parents,
Yours faithfully,
H.J. Bennett.[8]

The letter sparked a complaint in the House of Commons, forcing the home secretary to issue a statement confirming that convicted prisoners were not permitted to communicate directly with the press – '… such permission was, in this case, refused. It is impossible to prevent indirect communication.'[9]

In response to Herbert's request, the *Sun* launched a subscription, which it opened with 20 guineas. 'We shall welcome', the editor declared, 'from rich and poor alike, any sum which their hearts prompt them to give. With the sum subscribed we shall arrange an annuity through the Sun Life Insurance Company, Threadneedle Street, to meet the special needs of the case and shall take care that the full benefit of that annuity goes to Ruby Bennett.'[10] At the time, it was not unusual for newspapers to make appeals for money to support the victims of crime – the practice dated back to the

1870s.[11] In due course, Herbert's father, John Bennett, would write to the *Sun*, thanking them for launching the appeal. 'We are only poor people, and although we will always do our best for her in every way we can, we feel we cannot do for her what we would like if we were better off, and any sum collected by you would be taken care of in every way to her advantage. She is a dear, loving little child – one that anybody could love and care for, and we trust with God's help she will grow up a blessing in our home.'[12]

Undoubtedly pressed to do so by Marshall Hall, Herbert also wrote to Robert Allen requesting that the outstanding monies owed to him for the purchase of the piano and the bicycle be paid to his father.

Marshall Hall wrote personally to Lord Chief Justice Alverstone requesting a meeting to discuss Bennett's conviction. Alverstone's reply indicated that there was little hope for Bennett.

> DEAR MARSHALL HALL – my warm thanks for your very kind enquiry and your letter. You have nothing with which to reproach yourself. No man could have been more ably defended. I think you have let yourself regard the details too much, in your last letter, without considering the broad facts, which have to be dealt with. If Bennett could have given any account of where he was on the nights of the 15th and 22nd which would bear investigation, the case would be different. Or if he could bring anything to corroborate your theory that he did not know his wife had gone to Yarmouth. You see, the statements which were not evidence and were properly excluded, but which I think should be examined if they tell in favour of the prisoner, do not help him. If it is any comfort to you to come and see me, do so. I shall be quite free from two till four. Do exactly as you like.
>
> Very truly yours,
> ALVERSTONE.[13]

Despite meeting with both the Lord Chief Justice and the home secretary, Marshall Hall was unable to convince either man that there was any justification in commuting Bennett's sentence. Herbert may have escaped cross-examination, but his petition had left him open to a scathing rejection – the capital sentence would stand. With all avenues of appeal now closed to him, Marshall Hall had no choice but to accept that his valiant efforts to obtain mercy for his client had failed. On 19 March, he wrote one last letter. This one was addressed to the condemned man himself.

DEAR SIR, I should not like you to think that my interest in your case ceased with the verdict. Relying upon your repeated assurance of your innocence, I was able to do what I did at the trial on your behalf, and I have since felt it my duty to a fellow creature to see both the Home Secretary and the Lord Chief Justice, so that they should know all that you told me. As you have been informed, there is no hope for you, and the sentence of the law is to be carried out. If there is anything that you would wish to tell, or anything that you would desire done after your death, write me a few lines and any reasonable request that you may make I will endeavour to carry out.

May God in his great mercy grant you peace in the world to come . . .[14]

LAST WILL AND TESTAMENT

'I don't want to say anything at all'

I n the early hours of Wednesday, 6 March 1901, Herbert was transported to Norfolk by a newspaper train – one of the very trains that had transported the news of his conviction across the country. Two days later, Major Robert Jary, the newly appointed High Sheriff of Norfolk, set Thursday, 21 March, as his date of execution. According to the law, three clear Sundays had to elapse between a conviction and the passing of a capital sentence, which determined that Bennett's execution would take place during the week commencing 18 March. Two days after Herbert's sentencing, a telegram from Major Jary had joined the flurry of correspondence sent to the Home Office. Major Jary objected to Lord Alverstone's order that Herbert's execution should take place in Norfolk, expressing a fear that the press attention would add to the morbid excitement already gripping the county.[1] The High Sheriff appealed against Herbert's removal from Newgate Prison under the Central Criminal Court (Prisons) Act of 1881, which stated that when a death sentence was passed by the Central Criminal Court, judgment could be carried out in any prison in the Central Criminal Court district *or* in the county where the offence was committed. Major Jary's appeal was peremptorily disregarded, however, and arrangements were duly made for Bennett's transfer from Newgate Prison to Norwich Prison.

Accounts vary as to the circumstances surrounding Herbert's final two weeks. He reportedly suffered insomnia, was prone to 'violent outbursts', ate little and smoked excessively – a medley of behaviours that were perhaps unsurprising in a man haunted by the thought of his impending execution. He was said to have taken refuge in the ministrations of the prison chaplain, Evan Morgan, who was a frequent visitor to his cell in the days leading up to his execution. Herbert did not receive any other visitors and wrote no letters, save for one, which was passed to Chief Constable Parker. In all but name, it was his last will and testament. He asked that his personal property be sent to his father, John Bennett. There was no reference to Alice Meadows, or to the crime for which he would pay the ultimate price. The press reported that Parker had vowed to burn the letter when he had disposed of the property according to Bennett's wishes.[2]

Norwich Prison was still thought of by locals as the 'new prison' when Herbert found himself incarcerated there for the final time that March. The building, which had opened in 1887, sat on the northeastern boundary of the city, two miles from the centre of the town, in 'splendid and appropriate isolation'[3] on Mousehold Heath. Despite its brilliant red bricks, 'Mousehold', as it was known, was an imposing and uninviting building, lacking in architectural beauty and out of keeping with the other masonry of the cathedral city. Only one execution had taken place within the prison precincts since it had opened. George Watt, known as the 'Sprowston murderer', had been hanged there in 1898, after being found guilty of the shooting of his wife, Sophia. By the spring of 1901, Watt's body had lain in solitude in the southwest corner of the prison grounds for almost three years.

As Bennett waited in his cell, reporters clamoured for information about his incarceration. Prison officials remained tight-lipped following an order from Governor Bell not to give any reports to the press. One inquisitive reporter was referred to the chief warder, who would tell him nothing other than that Bennett would be hanged on the same scaffold as the murderer Watt three years before him.[4] The scaffold was constructed the day before the execution date in a low building at the east wing of the prison. The building, which was usually used as a coach house, was connected to the condemned man's cell by a corridor about 18 metres long. The notorious Victorian executioner James Billington, who had been a Home Office executioner since 1884, had been selected by the High Sheriff of Norfolk to undertake the task. Just two days before Herbert's sentence was due to be passed, Billington, and his son William, had carried out the execution of George Parker, the Southwest Railway murderer, at Wandsworth Prison.[5] When James Billington arrived at Norwich Prison the evening before Herbert's scheduled execution, he was accompanied by another son: Thomas. It was customary for the executioner to assess the condemned the day before their execution in order to estimate and measure the length of the drop, which was initially set by the High Sheriff based on a standard table of drops, first issued by the Home Office in 1892 following a series of botched hangings. The drop was calculated based on the height and weight of the prisoner. The Billingtons set Herbert's drop at 6 feet 9 inches.[6]

*

Thursday, 21 March 1901 began as a bright but bitterly cold morning. One solitary cloud threatened the vivid blue of the early-morning sky, hanging ominously over the prison compound. An icy wind blew in from the east, making its presence felt across the heath. A strong cordon of police officers had been put in place around the prison before the press had even made an appearance, limiting access to the private road leading up to the prison gates and keeping the public at least 90 metres from the prison walls.

As the hour of the execution drew nearer, reporters started gathering and were joined by members of the public. Soon, a small crowd had assembled, and it was not long before the private road leading up to the prison was lined with people. Their attention was firmly fixed on the flagpole that had been erected above the prison entrance. Since 1868, when executions in public were abolished, the hoisting of the black flag had become a symbol that the sentence of death had been carried out. Sensational as the Yarmouth murder case had been, the crowd that amassed outside the prison that morning was a modest one – the 'tamest ever witnessed at an execution in Norwich', lamented one reporter.⁷ The scene was certainly in stark contrast to those that had been common in the run-up to mid-century public executions at Norwich Castle. The castle had formed a central landmark, around which the public could congregate with ease, but the new prison, perched on the dizzying heights of Mousehold, was a steep climb from the city below.

The last public hanging in Norwich had been that of Hubbard Lingley, a gamekeeper from Barton Bendish, a small village in Norfolk. Lingley had been executed for the murder of his uncle, Benjamin Black, in 1867.⁸ Despite maintaining his innocence throughout his trial, Lingley was convicted primarily on the evidence that his gun, which was used in the killing, was found close to the scene of the crime. A reporter who was present outside the prison on the morning of Bennett's execution reflected on Norfolk's last public hanging for 'the benefit', he said, of those who still hankered for the 'good old times'.⁹ In reference to Lingley's hanging, the journalist wrote, '. . . every window within view had its complement of sightseers. Spyglasses and telescopes were brought into use by those further away, and it is no mere figure of speech to say that as the hands of the church clocks neared the hour of eight, the black gallows on the bridge was the cynosure of full five thousand eyes.'

The large crowds that had flocked to Castle Hill in 1867 had all vied for the best position to watch the wretched man Lingley's final moments. Many had come from miles around – some took to distant rooftops, clinging to the flimsiest of supports in hopes of catching the poor man's final moments of torment. The public houses did a roaring trade; pick-pockets worked the crowd. Cries of mercy for 'the poor devil' abounded, alongside cold-hearted exclamations denouncing him as a 'heartless war-mint as didn't oughter live'.[10] Women were there in force, some of whom had brought their babies and appeared to use them as levers to manoeuvre themselves into a good position in the crowd. A wild roar rang across Castle Hill as a trembling Lingley emerged onto the scaffold. His final moment was spent as a spectacle for a bloodthirsty crowd before the white cap was thrust over his head and he was sent falling into oblivion. The bulk of scaffold crowds tended to comprise mainly working people, from tradesmen to unskilled labourers and costermongers, but the so-called respectable classes, who tried to separate themselves from the noisy and potentially dangerous rabble by renting rooms overlooking the scaffold, also watched from their discreet viewpoints.[11]

In November 1849, novelist Charles Dickens and cartoonist John Leech had rented the upper half of a house overlooking Horsemonger Lane Gaol in order to watch the public execution of Maria and Frederick Manning. The Mannings, who had murdered Customs Officer Patrick O'Connor for money and buried him in a shallow grave in their kitchen, were the first married couple to hang since 1700. A crowd of 40,000 attended the execution. It was the peak of the broadside trade and the publication that was produced to mark the Mannings' execution sold 2.5 million sheets. Dickens later recalled being haunted for weeks by the images of 'those two forms dangling on the top of the entrance gateway', and a few days after the execution, he wrote a withering letter to *The Times*, attacking the behaviour of the scaffold crowd. 'I believe that a sight so inconceivably awful as the wickedness and levity of the immense crowd collected at that execution this morning could be imagined by no man.'[12] John Leech's illustration of the execution, published in *Punch* magazine,[13] was notable for its absence of both the scaffold and of the hanging bodies. The illustrator chose, as Dickens had, to focus on the raucous crowd. The broadsheets often reused generic woodcuts of executions, which some-times had gaps to allow for the insertion of different criminals. Facts did not necessarily matter to the scaffold crowd – the woodcut used for the Mannings' execution was a standard scene, with a solitary figure hang-ing from the gallows. A black silhouette had been crudely etched into the image beside the male figure to represent Mrs Manning.[14] Dickens would later immortalise Mrs Manning as Hortense, a lady's maid turned murderer, in *Bleak House*, first published as a serial between 1852 and 1853.

In the face of mounting disquiet over public executions, the House of Commons had launched a Select Committee in 1856, which ultimately decided that it was the scaffold crowd that posed the problem, not hanging itself. Eventually, in what was considered a civilising moment for the country, public execution was abolished – 'All must rejoice that the brutal spectacle afforded by a public hanging is put down,'[15] declared the *Express*. Interest in executions remained, however, and men, women and children continued to gather to bear witness to the passing of the most extreme penalty of the law. In the latter half of the nineteenth century, 'scaffold crowds', as they had once been known, came in waning numbers and exhibited a far more sombre mood than they had in the early part of the nineteenth century.

By nine o'clock on the morning of Herbert's execution, the crowd had swelled to well over 100 people. Groups of children on their way to school, labourers on their way to work, all paused to glance down the private road leading to the prison gate. As the crowd watched the prison clock, which was positioned on the main building facing the roadway, they discussed, with anticipation, the details of the crime. General opinion was that Bennett's fate was just. Among the crowd was James 'Jimmy' Crighton, a fairground cinematographer, who set up his cinematograph (a moving-picture camera) and promised onlookers a show at an upcoming exhibition.

The crowd watched with interest first the arrival of Dr Haynes Robinson – the police surgeon – and then Major Jary, the High Sheriff of Norfolk, with his assistant, Undersheriff Hansell. As the heavy doors of the prison entrance swung back to admit them, the crowd gained a stolen glimpse of the prison yard. Shortly afterwards, two representatives of the press, who had been hand-selected by Major Jary himself, presented themselves to the attendants at the prison gate. Newspapers from across the country had appealed to the High Sheriff for permission to attend the execution, but Major Jary had rejected all requests from Fleet Street journals and had instead chosen representatives from two local newspapers, the *Norfolk Daily Standard* and the *Eastern Daily Press*. Both men were subjected to careful scrutiny at the prison gate before being admitted and they were then taken to a small room just off the prison yard, which was only a short distance from the coach house where the scaffold had been erected.

Inside the prison, Reverend Morgan's ministrations filled the condemned man's cell. Bennett had sat in a trance-like state since he had been served his last meal of bread and tea at 7.30 a.m. (he had managed a little of the liquid, but none of the bread). He appeared gaunt and was decidedly thinner than he had been when he had stepped down from the dock at the Old Bailey almost three weeks earlier. The High Sheriff entered Herbert's cell to make the customary final visit to the prisoner. 'Do you wish to make a statement?' he asked.

'No, sir, I don't want to say anything at all,' replied Herbert, in a low, firm voice. As was procedure, the High Sheriff then gravely informed the prisoner that he must 'prepare to meet his doom', and Herbert rose to face his executioner, James Billington, who had just entered the cell. He stood upright and made no attempt to resist as the hangman pinioned his arms. The prisoner, chaplain and executioner were then joined by Herbert's prison warders, Governor Bell and the two pressmen. A moment later, the small group, led by Bell, began the walk to the scaffold. As they made their way down the short corridor, the chaplain recited passages of scripture. Herbert, who was wearing the same grey suit that he was alleged to have worn on the night of the murder, followed the chaplain, pale and glassy-eyed. Two warders were stationed on either side of him, should he falter, but he walked the few paces from the condemned cell to the scaffold un-supported and with a firm step, head erect, displaying a 'wonderful effort of self-control'.[16] He only stumbled once – as he passed through the door to the execution room and came face to face with the noose that would end his life. He recovered quickly, and a second later he had stepped fearlessly onto the trapdoor of the scaffold.

James Billington restrained Herbert's legs and positioned the rope around his neck. As the hangman was adjusting the noose, Herbert raised his chin and threw back his head to assist him. Meanwhile, the chaplain read the opening lines of the burial service. Herbert made no sound – he was ashen pale but stood unassisted. His eyes remained steadily riveted on the little knot of officials that had gathered beside the scaffold until the white cap was thrust over his head and the world around him was plunged into darkness. The hangman stepped back, and Thomas Billington pulled the lever of the scaffold. The trapdoor flung open, and Herbert fell into the pit with a dull thud as the words 'Lord, deliver this thy servant' tumbled from the chaplain's lips.

And so ended the life of Herbert John Bennett.

The prison bell began to toll; the condemned man had been put to death. The crowd failed to hear the steady ding over the howling of the wind. They did not, however, fail to miss the hoisting of the black flag. They watched in anticipation as the little piece of black cloth was run up the flagpole. Just as the cloth was about to unfurl, a strong gust of wind blew across the heath and lifted the flagstaff out of its socket. A loud gasp arose from the crowd as the prison officials clambered to reaffix it. Legend had it that if the flagpole snapped or dislodged when the flag was hoisted, an innocent person had been put to death. A few moments later, the black flag was fluttering gloomily in the wind, but the significance of the incident was not lost on the dispersing crowd.

Later that morning, the body of Herbert John Bennett was placed in a coffin and buried in an unmarked grave in the southwest corner of the prison compound next to the body of George Watt. The two men would lie together there, side by side, for a further seven years before another man was added to their number.

Towards the end of March, a memorial stone was placed on the grave that held the body of Mary Jane Bennett in the Kitchener Road cemetery, Great Yarmouth. Included on the epitaph was her name, age, date of death and a passage from the Book of Common Prayer.

'In the midst of life we are in death.'

A TRUE VICTORIAN CRIME

'CHAMBER OF HORRORS: Herbert Bennett and other notorious Criminals'[1]

T he *Norfolk Daily Standard* reporter who attended Herbert's execution would later write that Bennett had 'maintained the callous indifference he had shown since his arrest to the end, marking himself one of the most extraordinary criminals of the time'.[2]

It was this reputation that would ensure that Herbert would live on in popular culture for many years to come. While the Yarmouth Beach Murder may have fallen from the headlines following Bennett's execution, the story was set to seep into other forms of mass entertainment. With the ink barely dry on Bennett's execution notice, a new form of entertainment was about to take centre stage in Norwich, and the moving images depicting the dramatic hoisting of the black flag that signified Herbert's execution would be the star of the show . . .

In the early 1890s, American inventor Thomas Edison had started work on a moving picture machine. He was said to have been inspired by Eadweard Muybridge's pioneering work in photographic studies of motion. The result was the kinetoscope, the first moving-picture camera, capable of photographing film at 48 frames per second. By the mid 1890s, the Lumière brothers, Auguste and Louis, had developed a smaller, more advanced device that was capable of recording, developing and projecting moving images. They called it the cinématographe (cinematograph), and it paved the way for a new form of entertainment: cinema. The main restriction of the kinetoscope was that it only allowed one person to view film through its peephole viewing device, whereas the cinematograph's built-in projector made it possible for large crowds to view moving pictures simultaneously for the first time. Soon, a new breed of travelling showman had emerged, who created short films and exhibited them at fairgrounds, music halls and travelling shows – or bioscopes. Entry to the exhibitions was often as little as 2*d.* for adults, 1*d.* for children, making film accessible to the masses. 'Crighton Electrograph's "great draw" was a film of Coleman's [sic] workpeople leaving the [mustard] factory',[3] declared the *Showman*, a journal dedicated to travelling showmen, which launched in September 1900. The films were short (the running time was usually less than a minute) and silent. The flickering images would often cause headaches, but the public considered this a small price to pay for the chance to see themselves and their town on screen, and the films proved highly popular.[4] The *Showman* reveals extensive listings of reports of local films being exhibited at fairs and venues throughout the United Kingdom.[5]

The film James 'Jimmy' Crighton had captured outside Norwich Prison on the morning of Bennett's execution was exhibited alongside a series of local films of Norwich taken three weeks after Bennett was hanged: 'Bennet execution films ... are fine. These films are quite unique, and Crighton's takes [them] well.'[6]

The popularity of Bennett's execution film demonstrates that newspapers and popular literature were not the only leisure activities that early Edwardians turned to for their fix of sensation-horror. During the nineteenth century, as the working classes started to benefit from more leisure time and an increase in real wages, other forms of entertainment developed rapidly in Victorian culture. The latter half of the century saw an increase in the number and variety of leisure facilities and interests, including music halls, horse racing, theatre, parks, museums and exhibitions, notably the South Kensington Museum – renamed the Victoria and Albert Museum (V&A) in 1899 – which contained many of the exhibits from the Great Exhibition held at the Crystal Palace in 1851. Opening hours were specifically designed to cater for the working classes. Following the introduction of four regular bank holidays in the Bank Holidays Act of 1871, by the end of the century access to leisure activities had become cheaper. Crime and murder continued to be the main draw when it came to popular entertainment.

Throughout the century, many Victorians derived their fix of sensation-horror from museum-like displays of waxen effigies and plaster casts of heinous murderers.[7] Wax models had been exhibited in open-air shows since the seventeenth century, but it wasn't until the late 1700s/early 1800s that the practice of taking casts of criminals' heads to create effigies started to become popular. This macabre phenomenon was made famous in the nineteenth century by Madame Marie Tussaud (née Grosholtz), who had been taught the art of wax modelling in the late 1700s by Philippe Curtius, a Swiss physician who used wax models to illustrate anatomy. The popularity of Curtius's wax replicas inspired him to create portrait models, which he began exhibiting in Paris in 1770. In 1782, he opened a second exhibition on Boulevard du Temple, the Caverne des Grands Voleurs (Cave of the Great Thieves), which was said to be the precursor to Tussaud's Chamber of Horrors. Curtius died in 1793, bequeathing his wax exhibition to Marie.

In 1802, Marie, now Madame Marie Tussaud, transported her wax collection to London to begin what would become a thirty-year tour of Britain. The exhibition was a success and, with Curtius's Caverne des Grands Voleurs, and her experience of creating models from guillotined heads (in 1793, she had been forced to make the death mask of King Louis XVI to prove her loyalty to the Revolution), Marie established a permanent base in London's Baker Street at 'The Baker Street Bazaar'. At first, the room housed casts of the severed heads of the victims of the French guillotine, but later, Madame Tussaud began to add the figures of domestic murderers with whom her audiences were well acquainted.[8]

Madame Tussaud also collected and displayed relics of criminals and crime. Among these were the murderer Daniel Good's clogs, gruesome relics of the French Revolution and the Napoleonic dynasty, the suit in which murderer James Blomfield Rush was executed,[9] and latterly, the blood-stained trunk that had held the murdered body of the seventy-two-year-old victim of prostitute Marie Hermann, the first capital case that Marshall Hall had defended alone. The trunk had become the exhibition's chief attraction during the summer of 1894.

Madame Tussaud was a shrewd businesswoman, who transformed her artform into a respectable form of leisure. 'Education, rather than novelty or cheap thrills, was proclaimed to be at the centre of this entertainment, as patrons were introduced to important historical and contemporary figures with the aid of detailed guidebooks.'[10] The exhibition was deemed 'safe' for women and children and women 'patronized Madame Tussaud's as unselfconsciously as they devoured newspaper accounts of a bloody murder'.[11] By 1869, the Chamber of Horrors was enticing large crowds and it soon became as big an attraction as Westminster Abbey, St Paul's Cathedral and the Tower of London.[12] In 1884, the exhibition was removed to Marylebone Road, where it remains to this day. Joseph and François Tussaud, having inherited the business following their mother's death in 1850, continued to seek out the most notorious criminals to add to their now-famous Chamber of Horrors. They were led by sensation and public interest.

In November 1900, the *News of the World* reported that one of the Tussaud brothers had attended Bennett's magisterial hearing. 'Mr Tussaud, of Madame Tussaud's, was early in attendance, busily making notes.'[13] By the time of Bennett's police court hearing, talk of the Yarmouth murder was already widespread across the country. On 10 November, Ralph David Blumenfeld, an American journalist who would later become editor of the *Daily Express*, wrote in his diary, 'It is remarkable to note that people of all grades of society are more interested in crime mystery – particularly the murder of a woman – than in any other topic.'[14]

Bennett had become a perfect candidate for Madame Tussaud's Chamber of Horrors, and just over two weeks after Bennett's execution, advertisements for Madame Tussaud's 'new portrait model' began appearing in the newspapers:

MADAME TUSSAUD'S EXHIBITION – Open at 8 a.m. on Bank Holiday. – CHAMBER of HORRORS, Portrait Model of Herbert John Bennett and other notorious Criminals of the Century, the old Treadmill from York Castle Prison. &c. Admission 1s.; children under 12, 6d.; extra rooms 6d. Open at 8 a.m. on Bank Holiday.[15]

Tussaud's Exhibition which will open at 8am on Easter Monday, has many new remarkable models, such as Bennett, the Yarmouth murderer, the ubiquitous De Wet,[16] &c. In short, a wonderful show.[17]

The following month, the *London Evening Standard* published a review, which highlighted the *endless* popularity of the exhibition; there was, it said, 'no department more largely patronised yesterday than the Chamber of Horrors, which seems ever to possess a sort of grim fascination for holiday folk'.[18]

Images of victims were also a draw for macabre collectors of sensation-horror, as this advert, which appeared in the *Era* in December 1900, demonstrates:

WANTED, to sell. Yarmouth Murder. Correct model of the accused, from life; also of the dead woman, just as the body was found; also of the child, Ruby, and Alice Meadows and boy. We have the identical photographs taken of the dead woman in the mortuary, the authentic one. A good draw for the Horrors.[19]

In July 1901, a smaller, seedier wax exhibition opened on Great Yarmouth's Regent Road. The exhibition, which was clearly inspired by Tussaud's Chamber of Horrors, was housed in a dank cellar and featured 'five realistic tableaux, showing life sized portrait models of Bennett and his victim'.[20] The exhibition was operated by Clarence Barron, who later received a summons for using a 'vehicle to display advertisements without the written consent of the corporation, contrary to section 99 of the Corporation Act 1897'. The local authorities were appalled by the sordid exhibition and had pulled Barron up on a technicality. His cart – a four-wheeled bogie – had raised canvas sides on which the Yarmouth tragedy was advertised – 'Novel Exhibition, Regents Road'. Barron had already received a warning from Chief Constable Parker for using the word 'murder' to advertise the exhibition and he had been ordered to replace it with the word 'tragedy'. He had also been told to remove other advertisements from his shop front. In court, the tableaux were referred to as a 'heterogeneous collection of various shows in a partially finished shop, amid surroundings that made it about as degrading and demoralising as it could be'. Barron was given a fine and ordered to pay 20s. and costs.

The strong penalty came from the authorities' desire to disassociate the town from the murder. The tourist trade had already suffered irreparable damage thanks not only to the murder itself, but also to Marshall Hall's declaration that the killer was not Herbert Bennett, but one of the 'prowling brutes who haunted the shore at Yarmouth with their lust for greed and gold'.[21] His comments had been widely reported in the press at the time and had earned a rebuttal from the *Yarmouth Independent*, which advised the barrister 'not to venture a visit to the Town'.[22]

Some years later, Charles Leach, the son of Detective Inspector Alfred Leach – by then a retired detective inspector himself – would claim that the fateful bootlace used to kill Mary Jane Bennett had been put on display at the Black Museum in London, now known as the Crime Museum. 'One of the latter [exhibits] was a bootlace with which Bennett, the murderer, strangled his wife on the beach at Yarmouth. The visitors, particularly those from the USA and overseas, used to take a keen delight in handling this grim relic, and oftentimes, when we used to look around the museum at night and check-up to see whether everything was in order, the bootlace would be missing. So we simply used to put a fresh one in its place! There must be quite a number of people abroad who fondly imagine that they possess the famous bootlace. The real one, if I remember right, had disappeared long since.'[23]

The Black Museum had been established in the 1870s to collect and display prisoners' property in order to aid officers in their study of criminality. The collection, initially located in what was referred to as the 'identification room' of New Scotland Yard, 8–10 Broadway, formed a gruesome exhibition of relics from some of the most notorious crimes of the latter nineteenth century. A reporter wrote in 1877 that 'the building is, indeed, as it is called, a *Black Museum*, for it is associated with whatever is darkest in human nature and human destiny'.[24] The small, grim room contained the blood-stained clothing of murder victims, a wide variety of weapons (including numerous knives and pistols), death masks of murderers who had been hanged showing the rope marks around their necks, the actual ropes that had been used in executions, and the clothes of murder victims and criminals, including the coat worn by the 'Tichborne Claimant' – the man who falsely claimed to be the missing heir to the Tichborne baronetcy – during his trial in the 1870s. Among the drawings, plans and postcards (one allegedly written by Jack the Ripper) hanging from the walls were photographs that had featured in many celebrated cases, including the Yarmouth Beach Murder.[25]

Doubt remains over the accuracy of Charles Leach's account of the bootlace,[26] but there was clearly a strong appetite for collecting relics or souvenirs of crime at the time. In the 1820s, the hedge through which William Weare's murdered body was dragged was sold by the inch and the wooden cladding from the lower walls of the Red Barn – made famous as the place William Corder murdered his sweetheart Maria Marten and then buried her body – was picked apart by morbid souvenir hunters.[27]

As for the most famous exhibits in the Bennett case – Mary Jane's precious gold chain and the famous beach photograph – a desperate plea from William Clark for his daughter's 'clothes and wearing apparel' to be returned to him failed to convince Marshall Hall to give them up.[28]

The barrister added the exhibits to his personal collection of memorabilia from the cases he had defended, and they sat among a fearsome array of guns, knives, phials of poison and daggers,[29] which resided in his chambers at 3, Temple Gardens as a constant reminder, until his death in 1927, of the murder case that had enthralled the country.[30]

Postscript

In the early hours of 15 July 1912, the body of a young woman was found on Great Yarmouth's South Beach. A bootlace – tied with a reef knot – cut deeply into the skin of her neck. She was quickly identified as eighteen-year-old Dora May Grey, a waitress from one of Yarmouth's many lodging houses. As news of the tragedy spread throughout the town, comparisons were drawn to the murder that had gripped the nation twelve years earlier. Despite an extensive police hunt, led by Chief Constable Parker, Dora May's killer was never found. Her death was enough to convince those who still doubted Herbert Bennett's guilt that Mary Jane's killer still haunted the shores of Great Yarmouth ...

Conclusion

It has now been more than 120 years since that fateful night on the beach. In that time, the Clark and Bennett family lines have flourished. Little Ruby Elizabeth Bennett grew up in the home of Herbert's parents, with her great-grandfather, Henry Simmons, close by. She married at twenty-two, later emigrating to Australia, where she lived up until her death in 1993, aged ninety-four. Despite a traumatic start, hers was – for the most part – a happy life.

Poor Alice Meadows' story ended similarly well. Despite the devastation of Herbert's betrayal, Alice appears to have recovered quickly, and in the summer of 1902 she married another man. She and her husband went on to have four children together, three of whom survived infancy. The 1911 census has her widowed sister, May Lenson, living with the family. Never far from her side during the trial, May clearly continued to be a great support to Alice as she embarked on her new life.

As for the Rudrum family, life continued in much the same way after the trial as it had done before the murder. John returned to his work as a shoemaker, eventually rising in the ranks to become a 'salesman/shop-keeper' in the boot trade. By 1911, they had moved to a seven-roomed house in nearby Albion Road. Alice Rudrum, married for nine years by this point, was living in Row 103, the street adjacent to where she had grown up, with her husband and two children. As the Rudrums awoke to the news of another dead body on the morning of 15 July 1912, they would inevitably have recalled the events that had unfolded twelve years earlier, perhaps with a mixture of dread and excitement. John Rudrum had, after all, been forced to admit during the trial that the death of their lodger in 1900 had been the event of his life . . .

The Rudrums would not have been the only people to receive the news of Dora May Grey's death with interest. It is likely that Edward Marshall Hall would have considered the latest murder evidence that Mary Jane's killer was still at large, as he had once so vehemently argued. The barrister's certainty over Herbert Bennett's innocence would be brought into question four years later, however, when he was given cause to question another man's honesty ...

In the months following Herbert's execution, the public had formed its own opinion of Douglas Sholto Douglas. Orders for fancy boxes had dropped off and he had received several abusive and threatening letters, some of which were wittily addressed to the 'London Fancy Box and Alibi Manufacturing Company'. By 1916, however, the London Fancy Box Company had recovered from its drop in sales and was drawing in thousands of pounds a year. This success was marred by a series of 'disputes' between Sholto Douglas and fellow partner Andrew Lawson. The dispute ended in court proceedings, with Sholto Douglas accusing Lawson of defrauding the company. Lawson was defended by none other than Edward Marshall Hall, who would ultimately discover evidence that would lead to his client's acquittal. During the course of the trial, Lawson dramatically declared that there had been two attempts on his life, implying that Sholto Douglas was responsible. The newspapers reported the sensational news with delight: 'BY BOMB AND POISON: STORY IN COURT OF ATTEMPTS ON DEFENDANT'S LIFE'.[1,2]

Sholto Douglas was quick to deny any involvement in the conspiracies, but the case would certainly have given Marshall Hall pause for thought. In a particularly heated courtroom exchange, Marshall Hall made his thoughts about Sholto Douglas clear: 'I suggest that you are a gentleman suffering from a form of conceit which makes you imagine all sorts of things!'[3]

The sorry saga certainly brought Sholto Douglas's character into question and indicated that there may have been more to his relationship with Bennett than was first thought ...[4]

Standing on Great Yarmouth's South Beach today, it is hard to imagine that chilly night in September 1900 when Mary Jane met her untimely death. The sand dunes are still there, the marram grass still brushes against your legs as you stroll further down the beach towards the sea, but it is no longer the quiet, secluded spot it once was. Nine years after Mary Jane's body was discovered among the sand dunes, the area was turned into an amusement park, which is now known as the Great Yarmouth Pleasure Beach. Its gaudy neon lights and the loud chug-chug-chug-woosh of the nearby log flume fill the space. The joyous screams of children enjoying the amusements are a stark – and welcome – contrast to Mary Jane's cries for mercy that had, on that night, filled the air as she took her last, desperate breaths.

Over the years, the story of the Yarmouth Beach Murder has been resurrected several times, most recently in 2018 when the case featured in a new series, *Murder, Mystery and My Family*. The purpose of the series was to re-examine historical murder cases on behalf of living relatives, with the intention of testing the conviction of the accused. The question on everyone's mind was: had Herbert Bennett really killed his wife? The defence barrister assigned to the case – Jeremy Dein KC – attempted to prove otherwise, just like Marshall Hall had 100 years earlier. Despite the deployment of modern forensic techniques to test key evidence, the judge, David Radford, eventually found against the defence. Herbert Bennett's conviction was upheld. Herbert had, in effect, been found guilty of murdering his wife for the second time.

What I wanted to know was: where was Mary Jane's voice in all this? When I set out to write this book, I did so with two things in mind: to discover the truth about what really happened to my great-great-aunt, and to give Mary Jane her voice back.

I hope I have done her justice.

Notes

Introduction My Family Album

1 Mary Jane Bennett is referred to in text as the great-great-aunt of Kim Donovan. She was, in fact, her half great-great-aunt but for simplicity's sake, we have dropped the 'half'.

2 Barthes, R. (1993), *Camera Lucida*. (London: Vintage).

1 The Body on the Beach

1 The *Lowestoft Standard*, 29 September 1900.

2 UK Parliament (2021), 'Creating the nation's police force'. Available at: https://www.parliament.uk/about/living-heritage/transformingsociety/laworder/policeprisons/overview/nationspoliceforce/ [Accessed: 3 May 2021.]

3 Taylor, D. (1998), *Crime, Policing and Punishment in England, 1750–1914* (Basingstoke: Macmillan Education), p.89.

2 The Killer in Her Eyes

1 *Yarmouth Advertiser and Gazette*, 29 September 1900.

2 *Sun*, 24 November 1900.

3 Riley, B. (2011), *Great Yarmouth Row Houses and Greyfriars' Cloister* (London: English Heritage), p.28.

4 Ibid.

5 *Star*, 23 November 1900.

6 Riley, B. (2011), *Great Yarmouth Row Houses and Greyfriars' Cloister* (London: English Heritage), p.34.

7 Ibid.

3 The Letter in the Blue Envelope

1 Interview with Louisa Rudrum, *Sunday Express*, 5 February 1967.

2 *Yarmouth Independent*, 29 September 1900.

3 See: Dilnot, G., ed. (1929), *The Trial of Herbert John Bennett (The Yarmouth Beach Murder)* (London: Geoffrey Bles), p.98.

4 Interview with Louisa Rudrum, *Sunday Express*, 5 February 1967.

5 Warwick, P., and Spies, S.B. (1980), *The South African War: The Anglo-Boer War 1899–1902* (Harlow: Longman), p.21.

6 The 'Yarmouth beach photograph', as it would become known, cost 1*s*. 6*d*.

7 The Hippodrome was built on Marine Parade in 1903 and is still a popular entertainment venue today.

8 Interview with Louisa Rudrum, *Sunday Express*, 5 February 1967.

9 *Yarmouth Mercury*, 6 October 1900.

10 The Victoria Hotel is now the Bay Carlton Hotel.

11 The description that follows is taken from the depositions of Alfred Mason and Blanche Smith.

12 Hall, L.A. (2013), *Sex, Gender and Social Change in Britain Since 1880* (Basingstoke: Palgrave Macmillan), p.13.

13 Wiener, M. J. (2004), *Men of Blood: Violence, Manliness and Criminal Justice in Victorian England* (Cambridge: Cambridge University Press), p.122.

4 The Missing Bootlace

1 See: Dilnot, G., ed. (1929), *The Trial of Herbert John Bennett (The Yarmouth Beach Murder)* (London: Geoffrey Bles), p.185.

2 *News of the World*, 29 September 1900.

3 The description that follows is derived from the testimony and depositions of the two doctors.

4 The woman had a slight figure and weighed just over 8 stone.

5 The Mariner's Compass bar closed in 1904 and the site was redeveloped as council houses.

6 *Star*, 12 November 1900.

7 The description is derived from William Borking's deposition and testimony.

8 By 1904, over 60,000 sets of fingerprints had been registered with the police. The first people in Britain to be convicted of murder based on fingerprint evidence were Albert and Alfred Stratton, who were ultimately hanged for murdering Thomas and Ann Farrow during a robbery of their paint shop in 1905.

9 See: Dilnot, G., ed. (1929), *The Trial of Herbert John Bennett (The Yarmouth Beach Murder)* (London: Geoffrey Bles), p.185.

10 Goodman, R. (2014), *How to Be a Victorian* (London: Penguin Books), p.59.

5 A Murder a Day

1 See: *Norfolk Daily Standard, Eastern Evening News, Star* and *Morning Leader*, all 24 September 1900.

2 *Eastern Evening News*, 24 September 1900.

3 *Star*, 24 September 1900.

4 Curran, J. and Seaton, J. (2009), *Power Without Responsibility: The Press and Broadcasting in Britain* (London: Routledge), p.33.

5 Williams, K. (1998), *Get Me a Murder a Day! A History of Mass Communication in Britain* (London: Arnold), p.50.

6 Lee, A.J. (1976), *The Origins of the Popular Press in England: 1855–1914* (London: Croom Helm), p.59.

7 Shpayer-Makov, H. (2009), 'Journalists and Police Detectives in Victorian and Edwardian England: An Uneasy Reciprocal Relationship', *Journal of Social History*, 42(4), pp.963–987.

8 Ibid.

9 Ibid.

10 Ibid.

11 Reported in the *Yarmouth Mercury*, 29 September 1900.

12 *Evening News*, 26 September 1900.

13 *Star*, 27 September 1900.

14 Rowbotham, J. *et al.* (2013), *Crime News in Modern Britain: Press Reporting and Responsibility, 1820–2010* (Basingstoke: Palgrave Macmillan), p.103.

15 See: *Star*, 24 September 1900.

16 *Yarmouth Advertiser and Gazette*, 29 September 1900.

17 *Yarmouth Advertiser and Gazette*, 10 November 1900.

18 Williams, K. (1998), *Get Me a Murder a Day! A History of Mass Communication in Britain* (London: Arnold), p.53.

19 Clarke, B. (2004), *From Grub Street to Fleet Street: An Illustrated History of English Newspapers to 1899* (Aldershot: Ashgate), p.250.

20 *Weekly Dispatch*, 30 September 1900.

21 *Yarmouth Advertiser and Gazette*, 29 September 1900.

6 Call in Scotland Yard!

1 Leach, C.E. (1933), *On Top of the Underworld: The Personal Reminiscences of Ex-divisional Detective-Inspector Charles E Leach, Late of New Scotland Yard* (London: S. Low, Marston & Company Ltd), p.11.

2 *Yarmouth Advertiser and Gazette*, 3 November 1900.

3 Gleadle, K. (2001), *British Women in the Nineteenth Century* (Basingstoke: Palgrave), p.99.

4 *Weekly Dispatch*, 21 October 1900.

7 24, Dock Row

1 Spellings are interchangeable between 'Clarke' and 'Clark'. The surname is spelt 'Clarke' on the baptism record and some census records, but it more frequently appears as 'Clark'.

2 Sometimes 'Edmund.'

3 Rubenhold, H. (2019), *The Five: The Untold Lives of the Women Killed by Jack the Ripper* (London: Penguin), p.25.

4 This was not unusual: all adoptions were arranged on an informal basis until the Adoption Act was passed in England and Wales in 1926.

5 *The Times*, 5 March 1894.

6 Although we do not know for sure, it is likely that Herbert worked six days a week (with Sundays and Wednesday afternoons off, when the stores were closed). He could have worked anything from ten to twelve hours a day, or possibly even longer on some days.

7 *Star*, 10 November 1900.

8 *Evening News*, 10 November 1900.

9 *Star*, 10 November 1900.

10 *Weekly Times and Echo*, 11 November 1900.

11 Barret-Ducrocq, F. (1992), *Love in the Time of Victoria: Sexuality and Desire Among Working-class Men and Women in Nineteenth-century London* (London: Penguin), p.98.

12 Banns are an announcement in church of two people's intention to marry. Church of England marriages require banns to be read out for three Sundays during the three months before the wedding, partly to provide an opportunity for anyone who knows of a reason a marriage cannot legally take place to put forward an objection. Herbert's father objected to his son's marriage on the second reading of the banns, which put a stop to the wedding.

13 At the time, Herbert was in fact still seventeen, and would not turn eighteen until the start of the next month.

14 *Star*, 10 November 1900.

15 *Sun*, 10 November 1900.

8 Violins and Violence

1 *Star,* 13 November 1900.
2 Ibid.
3 The author's great-grandmother!
4 *Yarmouth Mercury,* 16 November 1900.
5 *Yarmouth Mercury Special,* 16 November 1900.
6 *Evening News,* 13 November 1900.
7 Baxter, A.L. (1899), BOOTH/B/366, Notebook: Police District 34 [Lambeth and Kennington], District 36 [Battersea East], District 37 [Battersea West], District 38 [Clapham]. Available at: https://booth.lse.ac.uk/notebooks/b366#?c=0&m=0&s=0&cv=0&z=-2832.4423%2C0%2C8689.8845%2C3618 [Accessed: 2 June 2021.]
8 Booth, C. Charles Booth's poverty map of London. LSE. Available at: https://booth.lse.ac.uk/map/14/-0.1174/51.5064/100/0 [Accessed: 2 June 2021.]
9 *Star,* 13 November 1900.
10 *Sun,* 13 November 1900.
11 *Evening News,* 13 November 1900.
12 *Exchange and Mart,* 18 August, 25 August and 1 September 1899.
13 In 1900, this would have been roughly the same as a skilled tradesman would have expected to earn for around fifteen days of work. See: https://www.nationalarchives.gov.uk/currency/.
14 Interview with Mrs Kato, *Evening News,* 13 November 1900.
15 *Star,* 12 November 1900.
16 Mrs Kato's surname is more commonly spelt 'Cato', but it is 'Kato' in official records.
17 *Lloyd's Weekly Newspaper,* 26 November 1899.
18 See: Dilnot, G., ed. (1929), *The Trial of Herbert John Bennett (The Yarmouth Beach Murder)* (London: Geoffrey Bles), p.171.
19 Gleadle, K. (2001), *British Women in the Nineteenth Century* (Basingstoke: Palgrave), p.136.
20 Ibid., p.133.
21 Rubenhold, H. (2019), *The Five: The Untold Lives of the Women Killed by Jack the Ripper* (London: Penguin), p.49.
22 *Evening News,* 13 November 1900.

9 A Graveyard of Canaries and a Curious Case of Arson

1 Reports of the fire appear in the *Evening News,* 12 November 1900, and the *Star,* 13 November 1900.
2 *Evening News,* 12 November 1900.
3 *People,* 3 April 1932.
4 Ibid.
5 Symes Thompson, E. (1888), *South Africa as a Health Resort* (Royal Colonial Institute). Available at: https://upload.wikimedia.org/wikipedia/commons/3/32/South_Africa_as_a_health_resort_%28IA_b22302347%29.pdf [Accessed: 3 August 2019.] A copy of this book was later found among Mary Jane's possessions.
6 They actually travelled under the names 'James' and 'Alice' Bennett. James Bennett was the name of Herbert's paternal grandfather.

10 Gold

1 Duckworth, G.H. (1900), BOOTH/B/376, George H. Duckworth's Notebook: Police

District 48 [Woolwich]. Available at: https://booth.lse.ac.uk/notebooks/b376#?cv=13&
c=0&m=0&s=0&z=1267.4673%2C739.368%2C1216.7958%2C527.4 [Accessed: 3 August
2021.]

2 *Daily Mail*, 12 November 1900.

3 *Evening Star*, 9 November 1900.

4 *Star*, 10 November 1900.

5 *Daily Mail*, 12 November 1900.

6 See: Dilnot, G., ed. (1929), *The Trial of Herbert John Bennett (The Yarmouth Beach Murder)* (London: Geoffrey Bles), p.88.

7 *Daily Mail*, 12 November 1900.

8 Bartlett was the name of the man who had bought the Bennetts' Stockwood Street business.

9 See 'Archives and local history', Bexley.gov.uk: https://www.bexley.gov.uk/discover -bexley/archives-and-local-history

10 Mrs Savage's witness testimony. See: Dilnot, G., ed. (1929), *The Trial of Herbert John Bennett (The Yarmouth Beach Murder)* (London: Geoffrey Bles), p.78.

11 UK Health Security Agency (2019), 'Are Victorian diseases making a comeback?' Available at: https://publichealthmatters.blog.gov.uk/2019/03/28/are-victorian-diseases -making-a-comeback/ [Accessed: 3 June 2021.]

12 Gough, W.C. (1927), *From Kew Observatory to Scotland Yard: Being Experiences and Travels in 28 years of Crime Investigation* (London: Hurst & Blackett), p.95.

13 Hope-Simpson, R.E. (1992), 'Epidemic Influenza, 1900–1932', in: *The Transmission of Epidemic Influenza* (Boston: Springer), pp. 23–32.

14 Powis Street remains a busy shopping street today, despite the closure of a number of large stores, including Garrett's in 1972, and the Royal Arsenal Co-operative Society in 1985.

15 Arkell, G.E. and Duckworth, G.H. (1899–1900), BOOTH/B/371, George E. Arkell and George H. Duckworth's Notebook: Police District 46 [Greenwich]; District 48 [Woolwich]. p.213. Available at: https://booth.lse.ac.uk/notebooks.

11 The Other Woman

1 There is no evidence to suggest that Comfort Pankhurst was any relation to the Suffragette and British political activist Emmeline Pankhurst.

2 The area got its name from the coal that was unloaded on the nearby wharves, which hung heavily in the air. The atmosphere made it a less desirable (and cheaper) place to live. The roughest areas were the north side of the high street between Nelson Street and Collingwood Street, a short walk from Union Street, where Herbert was lodging.

3 Arkell, G.E. and Duckworth, G.H. (1899–1900), BOOTH/B/371, George E. Arkell and George H. Duckworth's Notebook: Police District 46 [Greenwich]; District 48 [Woolwich]. p.157. Available at: https://booth.lse.ac.uk/notebooks.

4 Engelbach, F.G. (1899), Her Majesty's Ordnance Factories: Woolwich Arsenal. *The Navy and Army Illustrated*. 25 March 1899.

5 Arkell, G.E. and Duckworth, G.H. (1899–1900), BOOTH/B/371, George E. Arkell and George H. Duckworth's Notebook: Police District 46 [Greenwich]; District 48 [Woolwich]. p.157. Available at: https://booth.lse.ac.uk/notebooks.

6 'Frightful Explosion at Woolwich', reported in the *Cambrian*, 28 September 1883.

7 'Explosions', Royal Arsenal History. See: https://www.royal-arsenal-history.com.

8 Some have linked Herbert's job at the Arsenal with the Bennetts' mysterious trip to South Africa and have suggested that Herbert was working as a spy for the Boers.

While the suggestion is unsurprising given Herbert's character and activities, there is no evidence to support this assertion.

9 Goodman, R. (2014), *How to Be a Victorian* (London: Penguin Books), p.51.

10 Unknown (1910), *Every Woman's Encyclopaedia* (London: s.n.). Available at: https://archive. org/details/everywomansencyco1londuoft/page/166/mode/2up?ref=ol&view=theater [Accessed: 3 June 2021.] p.167.

11 Ibid.

12 Ibid.

13 *Weekly Dispatch*, 2 December 1900.

14 Unknown (1910), *Every Woman's Encyclopaedia* (London: s.n.). Available at: https://archive. org/details/everywomansencyco1londuoft/page/166/mode/2up?ref=ol&view=theater [Accessed: 3 June 2021.] p.167.

15 Herbert's grandfather had actually owned a public house.

16 The Bank Holidays Act of 1871 had established four bank holidays in England, Wales and Ireland: Easter Monday, Whit Monday, the first Monday in August and 26 December. The August bank holiday date moved to the last Monday of the month in 1971.

17 See: Dilnot, G., ed. (1929), *The Trial of Herbert John Bennett (The Yarmouth Beach Murder)* (London: Geoffrey Bles), p.82.

18 Ibid, p.94.

19 Rubenhold, H. (2019), *The Five: The Untold Lives of the Women Killed by Jack the Ripper* (London: Penguin), p.126.

20 Goodman, R. (2014), *How to Be a Victorian* (London: Penguin Books), p.350.

12 A Likely Story

1 Letter from Herbert Bennett to Alice Meadows, dated 23 September 1900. A.M.4. National Archives: HO 144/567/A62336.

2 Letter from Herbert to Alice Meadows, dated 21 September 1900. A.M.2. National Archives: HO 144/567/A62336.

3 *Daily News*, 22 September 1900.

4 *Eastern Evening News*, 22 September 1900.

5 The ABC, or Alphabetical Railway Guide, was a monthly timetable and guidebook to Britain's railways that was organised alphabetically by station. In 1936, Agatha Christie used it as a central prop in her book *The A.B.C. Murders*.

6 Jalland, P. (1996), *Death in the Victorian Family* (Oxford: Oxford University Press), p.143.

13 A Glass Too Many

1 *Echo*, 10 November 1900.

2 The date of the letter would later be disputed, but it was ultimately thought to have been written on either the Monday evening (24 September) or the Tuesday morning (25 September), as the postmark was dated 25 September, at 6.45 a.m.

3 Taylor, L. (1983), *Mourning Dress: A Costume and Social History* (London: Allen & Unwin), p.24.

4 Flanders, J. (2004), *The Victorian House: Domestic Life from Childbirth to Deathbed* (London: Harper Perennial), p.380.

5 Jalland, P. (1996), *Death in the Victorian Family* (Oxford: Oxford University Press), p.301.

6 Flanders, J. (2004), *The Victorian House: Domestic Life from Childbirth to Deathbed* (London: Harper Perennial), p.380.

7 *Yarmouth Independent*, 6 October 1900.

8 *Yarmouth Mercury*, 24 November 1900.

9 According to Dr Lettis, who performed the post-mortem examination (*Yarmouth Advertiser and Gazette*, 29 September 1900) Mary Jane's natural hair colour was 'fair, blonde'. It had, however, been dyed a golden colour, which may be why it appears darker in the photographs. It is unclear why Mary Jane dyed her hair, but it may have been as a way of disguising herself, or simply because fair hair was not very fashionable at the time.

10 Letter from Herbert Bennett to Alice Meadows, dated 3 October 1900. A.M.13. National Archives: HO 144/567/A62336.

11 Letter from Herbert Bennett to Alice Meadows, dated 6 October 1900. A.M.5. National Archives: HO 144/567/A62336.

12 Letter from Alice Meadows to Herbert Bennett, dated 6 October 1900. A.M.7. National Archives: HO 144/567/A62336.

13 Booth, C., Charles Booth's poverty map of London. LSE. Available at: https://booth.lse.ac.uk/map/14/-0.1174/51.5064/100/0 [Accessed: 2 June 2021.]

14 *The Times*, 29 October 1900.

15 Ibid.

16 Arkell, G.E. and Duckworth, G.H. (1899–1900), BOOTH/B/371, George E. Arkell and George H. Duckworth's Notebook: Police District 46 [Greenwich]; District 48 [Woolwich]. Available at: https://booth.lse.ac.uk/notebooks.

17 *Gravesend and Northfleet Standard*, 24 November 1900.

18 *Echo*, 10 November 1900.

14 A Victim of Vanity

1 Goodman, R. (2014), *How to Be a Victorian* (London: Penguin Books), p.34.

2 *Evening News*, 7 November 1900.

3 *Echo*, 10 November 1900.

4 *Yarmouth Advertiser and Gazette*, 7 November 1900.

5 *Yarmouth Independent*, 10 November 1900.

6 Chief Constable Parker would later claim that Alice had recognised the chain at once without being prompted. He denied making any reference to it at all.

15 A Swarm of Spectators

1 Photography in court was officially prohibited with the introduction of the Criminal Justice Act 1925.

2 *Daily Express*, 17 November 1900.

3 *Daily Mail*, 10 November 1900.

4 *Echo*, 14 November 1900.

5 Symons, J. (1960), *A Reasonable Doubt: Some Criminal Cases Re-Examined* (London: Cresset Press), p.98.

6 *Sun*, 12 November 1900.

7 *Yarmouth Advertiser and Gazette*, 7 November 1900.

8 *Suffolk Chronicle*, 9 November 1900.

9 Edward Marshall Hall. See: Dilnot, G., ed. (1929), *The Trial of Herbert John Bennett (The Yarmouth Beach Murder)* (London: Geoffrey Bles), p.178.

10 Rowbotham, J. *et al.* (2013), *Crime News in Modern Britain: Press Reporting and Responsibility, 1820–2010* (Basingstoke: Palgrave Macmillan), pp.70–71.

11 *Echo*, 10 November 1900.

12 Ibid.

13 *Daily Mail*, 12 November 1900.

14 *Evening News*, 12 November 1900. The *Daily Mail* and the *Evening News* were both owned by the Harmsworth brothers, Alfred and Harold, later Viscounts Northcliffe and Rothermere.

15 *Evening News*, 13 November 1900.

16 *Evening News*, 15 November 1900.

16 The Chain of (Circumstantial) Evidence

1 *Sun*, 16 November 1900.

2 See: Dilnot, G., ed. (1929), *The Trial of Herbert John Bennett (The Yarmouth Beach Murder)* (London: Geoffrey Bles), p.114, and *Yarmouth Mercury*, 2 March 1901.

3 *Weekly Dispatch*, 18 November 1900.

17 A Cloud of Witnesses

1 *Sun*, 16 November 1900.

2 Ibid.

3 *Norfolk Chronicle and Norwich Gazette*, 10 November 1900.

4 *Sun*, 16 November 1900.

5 Ibid.

6 *Norfolk Daily Standard,* 23 November 1900.

7 Quoted in: Altick, R.D., *Victorian Studies in Scarlet: Murders and Manners in the Age of Victoria* (New York: W.W. Norton & Company Ltd), p.42.

8 *Sun*, 15 November 1900.

9 *Yarmouth Advertiser and Gazette*, 16 November 1900.

10 *Gravesend & Northfleet Standard*, 24 November 1900.

11 *Evening News*, 17 November 1900.

12 *Sun*, 17 November 1900.

13 Ibid.

14 *Sun*, 16 November 1900.

15 Capon, P. (1965), *The Great Yarmouth Mystery: The Chronicle of a Famous Crime* (London: Harrap), p.137.

16 *Evening Star*, 12 November 1900.

17 *Sun*, 17 November 1900.

18 *Illustrated Police News*, 17 November 1900.

19 William Parritt was also in possession of a copy of the photograph, but it is most likely to have been William's copy that was used by the press, as one reporter claimed to have obtained the image from 'the deceased woman's father'.

20 *Weekly Dispatch*, 25 November 1900.

21 A 'clerical-cut vest' was a waistcoat that rose high on the chest, up to the neck (but could be unbuttoned to take on a different appearance). It was not in common use at the time, hence Borking's comment about it being a 'peculiar' cut.

18 An Alibi Disproved

1 *Sun*, 23 November 1900.

2 The courts of assize were periodic courts held in the main county towns of England and Wales and presided over by visiting judges from the higher courts in London.

3 *Yarmouth Mercury*, 24 November 1900.

4 *Weekly Dispatch*, 25 November 1900.

5 *Eastern Evening News*, 28 November 1900.

6 Alice later threatened to prosecute the newspaper with libel, but ultimately decided against proceedings.

19 The Old Bailey

1 The law changed in 1856. Dr William Palmer was accused of poisoning his friend and gambling partner, John Parsons Cook. His trial was removed from Staffordshire – where the crimes were committed – to the Old Bailey because Palmer was so well known in Staffordshire that it was thought a fair jury could not be found there. He was ultimately convicted of killing six people but suspected of killing as many as fourteen.

2 The trial dialogue has been taken from a mix of sources, including the judge's notes and other papers, the Dilnot text, and newspaper reports of the evidence, recorded as it was given.

3 The court is named after the street where it stands, which follows the line of the old fortified wall, which surrounded the 'bailey' of the city.

4 Eddington took the stand to claim she had gone to the shop with the intention of shooting herself in her sweetheart John Bellis's presence, but a struggle had taken place when Bellis tried to prevent her. The weapon discharged, inflicting a fatal wound to Bellis. The jury found Eddington not guilty of wilful murder, but guilty of attempted suicide, leading to a sentence of fifteen months hard labour. The case was heard by Mr Justice Phillimore.

5 *Eastern Daily Press*, 5 March 1901.

6 *Morning Leader*, 26 February 1901.

7 *Eastern Daily Press*, 25 February 1901.

8 *Gravesend & Northfleet Standard*, 2 March 1901. *Star*, 26 February 1901.

9 Hawley Crippen was an American doctor living in England, who was found guilty of murdering his music-hall-performer wife, Cora Turner, known as Belle Elmore, in 1910. Following the murder, Crippen fled to Canada with his lover, Ethel Le Neve, aboard a passenger ship. In his absence, police searched his house and found the dismembered body of his wife buried beneath some bricks in his cellar. Determined to catch Crippen and Le Neve, Scotland Yard detectives boarded a faster ship, intercepted them and returned them to England for trial. The case was hailed as one of the first to use wireless telegraphy to aid the capture of a criminal.

20 The Great Defender

1 Smith, S. (2016), *Marshall Hall: A Law unto Himself* (London: Wildy, Simmonds & Hill), p.60.

2 After Queen Victoria's death in January 1901, the new King decreed that all barristers in office would retain their original appointment. Therefore, the transition from QCs to KCs (King's Counsel) was gradual and happened as the King made new appointments. For this reason, the barristers in the Bennett case will be referred to as QCs.

3 The case of Annie Dyer, who was indicted for murdering her newborn baby. Marshall Hall convinced the jury that the death was accidental, and Annie was acquitted.

4 The case of Thomas Packman, a Brighton publican, who stood trial for the murder of his wife, Lucy. He was found guilty of manslaughter and sentenced to four years in prison.

5 Letter from Marshall Hall to Sir James Forrest Fulton, dated 11 March 1901. National Archives: HO 144/567/A62336.

6 *Weekly Dispatch*, 3 March 1901.

7 *Yarmouth Mercury*, 23 November 1900.

8 According to the National Archives currency converter, £300 to £400 would equate

to between £20,000 and £30,000 in today's money, although social historian Judith Flanders argues that relative values have altered so much that it is almost impossible to convert nineteenth-century prices into today's money. Based on historical records, £300 would have been what a skilled tradesman would have been paid for around 900 days of work in 1900. See http://www.nationalarchives.gov.uk/currency/.

9 *Norfolk Daily Standard*, 1 December 1900.
10 A guinea was a coin worth £1 and a shilling. The coin ceased circulation in 1813, but the term remained; 100 guineas at the time would have valued £105.
11 *Weekly Dispatch*, 3 March 1901.
12 *Daily Graphic*, 26 February 1901.
13 *Morning Leader*, 25 February 1901.

1 Although three weeks perhaps seems like a long time for a chief constable of a provisional police force to wait to consult Scotland Yard in a murder inquiry, at the time it was not the usual course of action to call upon 'Yard' detectives. In fact, the home secretary would not formally approve the practice until 1908.
2 *People*, 27 March 1932.

21 Spoiling for a Fight

1 *Echo*, 26 February 1901.
2 Foreign volunteers from several countries fought alongside the Boers against the British, including two military units from Ireland.
3 Marjoribanks, E. (1929), *The Life of Sir Edward Marshall Hall* (London: Victor Gollancz Ltd), p.160. There is no evidence to support Marshall Hall's theory and the most obvious motive for the Bennetts' trip remains that they were fleeing creditors and, potentially, the fear of prosecution following the fire at Westgate-on-Sea.
4 The report that Marshall Hall was referring to actually quoted Mrs Elliston as saying that the Bennetts 'had not the appearance or the manner of people who had come off a sea voyage' (see: *Evening News*, 12 November 1900). This was probably a fair observation given that they had been back in London for several days before taking lodgings with the Ellistons.
5 *Evening News*, 12 November 1901.
6 Ibid.
7 Smith, S. (2016), *Marshall Hall: A Law unto Himself* (London: Wildy, Simmonds & Hill), p.97.
8 *Yarmouth Mercury*, 2 March 1901.
9 The trilby hat was variously referred to in reports of the evidence as 'black' and 'dark'.
10 *Yarmouth Mercury*, 2 March 1901.

1 *Norfolk Daily Standard*, 7 March 1901.
2 Ibid.
3 The Aerated Bread Company (ABC) Café opened in the 1860s, serving hot drinks and snacks.
4 *Eastern Evening News*, 2 March 1901.

22 Cross-examination

1 *Lowestoft Standard*, 2 March 1901.

2 *Echo*, 27 February 1901.

3 Smith, S. (2016), *Marshall Hall: A Law unto Himself* (London: Wildy, Simmonds & Hill), p.67. The barrister would keep his connection to the spiritualist movement secret until the First World War, when spiritualism become more mainstream.

4 Of course, the contents of the letter had by now been widely reported in the newspapers and it was widely known that whoever wrote the letter had instructed 'Mrs Hood' to put her babe to bed and meet them by the 'big clock' at 9 p.m. on the evening of her murder.

23 A Voice in the Dark

1 *Illustrated Mail*, 24 November 1900.

2 *Eastern Evening News*, 28 February 1901.

3 Ibid. Reade was also described as a 'big burly looking Country waiter'. *Evening News*, 27 February 1901.

1 Wood, W. (1916), *Survivors' Tales of Famous Crimes* (London: Cassell & Company Ltd), p.193.

2 Ibid.

24 Doubt

1 *Eastern Evening News*, 1 March 1901.

25 One 'T' or Two?

1 *Eastern Evening News*, 28 February 1901.

2 *Eastern Evening News*, 2 March 1901.

3 *Sun*, 28 February 1901.

26 On Your Oath?

1 The chief constable's version was consistent with the newspaper reports of that day's proceedings before the magistrates.

2 *Eastern Evening News*, 1 March 1901.

27 Expert Testimony

1 Stereoscopic Photography creates the illusion of a three-dimensional image from a pair of two-dimensional images using depth perception. To create the illusion, the two images are printed side-by-side and viewed through a 'Stereo Viewer'.

2 May, B. (2006), 'Introduction to the London Stereoscopic Company'. See: https://www.londonstereo.com/introduction.html

1 Marshall Hall's conversation with Herbert was recounted by the barrister in a letter to his friend, Sir Arthur Pinero, dated 7 March 1901. See: Marjoribanks, E. (1929), *The Life of Sir Edward Marshall Hall* (London: Victor Gollancz Ltd), p.153.

28   Evidence of an Alibi

1   At the time, the defence was not required to give advance notice of an alibi as they are now.

2   *Yarmouth Mercury*, 9 March 1901.

3   Marjoribanks, E. (1929), *The Life of Sir Edward Marshall Hall* (London: Victor Gollancz Ltd), p.151.

4   Ibid., p.154.

5   *Daily Mail*, 2 March 1901.

6   The company still operates today under the name Pusterla 1880 UK Ltd, having been purchased by Pusterla 1880 SpA and fully incorporated into the Pusterla family in 2016. It is renowned for the manufacture of box packaging for luxury perfumes, such as Chanel and Estée Lauder, and DVD and CD cases for Sony, Universal and Warner.

7   ... and it arrived at the South Town station in Great Yarmouth at 8.28 p.m.

8   Zangwill, I. (2015), *The Big Bow Mystery* (London: Enhanced Media), p.96. (*The Big Bow Mystery* was first published in the *Star* in 1891 as a serial.)

9   It had been widely reported that Herbert wore a blue tie during his Yarmouth police court hearing, so blue was a good bet.

29   A Story for Half a Sovereign

1   *Eastern Daily Press*, 2 March 1901.

2   Ibid.

31   Is He Our Man?

1   *Evening News*, 2 March 1901.

2   Sir Edward Clarke was considered one of the leading barristers of the era.

3   See: Dilnot, G., ed. (1929), *The Trial of Herbert John Bennett (The Yarmouth Beach Murder)* (London: Geoffrey Bles), p.199.

4   Smith, S. (2016), *Marshall Hall: A Law unto Himself* (London: Wildy, Simmonds & Hill), p.96.

5   *People's Weekly Journal*, 9 March 1901.

6   Even modern experts have been unable to reach a conclusion on the identity of the chain from photographs alone – see: *Murder, Mystery and My Family*, series 1, episode 6, BBC One (5 March 2018), 09:15.

7   See: Dilnot, G., ed. (1929), *The Trial of Herbert John Bennett (The Yarmouth Beach Murder)* (London: Geoffrey Bles), p.200.

32   The Verdict

1   *Eastern Evening News*, 4 March 1901.

2   Ibid.

3   This was only the second such sentence he had delivered. The first was upon John Edward Cossey, the Stokesby murderer, who had been convicted by a jury the previous month of the murder of Thirza Kelly. See the *Leeds Times*, 2 February 1901. The death sentence was later reprieved.

4   *People's Weekly Journal*, 9 March 1901.

5   London papers were sent up to Yarmouth and the surrounding towns, but some local newspapers also published special editions. The *Yarmouth Mercury* published halfpenny evening 'specials' throughout Bennett's magisterial hearing.

6   The Maidstone by-election was triggered when the result of the previous year's vote was

made void after an investigation found evidence of bribery of electors by agents of the winning Liberal candidate, Sir John Barker. The vote took place on 1 March 1901, and despite the controversy that surrounded the party, they retained the seat with a win for Liberal candidate Sir Francis Evans.

7 *People's Weekly Journal*, 9 March 1901.

33 Trial by Press

1 *Eastern Daily Press*, 4 March 1901.

2 *Norfolk Daily Standard*, 7 March 1901.

3 *Echo*, 4 March 1901.

4 *Weekly Dispatch*, 3 March 1901.

5 National Archives: HO 144/567/A62336.

6 *Eastern Daily Press*, 5 March 1901.

7 *The Times*, reported in the *People's Weekly Journal*, 9 March 1901.

8 *Norwich Daily Standard*, 4 March 1901.

9 *Yarmouth Mercury*, 16 March 1901.

10 While awaiting trial, Bennett had shared a prison with three infamous murderers of the day: George Parker, who had been condemned to death for the murder of William Pearson and the attempted murder of Rhoda King, in a crime referred to as the 'train murder', at the Central Criminal Court the day before Bennett received his sentence; Samson Silas Salmon, who was convicted and later executed for the murder of his cousin, Lucy Salmon; and Barnet Abrahams, who was found guilty of the manslaughter of Whitechapel policeman Ernest Thompson. The *Illustrated Police News* published a sketch of the four men together in what appears to be the prison yard, but it is not clear if the men actually met, or if the image was invented by the newspaper to aid sensation mongering. See: *Illustrated Police News*, 16 March 1901.

11 *Referee*, 18 November 1900.

12 *Eastern Evening News*, 5 March 1901.

13 *Law Journal*, 9 March 1901.

14 Shattock, J., ed. (2017), *Journalism and the Periodical Press in Nineteenth-Century Britain* (Cambridge: Cambridge University Press), p.161.

15 Playbill for the Surrey Theatre, Monday 17 November 1823, Harvard Theatre Collection/ Playbills/ Surrey Theatre, quoted in: Crone, R. (2012), *Violent Victorians: Popular Entertainment in Nineteenth-century London* (Manchester: Manchester University Press), p.124.

16 *The King vs Williams and Romney* (1823), in: *The Law Journal for the Year 1824* (London: J.W. Paget), pp.30-31.

17 The case against the printer was dismissed on account of there being no evidence to connect him with the playbill other than the fact that his name was printed on it.

18 *Pall Mall Gazette*, 15 April 1896.

19 *Echo*, 12 March 1901.

20 *Eastern Evening News*, 19 January 1901.

21 David Allport and Louisa Chappell had been indicted for the attempted murder of David's son, Bertie, aged nine, through starvation. They were both found guilty and sentenced to fifteen years and five years in prison respectively.

22 See: *St James's Gazette*, 28 October 1901, and the *Morning Post*, 11 November 1901.

34 Appeal

1 See: Dilnot, G., ed. (1929), *The Trial of Herbert John Bennett (The Yarmouth Beach Murder)* (London: Geoffrey Bles), p.199.

2 The Court of Appeal was established in 1875.

3 The law would change in 1908, when the Court of Criminal Appeal was finally estab-lished, following an increase in public support, fostered by the press's representation of a series of miscarriage of justice cases. Heightened public support overrode contin-ued Treasury resistance, and the Criminal Appeal Act of 1907 abolished the Court for Crown Cases Reserved and replaced it with the new Court of Criminal Appeal.

4 Letter from Marshall Hall to Sir James Forrest Fulton, dated 11 March 1901. National Archives: HO 144/567/A62336.

5 Letter from Elvy Robb to Home Secretary Charles Ritchie, dated 14 March 1901. National Archives: HO 144/567/A62336.

6 Letter from Lord Chief Justice Alverstone to Marshall Hall, dated 15 March 1901. National Archives: HO 144/567/A62336.

7 Herbert Bennett petition. National Archives: HO 144/567/A62336.

8 Published in the *Sun*, 18 March 1901.

9 Reported in the *Yarmouth Mercury*, 16 March 1901.

10 The names 'Alice' and 'Eliza' appear beside each other on the list of subscribers, each giving one shilling. It is unclear whether this was Alice and Eliza Rudrum, but it seems fitting that they would want to contribute. See: *Sun*, 21 March 1901.

11 Curtis, L.P. (2001), *Jack the Ripper and the London Press* (London: Yale University Press), p.104.

12 Subscriptions to the Ruby Bennett fund closed in August 1901, having raised £358, which was eventually paid to Herbert's father and stepmother for the benefit of their granddaughter.

13 Letter from Lord Chief Justice Alverstone to Marshall Hall, dated 17 March 1901. National Archives: HO 144/567/A62336.

14 Letter from Marshall Hall to Herbert Bennett, dated 19 March 1901. Marjoribanks, E. (1929), *The Life of Sir Edward Marshall Hall* (London: Victor Gollancz Ltd), p. 164.

35 Last Will and Testament

1 Telegram from Under-Sheriff of Norfolk (on Behalf of High Sheriff) to the Home Office. National Archives: HO 144/567/A62336.

2 *Eastern Daily Press*, 22 March 1901.

3 *Echo*, 21 March 1901.

4 *Norfolk Daily Standard*, 21 March 1901.

5 George Parker's execution would be reported in the *Illustrated Police News* on 23 March, alongside a woodcut of Parker's final moments, a scene that had become synonymous with newspaper depictions of executions from across the country: the fearful face of the condemned, hangman poised, white cap in hand, while the police officials and digni-taries look on sombrely as the representative of the clergy – in this case the Reverend J. Phipps – recites passages from the Bible.

6 Herbert's height was 5 feet 9½ inches, and his build was described as 'proportionate'. According to the 1892 table, a prisoner assigned a drop of 6 feet 9 inches would have weighed around 125 pounds.

7 *Evening Star*, 22 March 1901.

8 See: *Trial, Confession & Execution of Hubbard Lingley*, 1867 (Norwich: Wilson). Available at: https://curiosity.lib.harvard.edu/crime-broadsides/catalog/46-990081188560203941 [Accessed: 25 September 2021.]

9 *Norfolk Daily Standard*, 21 March 1901.

10 Ibid.

11 Crone, R. (2012), *Violent Victorians: Popular Entertainment in Nineteenth-century London* (Manchester: Manchester University Press), p.81.

12 Dickens, C., 'Letters to the editor', *The Times*, 14 November 1849. See: https://www.bl.uk/romantics-and-victorians/articles/murder-as-entertainment

13 'The Great Moral Lesson at Horsemonger Lane Gaol, Nov. 13'. Published in *Punch*, 24 November 1849 (210).

14 See: 'Life of the Mannings', a broadside, at https://www.bl.uk/romantics-and-victorians/articles/murder-as-entertainment

15 *Express*, 14 August 1868.

16 *Eastern Daily Press*, 22 March 1901.

36 A True Victorian Crime

1 *The Times*, 3 August 1901.

2 *Norfolk Daily Standard*, 21 March 1901.

3 Toulmin, V. (2001), '"Local Films for Local People": Travelling Showmen and the Commissioning of Local Films in Great Britain, 1900–1902', *Film History* 13(2), pp.118–137.

4 Williams, K. (1998), *Get Me a Murder a Day! A History of Mass Communication in Britain* (London: Arnold), p.70.

5 Toulmin, V. (2001), '"Local Films for Local People": Travelling Showmen and the Commissioning of Local Films in Great Britain, 1900–1902', *Film History* 13(2), pp.118–137.

6 *Showman*, 12 April 1901, p.245.

7 Curtis, L.P. (2001), *Jack the Ripper and the London Press* (London: Yale University Press), p.78.

8 Crone, R. (2012), *Violent Victorians: Popular Entertainment in Nineteenth-century London* (Manchester: Manchester University Press), p.87.

9 James Blomfield Rush, a tenant farmer, was hanged in 1849 for the murder of his mortgage holder, Isaac Jermy, and Jermy's son, also Isaac. Staffordshire Potteries produced collectable figures of Rush and his accomplice Emily Sandford, as well as key locations connected to the murder. Rush's death mask now forms part of the Wellcome Collection.

10 Crone, R. (2012), *Violent Victorians: Popular Entertainment in Nineteenth-century London* (Manchester: Manchester University Press), p.87.

11 Altick, R.D. (1970), *Victorian Studies in Scarlet: Murders and Manners in the Age of Victoria* (New York: W.W. Norton & Company), p.101.

12 Curtis, L.P. (2001), *Jack the Ripper and the London Press* (London: Yale University Press), p.79.

13 *News of the World*, 25 November 1900.

14 Blumenfeld, R.D. (1930), *R.D.B.'s Diary 1887–1914* (London: William Heinemann Ltd). Available at: https://archive.org/details/rdbsdiary035086mbp/page/n153

15 *The Times*, 3 August 1901.

16 Christiaan Rudolf de Wet, Boer general, rebel leader and politician.

17 *Referee*, 7 April 1901.

18 *London Evening Standard*, 28 May 1901.

19 *Era*, 8 December 1900.

20 *Yarmouth Mercury*, 20 July 1901.

21 *Yarmouth Independent*, 9 March 1901.

22 Ibid.

23 Leach, C.E. (1933), *On Top of the Underworld: The Personal Reminiscences of Ex-divisional Detective-Inspector Charles E Leach, late of New Scotland Yard* (London: S. Low, Marston & Company Ltd), pp.17-18.

24 *Sussex Advertiser*, 24 April 1877.

25 Adam, H.L. (1920), *The Police Encyclopaedia*, Vol. IV (London: The Waverley Book Company).

26 There are no other records to confirm Leach's account, which throws doubt over whether the bootlace was ever added to the Crime Museum's notorious collection of murder weapons.

27 Crone, R. (2012), *Violent Victorians: Popular Entertainment in Nineteenth-century London* (Manchester: Manchester University Press), p.92.

28 William's request is recorded in official Home Office papers. National Archives: HO 144/567/A62336.

29 Smith, S. (2016), *Marshall Hall: A Law unto Himself* (London: Wildy, Simmonds & Hill), p.128.

30 The gold chain and the beach photograph have since been returned to the family.

Conclusion

1 *Sheffield Daily Telegraph*, 20 September 1916.

2 A package of poisoned fish patties was delivered to the Lawson house by hand in 1913. The whole family ate them and were all violently ill. The following year, a bomb that contained 10 ounces of gunpowder and an explosive fuse was delivered to the Lawson house by post, disguised as an ordinary package. Luckily, the bomb failed to explode when the package was opened.

3 *Sheffield Daily Telegraph*, 20 September 1916.

4 After he was acquitted of all charges, Lawson brought an action against Sholto Douglas to dissolve their partnership on the grounds that Sholto Douglas was embezzling money from the business. The case was heard in the Chancery Courts and was referred to by the judge, Mr Justice Younger, as 'one of the most remarkable cases ever brought before a court of equity'. Marshall Hall again acted on behalf of Lawson, and the partnership was eventually dissolved. Some years later, the Lawson family, who continued to own the company up until its sale to Pusterla in 2016, would claim that Sholto Douglas had fled the country after the ruling, without paying back any of the money that he owed.

List of Characters and Photographs

Mary Jane Bennett, *aged twenty-three in 1900.*
Herbert John Bennett, *husband of Mary Jane Bennett, aged twenty-one in 1900.*

FAMILY

Ruby 'Rose' Bennett, *daughter of Mary Jane and Herbert Bennett, aged two in 1900.*
William Clark, *father of Mary Jane Bennett.*
Mary Ann Clark (née Butler), *Mary Jane's mother.*
Selina Clark (née Durley), *Mary Jane's stepmother.*
William Clark Junior, *son of William and Selina Clark.*
Amy Elizabeth Edwards, *Mary Jane's grandmother.*
Edward Edwards, *Amy Edwards's second husband.*
John Bennett, *father of Herbert Bennett.*
Selina Bennett (née Meloy), *John Bennett's second wife, Herbert's stepmother.*
Henry Simmons, *Herbert Bennett's maternal grandfather.*

THE POLICE AND LEGAL REPRESENTATIVES

Edwin Manship, *Police Constable of Great Yarmouth.*
William Parker, *Chief Constable of Police, Great Yarmouth.*
Robert Lingwood, *Detective Inspector of Police, Great Yarmouth.*
Dr Thomas Lettis, *Police Surgeon of Great Yarmouth.*
Mr Charles O'Farrell, *Poor Law District Medical Officer of Great Yarmouth.*
Alfred Leach, *Chief Inspector of the Criminal Investigation Department (CID), Scotland Yard.*
Edward Marshall Hall QC, *defence barrister.*
Edward Elvy Robb, *solicitor for the defence.*
Charles Gill QC, *prosecution barrister.*
Charles J. Wiltshire, *solicitor for the prosecution.*

AT GREAT YARMOUTH

Eliza Rudrum, *landlady of lodging house, No. 3, Row 104, Great Yarmouth.*
John Rudrum, *landlord of lodging house, No. 3, Row 104, Great Yarmouth.*
Alice Rudrum, *daughter of John and Eliza Rudrum.*
William Borking, *landlord of the South Quay Distillery, Great Yarmouth.*
John Norton, *attendant at Hewett's Bathing Chalet, found the body.*
Blanche Smith, *machinist at Johnson & Sons factory, Great Yarmouth, eyewitness.*
Alfred Mason, *moulder at Crabtree & Co. engineering works, eyewitness.*
Edward Goodrum, *'boots' at the Crown and Anchor Hotel, Great Yarmouth.*
William Reade, *waiter at the Crown and Anchor Hotel, Great Yarmouth.*

LANDLADIES AND NEIGHBOURS

Susan Kato, *the Bennetts' landlady, Balham.*
Emma Elliston, *the Bennetts' landlady, Plumstead.*
Emma McDonald, *the Bennetts' neighbour, Woolwich Road.*
Lilian Langman, *Mary Jane Bennett's neighbour, Bexley Heath.*
Elizabeth 'Lizzie' Langman, *Mary Jane Bennett's neighbour, Bexley Heath.*
Comfort Pankhurst, *Herbert Bennett's landlady, Woolwich.*

FRIENDS AND ACQUAINTANCES

Alice Amelia Meadows, *parlourmaid, Hyde Park Terrace.*
John Cameron, *assistant at the Co-operative stores, Woolwich.*
William Parritt, *assistant at the Co-operative stores, Gravesend/Woolwich.*
Robert Allen, *assistant at the Co-operative stores, Woolwich.*
John Stevens, *lodger at the Pankhursts', Woolwich.*
Douglas Sholto Douglas, *fancy box manufacturer, alibi witness.*

Portrait of Mary Jane and Herbert Bennett, c. 1897, photograph by Frank Sayers' studio.

The 'beach photograph' – Mary Jane and Ruby Bennett, Great Yarmouth beach, September 1900. First published in the *Yarmouth Independent*, 29 September 1900. This copy is taken from the *Illustrated Mail*, 17 November 1900.

The spot on the beach where the body of Mary Jane Bennett was found. Original photograph by Frank Sayers, published in *The Police Encyclopaedia*, Vol. 2, by Hargrave L. Adam, 1920.

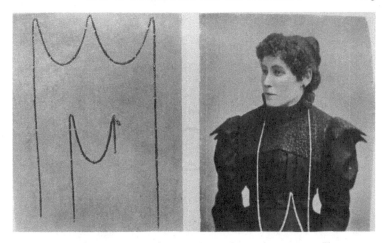

Left: The gold chain that was found among Herbert Bennett's possessions. The prosecution argued that this was the same watch chain that Mary Jane was pictured wearing in the beach photograph just days before her death. No other comparable chain was ever recovered from Great Yarmouth, nor from Mary Jane's house in London. From *The Police Encyclopaedia*, Vol. 2, by Hargrave L. Adam, 1920.

Right: Photograph of Mary Jane Bennett, wearing a gold watch chain, 1899, known as the 'Taylor photograph'. Originally taken by the firm A & G Taylor Photographers, and republished in *The Police Encyclopaedia*, Vol. 2, by Hargrave L. Adam, 1920.

The once unmarked grave of Mary Jane and now a fitting tribute to her life, situated in Great Yarmouth Old Cemetery.

William and Selina Clark – Mary Jane Bennett's father and stepmother. Date unknown. The author's great-great-grandparents. From the author's private collection.

William Clark Jr, c. 1915. This image was printed on the back of a postcard in memoriam of 'Able Seaman W.G. Clarke', who died on the HMS *Queen Mary* during the Battle of Jutland, 1916. William was thirty-one years old. The photograph was cut out by William's family, presumably for display. From the author's private collection.

Ruby Elizabeth Fitchett (née Bennett), aged seventy-two, Australia, 1970. From the author's private collection.

Sources

NEWSPAPERS

Local and Regional

Birmingham Daily Mail
Eastern Daily Press
Eastern Evening News
Gravesend & Northfleet Standard
Gravesend Reporter
Kentish Independent
Leeds Times
Lowestoft Standard
Norfolk Chronicle and Norwich Gazette
Norfolk Daily Standard
Norfolk News
Norfolk Weekly Standard
Norwich Mercury
Sheffield Daily Telegraph
Suffolk Chronicle
Suffolk Mercury
Yarmouth Advertiser & Gazette
Yarmouth Independent
Yarmouth Mercury

London Daily

Daily Chronicle
Daily Express
Daily Graphic
Daily Mail
Daily News
Daily Telegraph
The *Echo*
Evening News
Evening Standard
Evening Star
Express
The *Globe*
The *Guardian*
Morning Leader
Morning Post
Pall Mall Gazette

St James's Gazette
The *Star*
The *Sun*
The Times
Westminster Gazette

London Weekly

Illustrated Mail
Illustrated Police News
Lloyd's Weekly Newspaper
News of the World
The *Observer*
Penny Illustrated Paper
The *People*
People's Weekly Journal
The *Referee*
Reynolds News
Sunday Express
Sunday Special
Sunday Sun
Sunday Times
Weekly Dispatch
Weekly Times & Echo

Miscellaneous

Cape Times
The *Bazaar, Exchange and Mart*
Law Journal
The *Showman*

ARCHIVAL DOCUMENTS

The National Archives

CRIM 1/65/2 – Central Criminal Court: Depositions
HO 144/567/A62336 – Home Office: Registered Papers, Supplementary, Judge's notes, Marshall Hall letters.
COPY 1/762 no.33118 – (23 Jan 1901) –The Yarmouth murder case penny pamphlet.

Hackney Archives

M3940/1 – The Fancy Box Company: Agreement between Frederick William Bateman (as the owner of the Company), Douglas Sholto Douglas.

UK Census Collection

Census Returns of England and Wales, 1851–1901.
Birth, Marriage and Death records.

Charles Booth's London: Poverty Maps and Police Notebooks: https://booth.lse.ac.uk

SECONDARY SOURCES

Adam, H.L. (1920), *The Police Encyclopaedia* (London: Waverley Book Company).

Adam, H.L. (1931), *Murder by Persons Unknown* (London: W. Collins, Sons & Company).

Altick, R.D. (1970), *Victorian Studies in Scarlet: Murders and Manners in the Age of Victoria* (New York: W.W. Norton & Company).

Alverstone, R.E. (1914), *Recollections of Bar and Bench* (London: Edward Arnold).

Barret-Ducrocq, F. (1992), *Love in the Time of Victoria: Sexuality and Desire Among Working-class Men and Women in Nineteenth-century London* (London: Penguin).

Beeton, I. (1906), *Mrs Beeton's Book of Household Management* (London: Ward, Lock & Company Ltd).

Brook, A. (1948), *A Casebook of Crime* (London: Rockcliff).

Capon, P. (1965), *The Great Yarmouth Mystery: The Chronicle of a Famous Crime* (London: Harrap).

Clarke, B. (2004), *From Grub Street to Fleet Street: An Illustrated History of English Newspapers to 1899* (Aldershot: Ashgate).

Crone, R. (2012), *Violent Victorians: Popular Entertainment in Nineteenth-century London* (Manchester: Manchester University Press).

Curran, J. and Seaton, J. (2009), *Power Without Responsibility: The Press and Broadcasting in Britain*, 7th edition (London: Routledge).

Curtis, L.P. (2001), *Jack the Ripper and the London Press* (New Haven/London: Yale University Press).

Dearden, H. (1934), *Death Under the Microscope: Some Cases of Sir Bernard Spilsbury and Others* (London: Hutchinson & Company Ltd).

Dilnot, G., ed. (1929), *The Trial of Herbert John Bennett (The Yarmouth Beach Murder)* (London: Geoffrey Bles).

Engelbach, F.G. (1899), 'Her Majesty's Ordnance Factories: Woolwich Arsenal', *The Navy and Army Illustrated*.

Felstead, S. (1926), *Sir Richard Muir: The Memoirs of a Public Prosecutor* (London: John Lane The Bodley Head Ltd).

Flanders, J. (2004), *The Victorian House: Domestic Life from Childbirth to Deathbed* (London: Harper Perennial).

Flanders, J. (2014), *The Invention of Murder: How the Victorians Revelled in Death and Detection and Created Modern Crime* (London: St Martin's Griffin).

Fowler, S. (2007), *Workhouse: The People, the Places, the Life Behind Doors* (Kew: National Archives).

Gatrell, V.A.C. (1996), *The Hanging Tree: Execution and the English People, 1770–1868* (Oxford: Oxford University Press).

Gleadle, K. (2001), *British Women in the Nineteenth Century* (Basingstoke: Palgrave).

Goodman, R. (2014), *How to Be a Victorian* (London: Penguin).

Gough, W.C. (1927), *From Kew Observatory to Scotland Yard* (London: Hurst and Blackett).

Hall, L.A. (2013), *Sex, Gender and Social Change in Britain Since 1880*, 2nd edition (Basingstoke: Palgrave Macmillan).

Hope-Simpson, R.E. (1992), 'Epidemic Influenza, 1900–1932', in *The Transmission of Epidemic Influenza* (Boston, MA: Springer US).

Jalland, P. (1996), *Death in the Victorian Family* (Oxford: Oxford University Press).

Laurence, J. (1931), *Seaside Crimes* (London: Sampson Low & Company).

Leach, C.E. (1933), *On Top of the Underworld: The Personal Reminiscences of Ex-divisional*

Detective-Inspector Charles E. Leach Late of New Scotland Yard (London: Sampson Low, Marston & Company Ltd).

Lee, A.J. (1976), *The Origins of the Popular Press in England, 1855–1914* (London: Croom Helm).

Marjoribanks, E. (1929), *The Life of Sir Edward Marshall Hall* (London: Victor Gollancz Ltd).

Meier, A.C. (2018), 'Finding a murderer in a victim's eyes', *JSTORDaily*. Available at: https://daily.jstor.org/finding-a-murderer-in-a-victims-eye/.

Perkin, J. (1993), *Victorian Women* (London: Murray).

Riley, B. (2011), *Great Yarmouth Row Houses and Greyfriars' Cloister* (London: English Heritage).

Rowbotham, J., Pegg, S. and Stevenson, K. (2013), *Crime News in Modern Britain: Press Reporting and Responsibility, 1820–2010* (Basingstoke: Palgrave Macmillan).

Rubenhold, H. (2020), *The Five: The Untold Lives of the Women Killed by Jack the Ripper* (London: Black Swan).

Shattock, J., ed. (2017), *Journalism and the Periodical Press in Nineteenth-Century Britain* (Cambridge: Cambridge University Press).

Shew, E.S. (1960), *A Companion to Murder* (London: Cassell).

Shpayer-Makov, H. (2009), 'Journalists and Police Detectives in Victorian and Edwardian England: An Uneasy Reciprocal Relationship', *Journal of Social History*, 42(4).

Skilton, D. and Dennis, B. (1987), *Reform and Intellectual Debate in Victorian England* (Beckenham: Croom Helm).

Smith, S. (2016), *Marshall Hall: A Law unto Himself* (London: Wildy, Simmonds & Hill).

Stone, L. (1990), *The Family, Sex and Marriage in England, 1500–1800.* Abridged edition (London: Penguin).

Stone, L. (1990), *Road to Divorce: England 1530–1987* (Oxford: Oxford University Press).

Symes Thompson, E. (1888), *South Africa as a Health Resort* (Royal Colonial Institute).

Symons, J. (1960), *A Reasonable Doubt: Some Criminal Cases Re-examined* (London: Cresset Press).

Taylor, D. (1998), *Crime, Policing and Punishment in England, 1750–1914* (Basingstoke: Macmillan Education).

Taylor, L. (1983), *Mourning Dress: A Costume and Social History* (London: Allen & Unwin).

Tosh, J. (2007), *A Man's Place: Masculinity and the Middle-class Home in Victorian England* (London: Yale University Press).

UK Parliament (2021), 'Creating the nation's police force'. Available at: https://www.parliament.uk/about/living-heritage/transformingsociety/laworder/policeprisons/overview/nationspoliceforce/ [Accessed: 3 May 2021.]

Unknown (1910), *Every Woman's Encyclopaedia* (London: s.n.).

Wallace, E. (1924), *The Murder on Yarmouth Sands* (London: George Newnes Ltd).

Warwick, P. and Spies, S.B. (1980), *The South African War: The Anglo-Boer War 1899–1902* (Harlow: Longman).

Wiener, J.H. (2011), *The Americanization of the British press, 1830s–1914: Speed in the Age of Transatlantic Journalism* (Basingstoke: Palgrave Macmillan).

Wiener, M.J. (2004), *Men of Blood: Violence, Manliness and Criminal Justice in Victorian England* (Cambridge: Cambridge University Press).

Williams, K. (1998), *Get Me a Murder a Day! A History of Mass Communication in Britain* (London: Arnold).

Wilson, C. and Pitman, P. (1961), *Encyclopaedia of Murder* (London: Arthur Barker Ltd).

Wood, W. (1916), *Survivors' Tales of Famous Crimes* (London: Cassell & Company Ltd).

Zangwill, I. (1892), *The Big Bow Mystery* (London: Enhanced Media).

Acknowledgements

I have spent many a happy hour rooting around in libraries and archives in search of Mary Jane's story and I am delighted to have been able to bring it alive on the page. I am extremely grateful to everyone who has helped me along the way.

My sincerest thanks must first go to the wonderful Wendy Moore, who gave me the confidence to believe that this book was worthy of publication. Words cannot express how grateful I am to you, Wendy, for believing in me as a writer and for seeing the potential in this book.

My deepest thanks to my uncle, Joe, who was the first person I trusted with a complete first draft of the manuscript: thank you for your thoughtful and considered advice.

To my award-winning powerhouse of an agent, Hannah Schofield, who saw the book's potential as soon as she picked it up and who worked tirelessly to find it its perfect home: thank you for your advice and enthusiasm. I couldn't have wished for a better champion for my book.

It has been an absolute joy to work with Beth Eynon, who 'got' the book from our very first conversation. As an author, finding an editor who not only understands but shares your vision is beyond important, especially when working on such a personal project. Thank you, Beth, for working so hard to realise this vision. Thank you to Jo Roberts-Miller for expertly keeping the project on track, and to all of the team at Seven Dials who have worked on the project.

I would like to say a big thank you to all the staff who keep the country's history and heritage safe and well cared for in our libraries and archives, and those who work hard to preserve and digitise materials for future generations. Without their work, the research that went into creating this book may not have been possible. Particular thanks go to the staff at the British Library – including the wonderful Lucy Rowland – the National Archives, the Great Yarmouth public library and the Bodleian.

I am extremely lucky to work in a supportive and creative environment where the expression and discussion of ideas is encouraged. To Julia, Paula,

Iestyn and Joe, thank you for encouraging me to believe in this book when it was just an idea.

This book wouldn't have been possible if it weren't for the people who are always by my side cheering me on. Special thanks to my family, especially to my parents, Deborah and John, for always believing in me. To Elsie and Harrison, who not only keep the Clark line burning bright but are two of the brightest beacons in my life: thank you for bringing me so much laughter and joy. Never let anyone dim your light.

To Matt, who embraces my many idiosyncrasies and listens to my constant stream of questions (the prerogative of a writer): thank you. You mean the world to me.

Finally, to all of my brilliant friends and colleagues, particularly Vicky, Jed, Lisa, Rich and Maggie, who have supported me along the way, listened to my constant ramblings, and waited in patient anticipation for the book to be published because it had to be 'finished' before they could read any of it: thank you.